GW01231021

LIVERPOOL FC
THE OFFICIAL GUIDE
2008

Sport Media
A Trinity Mirror Business

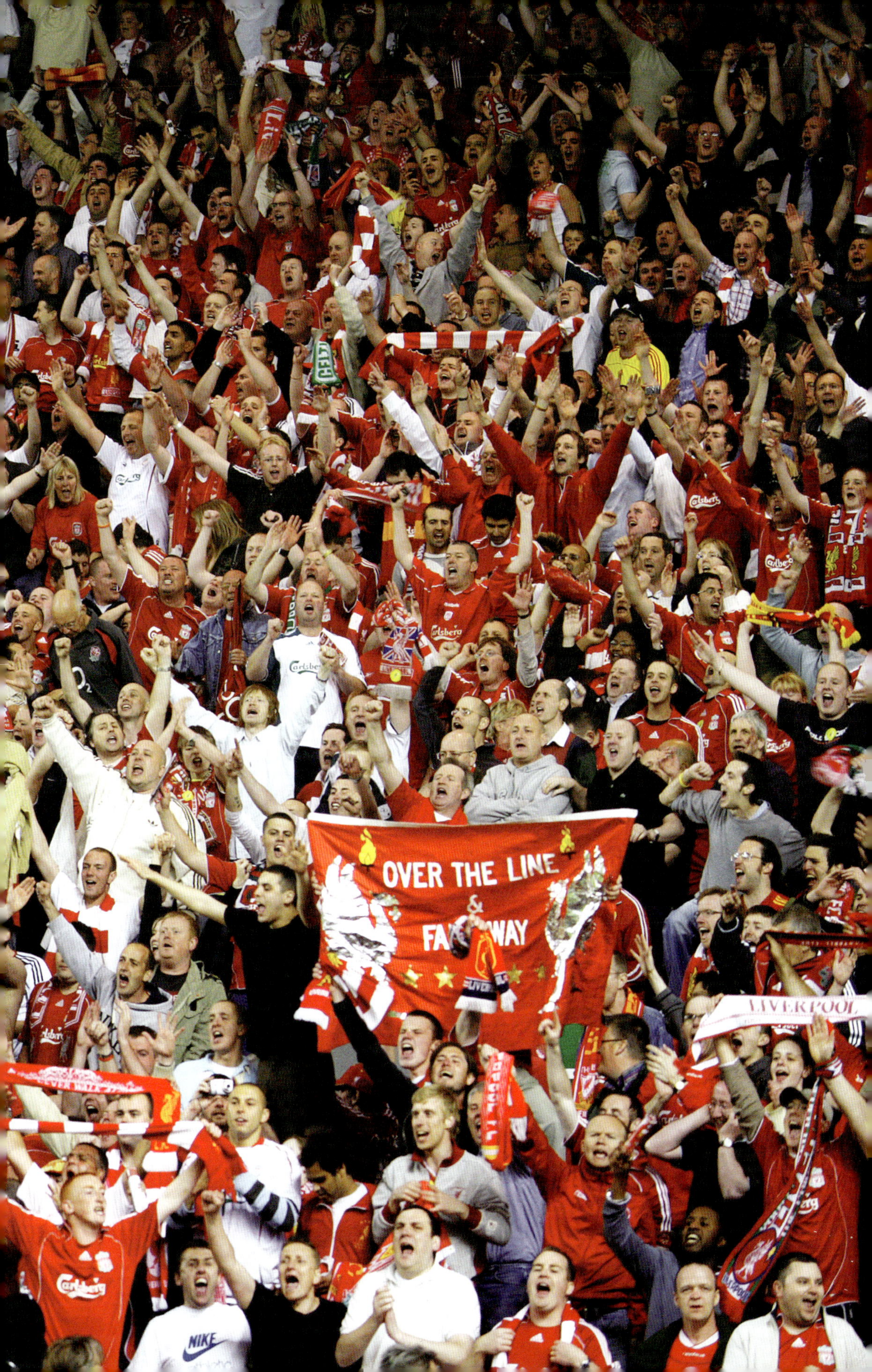
OVER THE LINE
&
LIVERPOOL

HONOURS

LEAGUE CHAMPIONSHIP (18)
1900/01, 1905/06, 1921/22,1922/23, 1946/47, 1963/64, 1965/66, 1972/73, 1975/76, 1976/77, 1978/79, 1979/80, 1981/82,1982/83, 1983/84, 1985/86,1987/88, 1989/90

DIVISION TWO WINNERS (4)
1893/94, 1895/96, 1904/05, 1961/62

FA CUP WINNERS (7)
1964/65, 1973/74, 1985/86, 1988/89, 1991/92, 2000/01, 2005/06

LEAGUE CUP WINNERS (7)
1980/81, 1981/82, 1982/83, 1983/84,1994/95, 2000/01, 2002/03

EUROPEAN CUP /UEFA CHAMPIONS LEAGUE WINNERS (5)
1976/77, 1977/78, 1980/81, 1983/84, 2004/05

UEFA CUP WINNERS (3)
1972/73, 1975/76, 2000/01

EUROPEAN SUPER CUP WINNERS (3)
1977/78, 2001/02, 2005/06

FA CHARITY SHIELD WINNERS/FA COMMUNITY SHIELD WINNERS (10)
1966, 1974, 1976, 1979, 1980,1982, 1988, 1989, 2001, 2006

FA CHARITY SHIELD WINNERS/FA COMMUNITY SHIELD SHARED (5)
1964, 1965, 1977, 1986, 1990

SUPER CUP WINNERS
1986/87

LANCASHIRE LEAGUE WINNERS (1)
1892/93

INTRODUCTION

Liverpool FC : The Official Guide 2008 is the bible of club information for Reds fans everywhere. From contact numbers to essential club information, player profiles to club records, everything and more is included in this invaluable publication.

Now in its third year, the Guide is again packed full of facts and statistics about the Reds. To achieve this we have again utilised the finest statisticians and club experts to provide as much up-to-date information as possible that deadlines have allowed, prior to the new campaign and taking into account the summer transfer deadline at the end of August 2007.

We continue to strive to improve and develop the publication, and the changes to this edition again reflect the progress made by Rafael Benitez's side. Jamie Carragher's 10 years as an Anfield first-teamer are recognised as we reflect on Carra's full career stats, while clean sheets are analysed as we breakdown a new record set by Pepe Reina, that of the most clean sheets kept by a Liverpool goalkeeper in his first 50 games. A new edition to the records section also sees Steven Gerrard at the head of the list of Liverpool's record goalscorers in the European Cup.

Other additions to look out for include the final Liverpool career statistics of Robbie Fowler, a full rundown of the club's league record against every team, league sequences, debut goalscorers (three additions from season 2006/07), super subs and a return for Liverpool FC hat-trick men, Peter Crouch being the newest addition to the list.

All new signings have been included in the squad section, although please note that the criteria we have used is that they must have been awarded an official squad number. You'll also find some additional information on Liverpool Ladies, plus details of the victorious Reds youth team who secured back-to-back FA Youth Cup glory in 2007.

The ultimate aim of this title is to strive to make this series the kind of book that you will take down from your bookshelf time and again as a source of reference. We pride ourselves on our accuracy and reflecting the constant changes in and around the club. We hope you continue to enjoy it.

WRITERS

Ged Rea and Dave Ball are Liverpool FC's official statisticians. Ged's Liverpool FC records are second-to-none, while Dave is a key researcher for long-running BBC TV show *A Question of Sport*. James Cleary has played a major role in researching and writing key information.

Sport Media
A Trinity Mirror Business

Executive Editor: KEN ROGERS Editor: STEVE HANRAHAN
Art Editor: RICK COOKE Production Editor: PAUL DOVE
Sub Editor: ROY GILFOYLE
Editorial Assistant: JAMES CLEARY
Sales and Marketing Manager: ELIZABETH MORGAN
Design Team: BARRY PARKER, COLIN SUMPTER, GLEN HIND, LEE ASHUN, ALISON GILLILAND, JAMIE DUNMORE, JAMES KENYON
Liverpool FC Writers: CHRIS McLOUGHLIN, DAVID RANDLES, GAVIN KIRK, JOHN HYNES

All Rights Reserved. No part of this publication may be reproduced, stored in a retrieval system, or transmitted in any form, or by any means, electronic, mechanical, photocopying, recording or otherwise without the prior permission in writing of the copyright holders, nor be otherwise circulated in any form of binding or cover other than in which it is published and without a similar condition being imposed on the subsequent publisher.
ISBN 978 1 9052 66333
Printed and finished by Scotprint, Haddington, Scotland

Liverpool FC : The Official Guide 2008

CLUB TELEPHONE NUMBERS

Main Switchboard   0151 263 2361

Customer Services   0844 844 2005

Ticket Office   0844 844 0844

Mail Order Hotline (UK)   0870 6000532
International Mail Order Hotline   + 44 1386 852035
Club Store (Anfield)   0151 263 1760
Club Store (City Centre)   0151 330 3077
Club Store (Chester)   01244 344608

Conference and Banqueting (for your events at Anfield)   0151 263 7744
Corporate Sales   0151 263 9199
Development Association   0151 263 6391
Community Department   0151 264 2316
Museum & Tour Centre   0151 260 6677
Membership Department   0844 499 3000
Public Relations (including all charity requests)   0151 260 1433

BECOME A MEMBER OF THE **OFFICIAL LIVERPOOL SUPPORTERS CLUB**
To join, please call: 0844 499 3000
International: +44 151 261 1444

SUBSCRIBE TO THE OFFICIAL **LFC PROGRAMME AND WEEKLY MAGAZINE**
To take out a subscription please call: 0845 1430001

LIVE AND BREATH LFC 24/7
Official Club Media

www.liverpoolfc.tv - the official website. News, views, match coverage, interviews, statistics, history and more.

e-Season Ticket – FAPL & CL video highlights, video interviews, Kop classics + LIVE match commentary.

LFC TV – The Official Club TV Channel. Available as part of the Setanta sports package and simulcast on e-Season Ticket.

LFC Mobilezone – LFC downloads, SMS & videos through www.liverpoolfc.tv or visit the LFC mobile site at wap.liverpoolfc.tv (UK)
For News, Team Sheet, Goals & Results to your mobile simply text
LFC 4U to 61718 (UK) / 53235 (ROI) .
Full range of packages and T&Cs at www.liverpoolfc.tv.

LFC Save & Support Account with Britannia
For more information visit www.britannia.co.uk/lfc, call 0800 915 0503 or visit any Britannia branch.

Liverpool FC Credit Card in Association with MBNA
For more information call 0800 776 262.

CONTENTS

	Pages
Liverpool honours list	4
Introduction	5
Club telephone numbers	6
Foreword: Rick Parry	9
Key dates 07/08	10-11
Fixture list 07/08	12-13
Anfield past and present	14-15
Anfield future	16-17

THE BOSS — 18-27
Full managerial statistics for Rafael Benitez updated until the end of 2006/07, while we also look at the record of the Liverpool boss compared to other overseas managers in the top flight. There is also the added bonus of comparisons between Rafa's record in Champions League final campaigns and that of other twice Champions League finalists.

THE PLAYERS 07/08 — 28-49
A complete guide to this season's squad, including honours won, appearances and goals. Reserve, Academy and Ladies statistics are also present, while a rundown of the victorious 2007 FA Youth Cup-winning players is also included.

THE TOP 10 MOMENTS 06/07 — 50-57
The games and goals included as a pictorial reminder of the campaign.

THE ROAD TO ATHENS — 58-91
From Maccabi Haifa in August all the way through to AC Milan in May – each game is documented. A full list of European results is also included, plus Liverpool's club-by-club record in Europe.

THE 2006/07 SEASON — 92-119
An in-depth look back at the campaign, including pictures, results, quotes, ins and outs plus the usual gems of wisdom from Rafael Benitez.

THE TOP FLIGHT — 120-131
Full Premier League statistics and Football League records included together. New additions include Premier League captains, unbeaten records and league sequence records.

THE CUPS — 132-155
Full complement of cup statistics from every domestic competition, plus the Club World Championship.

THE RECORDS — 156-177
Appearance and goals records come as standard, but there are several new additions including 'super subs', 'debut goalscorers', 'Liverpool hat-trick men' and 'clean sheet records.'

PREMIERSHIP OPPONENTS — 178-189
Our analysis of who the Reds will be facing in the 2007/08 season, with useful information on each opposing stadium, travel details and past Liverpool records against each team.

CLUB ESSENTIALS — 190-208
Updated club information including ticket details and how to join the Reds' supporters club, to travel information and other Liverpool products – essential info for following the Reds.

Liverpool FC : The Official Guide 2008

FOREWORD

RICK PARRY
CHIEF EXECUTIVE

Welcome to our third edition of Liverpool FC : The Official Guide.

We are into our stride in another fascinating campaign, having further strengthened our squad in the summer to give us the best possible chance of turning your hopes and dreams into more silverware.

Once again, this Guide highlights our rich history and reflects the passion of our supporters, who clearly want to know everything about our famous club.

We work tremendously hard to keep you informed across a range of mediums.

* Our official magazine – *LFC* – is still the ONLY official weekly club publication in the country. It is now firmly established as a fans' favourite, bringing you exclusive news, information and interviews from the very heart of the club.
* Our website – liverpoolfc.tv – provides all breaking news from the club and is acknowledged as one of world football's leading sites. This, in itself, is a tribute to your daily need to keep in touch with everything that is happening at Anfield and Melwood.
* Our quarterly *Official Liverpool Poster Magazine* reaches out to our younger fanbase and our award-winning *This Is Anfield* matchday programme is one of the best in the country, always moving forward with innovative new ideas.
* Liverpool FC's worldwide fanbase is catered for through exclusive quarterly glossy magazines for both our junior and senior Official Liverpool Supporters' Club members. These publications provide a different content agenda focused on the fans themselves and how the club operates on a daily basis.

The Liverpool FC : Official Guide 2008 will tell you everything you need to know about the club. Many supporters collect every edition, each providing new statistics and updated information. The Guide is the definitive information package for Anfield fans.

Once again, many thanks for your passionate and loyal support.

Rick Parry

KEY DATES 2007-08
(Dates are subject to change)

August 2007

3	UEFA Champions League third qualifying round draw
11	Barclays Premier League kick-off
14/15	UEFA Champions League third qualifying round, first leg
28/29	UEFA Champions League third qualifying round, second leg
30	UEFA Champions League group stage draw
31	UEFA Cup first-round draw
31	Transfer window closes

September 2007

18/19	UEFA Champions League group stage matchday 1
20	UEFA Cup first round, first leg
24 (w/c)	Carling Cup third round

October 2007

2/3	UEFA Champions League group stage matchday 2
4	UEFA Cup first round, second leg
9	UEFA Cup group stage draw (11am)
23/24	UEFA Champions League group stage matchday 3
25	UEFA Cup group stage matchday 1
29 (w/c)	Carling Cup fourth round

November 2007

6/7	UEFA Champions League group stage matchday 4
8	UEFA Cup group stage matchday 2
27/28	UEFA Champions League group stage matchday 5
29	UEFA Cup group stage matchday 3

December 2007

2	European Championship finals draw
5	UEFA Cup group stage matchday 4
11/12	UEFA Champions League group stage matchday 6
17 (w/c)	Carling Cup quarter-final
20	UEFA Cup group stage matchday 5
21	UEFA Champions League first knockout stage draw (11am)
21	UEFA Cup round of 32 & round of 16 draw (12pm)
31	Transfer window re-opens

January 2008

5	FA Cup third round
7 (w/c)	Carling Cup semi-final 1st leg

KEY DATES 2007-08
(Dates are subject to change)

January 2008

21 (w/c)	Carling Cup semi-final 2nd leg
26	FA Cup fourth round
31	Transfer window closes (5pm)

February 2008

13/14	UEFA Cup round of 32, first leg
16	FA Cup fifth round
19/20	UEFA Champions League first knockout round, first leg
21	UEFA Cup round of 32, second leg
24	Carling Cup final (Wembley Stadium, London)

March 2008

4/5	UEFA Champions League first knockout round, second leg
6	UEFA Cup round of 16, first leg
8	FA Cup quarter-finals
13	UEFA Cup round of 16, second leg
14	UEFA Champions League quarter-finals and semi-finals draw (11am)
14	UEFA Cup quarter-finals and semi-finals draw (12pm)

April 2008

1/2	UEFA Champions League quarter-finals, first leg
3	UEFA Cup quarter-finals, first leg
5	FA Cup semi-finals
8/9	UEFA Champions League quarter-finals, second leg
10	UEFA Cup quarter-finals, second leg
22/23	UEFA Champions League semi-finals, first leg
24	UEFA Cup semi-finals, first leg
29/30	UEFA Champions League semi-finals, second leg

May 2008

1	UEFA Cup semi-finals, second leg
11	Barclays Premier League final day
14	UEFA Cup final (City of Manchester Stadium, Manchester, England)
17	FA Cup final (Wembley Stadium, London)
21	UEFA Champions League final (Luzhniki Stadium, Moscow, Russia)

June 2008

7	European Championship finals begin (St. Jakob-Park, Basle)

FIXTURE LIST 2007-08

August 2007

11	Aston Villa	(A)	-	5.15pm
15	Toulouse UEFA C. LGE Q. 1	(A)		
19	Chelsea	(H)	-	4pm
25	Sunderland	(A)	-	12.45pm
28	Toulouse UEFA C. LGE Q. 2	(H)		

September 2007

1	Derby County	(H)	-	3pm
15	Portsmouth	(A)	-	12.45pm
18/19	UEFA CHAMPIONS LEAGUE GROUP STAGE MATCHDAY 1			
22	Birmingham City	(H)	-	3pm
25/26	CARLING CUP THIRD ROUND			
29	Wigan Athletic	(A)	-	3pm

October 2007

2/3	UEFA CHAMPIONS LEAGUE GROUP STAGE MATCHDAY 2			
7	Tottenham Hotspur	(H)	-	3pm
20	Everton	(A)	-	12.45pm
23/24	UEFA CHAMPIONS LEAGUE GROUP STAGE MATCHDAY 3			
28	Arsenal	(H)	-	4pm
30/31	CARLING CUP FOURTH ROUND			

November 2007

3	Blackburn Rovers	(A)	-	5.15pm
6/7	UEFA CHAMPIONS LEAGUE GROUP STAGE MATCHDAY 4			
10	Fulham	(H)	-	5.15pm
24	Newcastle United	(A)	-	12.45pm
27/28	UEFA CHAMPIONS LEAGUE GROUP STAGE MATCHDAY 5			

December 2007

1	Bolton Wanderers	(H)	-	3pm
8	Reading	(A)	-	3pm
11/12	UEFA CHAMPIONS LEAGUE GROUP STAGE MATCHDAY 6			
15	Manchester United	(H)	-	12pm
18/19	CARLING CUP QUARTER-FINALS			
22	Portsmouth	(H)	-	3pm
26	Derby County	(A)	-	3pm
29	Manchester City	(A)	-	3pm

January 2008

1	Wigan Athletic	(H)	-	3pm
5	FA CUP THIRD ROUND			
8/9	CARLING CUP SEMI-FINALS, FIRST LEG			
12	Middlesbrough	(A)	-	3pm
19	Aston Villa	(H)	-	3pm
22/23	CARLING CUP SEMI-FINALS, SECOND LEG			

FIXTURE LIST 2007-08

January 2008

26	FA CUP FOURTH ROUND			
29	West Ham United	(A)	-	7.45pm

February 2008

2	Sunderland	(H)	-	3pm
9	Chelsea	(A)	-	3pm
16	FA CUP FIFTH ROUND			
19/20	UEFA CHAMPIONS LEAGUE FIRST KNOCKOUT STAGE, FIRST LEG			
23	Middlesbrough	(H)	-	3pm
24	CARLING CUP FINAL			

March 2008

1	Bolton Wanderers	(A)	-	3pm
4/5	UEFA CHAMPIONS LEAGUE FIRST KNOCKOUT STAGE, SECOND LEG			
8	Newcastle United	(H)	-	3pm
8	FA CUP QUARTER-FINALS			
15	Reading	(H)	-	3pm
22	Manchester United	(A)	-	12pm
29	Everton	(H)	-	3pm

April 2008

1/2	UEFA CHAMPIONS LEAGUE QUARTER-FINALS, FIRST LEG			
5	Arsenal	(A)	-	3pm
5	FA CUP SEMI-FINALS			
8/9	UEFA CHAMPIONS LEAGUE QUARTER-FINALS, SECOND LEG			
12	Blackburn Rovers	(H)	-	3pm
19	Fulham	(A)	-	3pm
22/23	UEFA CHAMPIONS LEAGUE SEMI-FINALS, FIRST LEG			
26	Birmingham City	(A)	-	3pm
29/30	UEFA CHAMPIONS LEAGUE SEMI-FINALS, SECOND LEG			

May 2008

3	Manchester City	(H)	-	3pm
11	Tottenham Hotspur	(A)	-	3pm
14	UEFA CUP FINAL			
17	FA CUP FINAL			
21	UEFA CHAMPIONS LEAGUE FINAL			
TBA	West Ham United	(H)		

Copyright © The FA Premier League Ltd and The Football League Ltd 2007.
Compiled in association with Atos Origin. All fixtures and kick off times subject to change.
Home UEFA Champions League matches kick off at 7.45pm.
FA Cup and Carling Cup kick off times to be confirmed.
All information correct at time of press -August 2007.

Please note all fixtures, kick-off times and dates are subject to change

ANFIELD PAST AND PRESENT

Since Liverpool's formation in 1892, there have been a host of changes to the stadium which now resides on Anfield Road. Originally inaugurated in 1884 with a capacity of 20,000 when the Reds first played there as hosts eight years later, extensive redevelopment, beginning particularly in the Bill Shankly era, has seen Anfield hold upwards of 60,000. The ground, which hosted European Championship games in 1996 and is rated a 4-star stadium by UEFA, currently holds 45,522 – with this figure taking into account the Press and disabled areas and all seating, some of which is not used due to segregation at the Anfield Road end.

THE KOP GRANDSTAND - Capacity 12,409

Built in 1906 after the Reds won the league championship for a second time. It was, of course, named 'The Spion Kop' after a South African hill in Natal which was the scene of a bloody Boer War battle. In 1928 it was rebuilt and a roof was added with the capacity reaching close to 30,000 - the largest covered terrace in the Football League at that time. It was rebuilt in summer 1994 to its current splendour after an emotional 'last stand' against Norwich City at the end of the 1993/94 campaign.

CENTENARY STAND - Capacity 11,414

The original Kemlyn Road Stand incorporated a barrel roof and was fronted by an uncovered paddock. It was demolished in 1963 to make way for a new cantilever stand. In 1992 a second tier was added and the stand was renamed to mark the club's 100th anniversary.

MAIN STAND/PADDOCK - Capacity 12,277

The original structure was erected in the late 19th century, a 3,000-capacity stand with a distinctive red and white tudor style with the club's name in the centre. In 1973 it was redeveloped with a new roof and officially opened by HRH the Duke of Kent. Seats were added to the Paddock seven years later.

ANFIELD ROAD STAND - Capacity 9,045

In 1903 the first Anfield Road stand was built. Once a simple one-tier stand which contained a covered standing enclosure (the roof was first added in 1965), it was demolished to make way for a two-tier development in 1998 – the stand having been originally altered to accomodate multi-coloured seating in the early 1980s.

RECORD ANFIELD ATTENDANCES (Highs)

Overall: 61,905 v Wolves, 2/2/1952, FA Cup fourth round
League: 58,757 v Chelsea, 27/12/1949, Division One
League Cup: 50,880 v Nottingham Forest, 12/2/1980, semi-final second leg
Europe: 55,104 v Barcelona, 14/4/1976, Uefa Cup semi-final second leg

RECORD ANFIELD ATTENDANCES (Lows)

Overall: 1,000 v Loughborough Town, 7/12/1895, Division Two
League (post-war): 11,976 v Scunthorpe United, 22/4/1959, Division Two
FA Cup: 4,000 v Newton, 29/10/1892, second qualifying round
FA Cup (post-war): 11,207 v Chester City, 9/1/1946, third round, second leg
League Cup: 9,902 v Brentford, 25/10/1983, second round, second leg
Europe: 12,021 v Dundalk, 28/9/1982, European Cup first round, first leg

Top: Aerial view of Anfield, Goodison Park and Stanley Park area – including the proposed site for The New Anfield. **Above:** View from the corner of The Kop towards the Anfield Road Stand

ANFIELD FUTURE

Original plans for a new stadium had been approved as early as 2003 but it was not until July 2007 when the latest pictures of The New Anfield were released. With the stadium hoped to be ready in time for the 2010/2011 season, the 60,000 all-seater stadium – with plans to add up to a further 18,000 seats – will be built just a goal-kick away from the existing ground, next to Stanley Park. Indeed, it is this capacity figure which has been assigned to a huge, single-tier Kop, which will act as the heart of the stadium. Another striking feature will see the South East and South West corners of the stadium be visually open, providing views from the park.

Regeneration in the area is expected to include changing facilities for amateur players who use the existing pitches in the park, facilities for the Anfield Sport and Communitiy Centre and Liverpool Hope University, the development of gardens in the tradition of Stanley Park, tennis courts, a multi-use games area and a new Anfield plaza development.

Plans for the original Anfield is for all four stands to be demolished, with the pitch retained as a garden of remembrance.

NEW STADIUM STATISTICS

Capacity:	60,000
New Kop Capacity:	18,000
Estimated Cost:	£300m
Scheduled Opening:	2010
Stadium Architects:	HKS

NEW STADIUM QUOTES - JULY 2007

Tom Hicks (Liverpool co-owner)
"The design is now final. It's spectacular...I think our fans will love it. It's very creative architecture, very contemporary but also unique to Liverpool. It is all centred around the Kop – it will be the symphony stage that plays to the symphony hall."

Rick Parry (Liverpool chief executive)
"We're creating a stadium that not only the club and supporters can be proud of, but something the whole city can be proud of. Liverpool as a city is on the move and deserves world-class developments like this."

Rafael Benitez (Liverpool manager)
"The facilities the new stadium will provide are going to ensure that the future of this club is a great one and this is what our fans deserve."

Steven Gerrard (Liverpool captain)
"I knew it was going to be great but after spending five minutes looking at the plans I was just completely blown away by it. We are Liverpool Football Club and we expect the best and this will be the best."

Jamie Carragher (Liverpool vice-captain)
"Everyone is excited by the new plans. They are spectacular. We've got a great stadium at the minute at Anfield, but the designers have come up with something completely unique. I've never seen a football ground like it and that's what makes it so special."

Anfield Future

Proposed shots of the club's new stadium. Top: The South East view, and above, view of the Kop

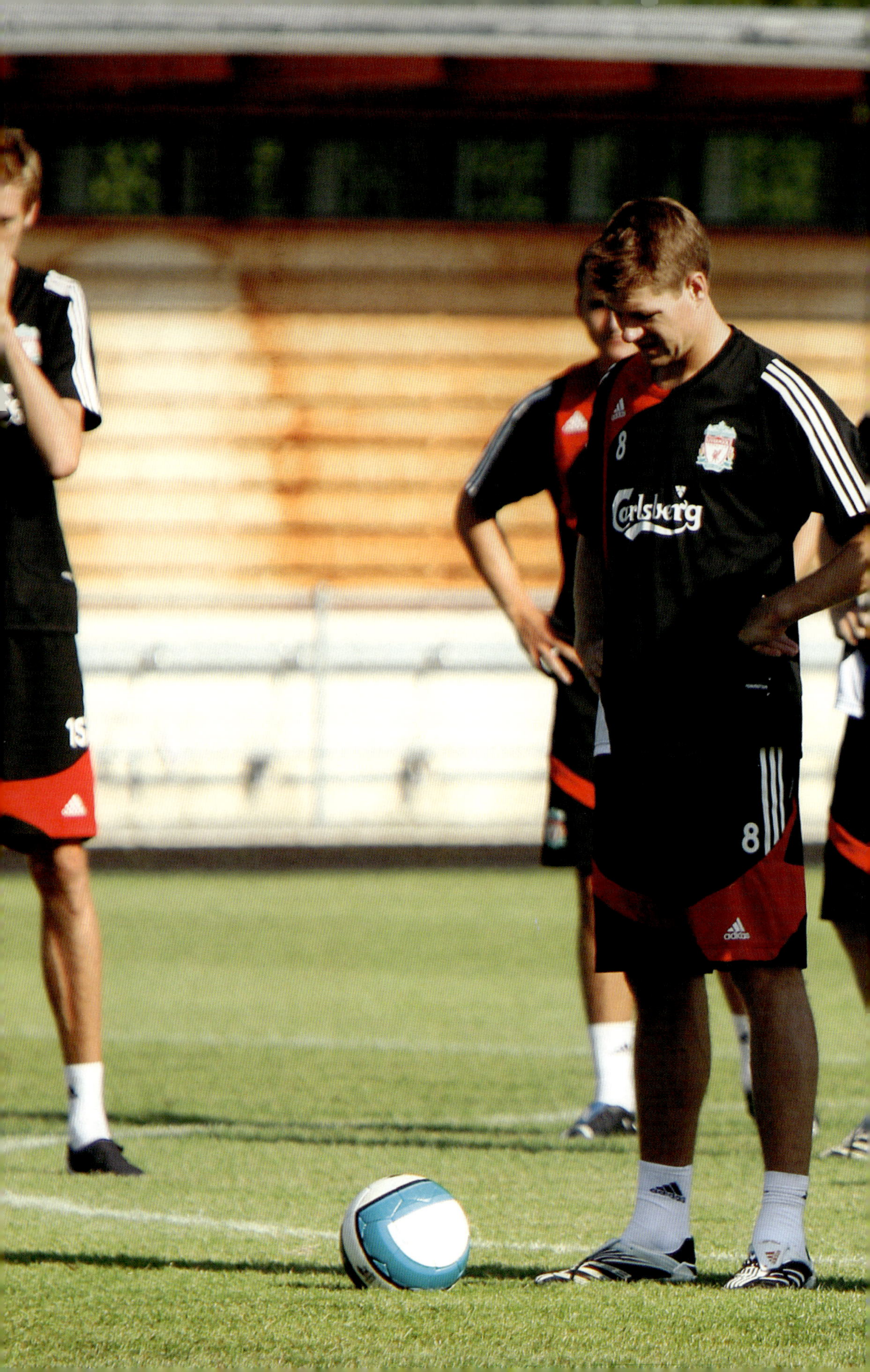
Carlsberg

THE BOSS

LIVERPOOL'S MANAGERS

RAFAEL BENITEZ	**June 2004-Present**
PHIL THOMPSON (caretaker)	October 2001-March 2002
GERARD HOULLIER	November 1998-May 2004
ROY EVANS (joint manager with Gerard Houllier)	July 1998-November 1998
ROY EVANS	January 1994-November 1998
GRAEME SOUNESS	April 1991-January 1994
RONNIE MORAN (caretaker)	February 1991-April 1991
KENNY DALGLISH	May 1985-February 1991
JOE FAGAN	May 1983-May 1985
BOB PAISLEY	July 1974-May 1983
BILL SHANKLY	December 1959-July 1974
PHIL TAYLOR	May 1956-November 1959
DON WELSH	March 1951-May 1956
GEORGE KAY	May 1936-February 1951
GEORGE PATTERSON	February 1928-May 1936
MATT McQUEEN	February 1923-February 1928
DAVID ASHWORTH	December 1919-February 1923
TOM WATSON	August 1896-May 1915
JOHN McKENNA	August 1892-August 1896

RAFAEL BENITEZ'S RECORD

Despite the disappointment of defeat in the Champions League final at the hands of AC Milan back in May, 2006/07 saw the Reds boss continue to enhance his reputation. Beginning with silverware in the form of the FA Community Shield, European progress proved smooth although early-season stumbles in the league meant a first title in 17 years was rarely within sight.

Although domestic cup disappointment overshadowed matters somewhat in January, Benitez still scooped the Premiership's Manager of the Month award. Memorable Champions League progress came against holders and favourites Barcelona, PSV Eindhoven and Chelsea before Carlos Ancelotti's side claimed revenge for 2005 in Athens.

The following statistics are a breakdown of Rafa Benitez's three seasons at the helm, and are up-to-date to the end of the 2006/07 campaign.

SEASON BY SEASON (ALL COMPETITIONS)

	Pld	W	D	L	F	A	% Wins
SEASON 2004/2005	60	31	10	19	82	56	52
SEASON 2005/2006	62	41	10	11	104	44	66
SEASON 2006/2007	58	32	10	16	90	52	55
TOTAL	**180**	**104**	**30**	**46**	**276**	**152**	**58%**

SEASON 2004/2005

	Pld	W	D	L	F	A	Pts
LEAGUE	38	17	7	14	52	41	58
FA CUP	1	0	0	1	0	1	-
LEAGUE CUP	6	5	0	1	10	4	-
EUROPEAN CUP	15	9	3	3	20	10	-
TOTAL	**60**	**31**	**10**	**19**	**82**	**56**	**-**

SEASON 2005/2006

	Pld	W	D	L	F	A	Pts
LEAGUE	38	25	7	6	57	25	82
FA CUP	6	6	0	0	20	8	-
LEAGUE CUP	1	0	0	1	1	2	-
EUROPEAN CUP	14	8	3	3	20	7	-
EUROPEAN SUPER CUP	1	1	0	0	3	1	-
WORLD CLUB C'SHIP	2	1	0	1	3	1	-
TOTAL	**62**	**41**	**10**	**11**	**104**	**44**	**-**

SEASON 2006/2007

	Pld	W	D	L	F	A	Pts
LEAGUE	38	20	8	10	57	27	68
FA CUP	1	0	0	1	1	3	-
LEAGUE CUP	3	2	0	1	8	9	-
FA COMMUNITY SHIELD	1	1	0	0	2	1	-
EUROPEAN CUP	15	9	2	4	22	12	-
TOTAL	**58**	**32**	**10**	**16**	**90**	**52**	**-**

OVERSEAS MANAGERS

With the prominent influence of foreign coaches in the top flight, three seasons seems an ideal opportunity to compare the record of Rafa Benitez with three other high-profile managers who began the season in the Barclays Premiership.
With Sven-Goran Eriksson a newcomer to English football club management at Manchester City, comparisions will be made with the long-serving Arsene Wenger at Arsenal, Jose Mourinho at Chelsea and Tottenham Hotspur's Martin Jol.

ARSENE WENGER RECORD

	Pld	W	D	L	Pts	% Wins	Points per game
LEAGUE	410	240	103	67	823	58.54	2.01
FA CUP	60	42	11	7	-	70	-
LEAGUE CUP	36	20	4	12	-	55.56	-
EUROPE	102	47	28	27	-	46.08	-
CH./CO. SHIELD	6	4	0	2	-	66.67	-
TOTAL	614	353	146	115	-	57.49	-

ARSENE WENGER: Appointed 1st October 1996
TROPHIES WON (11)
League: 1997/98, 2001/02, 2003/04
FA Cup: 1997/98, 2001/02, 2002/03, 2004/05
FA Charity Shield/ FA Community Shield: 1998, 1999, 2002, 2004

English football's longest-serving overseas manager, Wenger is also the most successful in terms of silverware. The league statistics include the record 49-match unbeaten run, taking in the whole of the 2003/04 season. The FA Cup has seen the Frenchman garner most win success – although the Gunners were downed by Liverpool during Wenger's tenure in the 2001 FA Cup final at the Millennium Stadium.

JOSE MOURINHO RECORD

	Pld	W	D	L	Pts	% Wins	Points per game
LEAGUE	114	82	23	9	269	71.93	2.36
FA CUP	16	12	2	2	-	75	-
LEAGUE CUP	13	10	2	1	-	76.92	-
EUROPE	32	16	8	8	-	50	-
CO. SHIELD	2	1	0	1	-	50	-
TOTAL	177	121	35	21	-	68.36	-

JOSE MOURINHO: Appointed 2nd June 2004
TROPHIES WON (6)
League 2004/05, 2005/06
FA Cup 2006/07
League Cup 2004/05, 2006/07
FA Community Shield: 2005

By far the biggest spender of the four managers, the former Chelsea supremo had also been the most successful in terms of win percentage and points per game. It is only really in European competition where the Portuguese fell down, winning only half his games in charge and failing to reach a final in three years of Champions League participation.

OVERSEAS MANAGERS

MARTIN JOL RECORD

	Pld	W	D	L	Pts	% Wins	Points per game
LEAGUE	102	46	26	30	164	45.10	1.61
FA CUP	13	6	4	3	-	46.15	-
LEAGUE CUP	8	4	1	3	-	50	-
EUROPE	10	8	1	1	-	80	-
TOTAL	133	64	32	37	-	48.12	-

MARTIN JOL: Appointed 8th November 2004

The only manager of the four who has failed to yield any silverware for his club, Jol has managed to stabilise and improve on-field matters at White Hart Lane. The club's run to the Uefa Cup quarter-final in 2006/07 is magnified in the above statistics.

RAFAEL BENITEZ RECORD

	Pld	W	D	L	Pts	% Wins	Points per game
LEAGUE	114	62	22	30	208	54.39	1.82
FA CUP	8	6	0	2	-	75	-
LEAGUE CUP	10	7	0	3	-	70	-
EUROPE	45	27	8	10	-	60	-
CH./CO. SHIELD	1	1	0	0	-	100	-
WORLD C. C'SHIP	2	1	0	1	-	50	-
TOTAL	180	104	30	46	-	57.78	-

RAFAEL BENITEZ: Appointed 16th June 2004
TROPHIES WON (4)
FA Cup: 2005/06
European Cup: 2004/05
European Super Cup: 2005/06
FA Community Shield: 2006

Continued improvement has been the hallmark of Rafael Benitez's Anfield spell, while a run to two Champions League finals in three seasons has rarely been matched in history. A clutch of silverware and impressive domestic cup statistics bodes well as the club look to further success.

MOST SUCCESSFUL PREMIER LEAGUE OVERSEAS MANAGER (ALL COMPETITIONS)

RATING	MANAGER	% Wins
1	MOURINHO	68.36
2	BENITEZ	57.78
3	WENGER	57.49
4	JOL	48.12

MOST SUCCESSFUL PREMIER LEAGUE OVERSEAS MANAGER (LEAGUE)

RATING	MANAGER	% Wins	POINTS PER GAME
1	MOURINHO	71.93	2.36
2	WENGER	58.54	2.01
3	BENITEZ	54.39	1.82
4	JOL	45.10	1.61

TWICE EUROPEAN FINALISTS

Rafael Benitez's achievement in leading Liverpool to a second European Cup final in three seasons in 2006/2007 is duly recognised in the following pages, as we compare the current Reds boss with some of the legends of yesteryear, as well as his compatriots who have made their mark on the competition in its current guise as the Champions League.

Only four managers have led English clubs to two or more European Cup finals, namely Bob Paisley, Brian Clough, Joe Fagan and Benitez, with the latter the only man to achieve the feat in the modern Champions League era.

BOB PAISLEY - LIVERPOOL

	Pld	W	D	L	F	A	OUTCOME
1976/1977	9	7	0	2	22	5	WON
1977/1978	7	5	0	2	17	7	WON
1980/1981	9	6	3	0	24	4	WON
TOTAL	25	18	3	4	63	16	

The most successful manager in Liverpool history and one of the most decorated in British football, Paisley led the club to three of their five European crowns. With ties played as a knockout over two legs and only the champions of each country allowed to enter the tournament (as well as the holders if they had failed to win their league), only five teams were met during each run (only four in 1977/1978, as the Reds were given a bye in round one due to their status as holders). A win percentage of 72% overall is impressive however, and the Reds' defence only let in an average of 0.64 goals a game during the three seasons of success.

BRIAN CLOUGH - NOTTINGHAM FOREST

	Pld	W	D	L	F	A	OUTCOME
1978/1979	9	6	3	0	19	7	WON
1979/1980	9	6	1	2	13	5	WON
TOTAL	18	12	4	2	32	12	

Brian Clough's legendary status at the City Ground was established in the mid-to-late 1970s, as he led unfashionable Nottingham Forest from the lower reaches of the Second Division to twice European champions, also claiming the League Championship and League Cup during this period.

JOE FAGAN - LIVERPOOL

	Pld	W	D	L	F	A	OUTCOME
1983/1984	9	8	1	0	16	3	WON
1984/1985	9	6	1	2	18	5	LOST
TOTAL	18	14	2	2	34	8	

Following on from Bob Paisley, Joe Fagan appeared to have inherited a thankless situation in the summer of 1983 following the great man's retirement. The transition was seamless however, as Fagan became the first manager to win a 'treble' with an English club, that of First Division, League Cup and European Cup. Unfortunately, a season later and defeat to Juventus at Heysel in the final and the subsequent tragedy brought a sad end for Fagan, who would step down.

RAFAEL BENITEZ - LIVERPOOL

	Pld	W	D	L	F	A	OUTCOME
2004/2005	15	9	3	3	20	10	WON
2006/2007	15	9	2	4	22	12	LOST
TOTAL	30	18	5	7	42	22	

The only one of the four managers to achieve the feat in the modern era, Benitez reached two finals playing five more fixtures than Paisley needed to win three European Cups. The statistics do not necessarily do full justice to the Spaniard too, in that games like Grazer AK at home (in 2004/2005 – Liverpool had already all but sealed third qualifying round progress) and Galatasaray away (2006/2007 – qualification from the group phases had already been confirmed), both of which were defeats, did not hinder the club's progress in either season's competition.

Bob Paisley (above) and his 'apprentice', Joe Fagan (below) – two of only four managers to lead an English club side to two European Cup finals

TWICE EUROPEAN FINALIST

The following statistics document the records of every club manager who has led their side to two UEFA Champions League finals since the competitions' inception in 1992, Rafael Benitez becoming the eighth member of that exclusive club in 2007. Interestingly, only Ottmar Hitzfeld as achieved the feat with two different clubs, whilst only Vicente Del Bosque achieved successes in each final.

FABIO CAPELLO – AC MILAN

	Pld	W	D	L	F	A	OUTCOME
1992/1993	11	10	0	1	23	2	LOST
1993/1994	12	7	5	0	21	2	WON
1994/1995	11	6	2	3	11	6	LOST
TOTAL	34	23	7	4	55	10	

The legendary Italian coach, who won the competition by guiding AC Milan to victory over Barcelona in 1994, has the distinction of winning the domestic league title with every team he has managed. His Milan side of the 1990s, nicknamed 'the invincibles', won four Serie A titles in five seasons including going an entire season unbeaten.

LOUIS VAN GAAL – AJAX AMSTERDAM

	Pld	W	D	L	F	A	OUTCOME
1994/1995	11	7	4	0	18	4	WON
1995/1996	11	8	1	2	22	3	LOST
TOTAL	22	15	5	2	40	7	

Van Gaal, who was able to mould a mainly homegrown side before the Bosman ruling really took effect, guided the Amsterdam side to victory over Capello's Milan in 1995, having also helped the club to UEFA Cup glory three years earlier. Ajax would also win a hat-trick of league titles during this period, as well as winning the Intercontinental Cup.

MARCELLO LIPPI – JUVENTUS

	Pld	W	D	L	F	A	OUTCOME
1995/1996	11	7	1	3	22	9	WON
1996/1997	11	8	2	1	21	7	LOST
1997/1998	11	6	1	4	23	15	LOST
2002/2003	17	8	3	6	30	19	LOST
TOTAL	50	29	7	14	96	50	

Another giant in Italian football, Lippi, who guided Italy to World Cup glory in 2006, led Juventus to three successive finals in his first spell with the club, before taking them to another final in the early 2000s. He won five Serie A titles and his one success in the competition came against Ajax in 1996.

OTTMAR HITZFELD – BORUSSIA DORTMUND

	Pld	W	D	L	F	A	OUTCOME
1996/1997	11	9	1	1	23	10	WON

OTTMAR HITZFELD – BAYERN MUNICH

	Pld	W	D	L	F	A	OUTCOME
1998/1999	13	7	4	2	25	12	LOST
2000/2001	17	12	3	2	24	12	WON
TOTAL	41	28	8	5	72	34	

The only manager to coach two different sides in the Champions League final, Hitzfeld, the most successful coach in German football, guided Borussia Dortmund to victory over Juventus in 1997 and then helped Bayern Munich see off Valencia in 2001. His first success with Dortmund, the 1995 Bundesliga, was the Rhine clubs' first trophy since 1966.

TWICE EUROPEAN FINALIST

VICENTE DEL BOSQUE - REAL MADRID							
	Pld	W	D	L	F	A	OUTCOME
1999/2000	17	10	3	4	35	23	WON
2001/2002	17	12	3	2	35	14	WON
TOTAL	34	22	6	6	70	37	

Having served the club since 1964 (he played against Liverpool in the European Cup final of 1981), Del Bosque rose through the club ranks to take charge for four seasons from 1999, the most successful spell in Real Madrid's modern history. Wins in the final of 2000 over Valencia and against Bayer Leverkusen make him the only man to win every Champions League final he has took charge in.

HECTOR CUPER - VALENCIA							
	Pld	W	D	L	F	A	OUTCOME
1999/2000	19	10	4	5	31	18	LOST
2000/2001	17	9	5	3	23	9	LOST
TOTAL	36	19	9	8	54	27	

Cuper enjoyed a two-year tenure with Valencia, during which he managed to reach the Champions League final in both seasons – against Real Madrid and Bayern Munich respectively, the latter opposition only winning on penalties.

CARLO ANCELOTTI - AC MILAN							
	Pld	W	D	L	F	A	OUTCOME
2002/2003	19	11	3	5	23	16	WON
2004/2005	13	9	1	3	23	9	LOST
2006/2007	15	9	3	3	23	11	WON
TOTAL	47	29	7	11	69	36	

A winner and loser against Liverpool, Ancelotti also enjoyed success in 2003 on penalties against Juventus. He is only the fifth man to win the European Cup as both a player and manager, and is viewed as one of the most successful Italian coaches of all time.

RAFAEL BENITEZ - LIVERPOOL							
	Pld	W	D	L	F	A	OUTCOME
2004/2005	15	9	3	3	20	10	WON
2006/2007	15	9	2	4	22	12	LOST
TOTAL	30	18	5	7	42	22	

Catching the eye of Liverpool in 2004 following his successful stint with Valencia which included two La Liga titles and a UEFA Cup success, victory in the Champions League in 2005 meant he was only the third man after Bob Paisley and Jose Mourinho to win the UEFA Cup and European Cup in succesive seasons. He was also the first coach to achieve this with two different clubs.

MOST SUCCESSFUL MANAGER IN UEFA CHAMPIONS LEAGUE FINAL CAMPAIGNS (TWO FINALS MINIMUM)			
RATING	MANAGER	% Wins	FINALS WON
1	HITZFELD	68.29	2001
2	VAN GAAL	68.18	1995
3	CAPELLO	67.65	1994
4	DEL BOSQUE	64.71	2000, 2002
5	ANCELOTTI	61.70	2003, 2007
6	BENITEZ	60	2005
7	LIPPI	58	1996
8	CUPER	52.78	

The above table makes for interesting reading in terms of percentage performance, although in reality win percentage is not necessarily an accurate indicator, with 'dead rubber' games being included while two-time winners Del Bosque and Ancelotti only lie in mid-table.

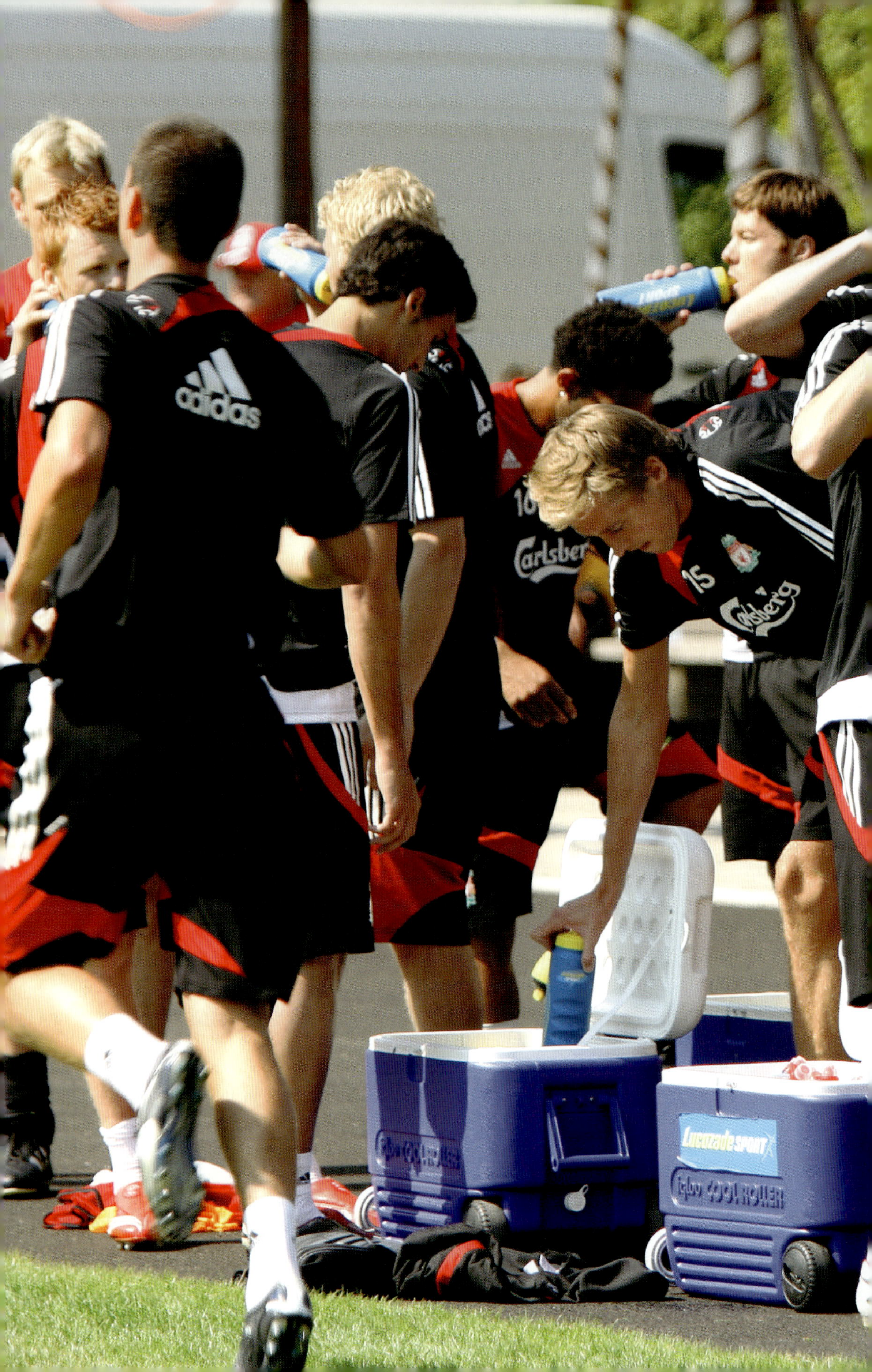
adidas
15
Carlsberg
Lucozade SPORT
Igloo COOL ROLLER

THE PLAYERS 07/08

THE SQUAD 2007/08

Scott Carson (on loan to Aston Villa)

Position	Goalkeeper
Born	Whitehaven
Age (at start of 07/08)	21
Birth date	03/09/85
Height	6ft 3ins
Other clubs	Leeds U, Sheffield Wed, Charlton Athletic
Honours	2005 Champions League, 2005 European Super Cup
Liverpool debut	05/03/05 v Newcastle United
Liverpool appearances	9
Liverpool goals	0

Charles-Hubert Itandje - Squad number 30

Position	Goalkeeper
Born	Bobigny, France
Age (at start of 07/08)	24
Birth date	02/11/82
Height	6ft 4ins
Other clubs	Red Star 93, Lens
Honours	-
Liverpool debut	-
Liverpool appearances	-
Liverpool goals	-

David Martin - Squad number 40

Position	Goalkeeper
Born	Romford
Age (at start of 07/08)	21
Birth date	22/01/86
Height	6ft 1ins
Other clubs	Milton Keynes Dons, Accrington Stanley
Honours	2006, 2007 FA Youth Cup
Liverpool debut	-
Liverpool appearances	-
Liverpool goals	-

The Players 2007/08

Jose Manuel Reina Paez - Squad number 25

Position	Goalkeeper
Born	Madrid, Spain
Age (at start of 07/08)	24
Birth date	31/08/82
Height	6ft 2ins
Other clubs	Barcelona, Villarreal
Honours	2004, 2005 UEFA Intertoto Cup, 2005 European Super Cup, 2006 FA Cup, 2006 FA Community Shield
Liverpool debut	13/07/05 v TNS
Liverpool appearances	104
Liverpool goals	0
International caps	6 (0 goals)

Daniel Agger - Squad number 5

Position	Central Defence
Born	Hvidovre, Denmark
Age (at start of 07/08)	22
Birth date	12/12/84
Height	6ft 3ins
Other clubs	Rosenhoj, Brondby
Honours	2005 Danish League, 2005 Danish Cup, 2006 FA Comm. Shield
Liverpool debut	01/02/06 v Birmingham
Liverpool appearances	43 + 4 as substitute
Liverpool goals	3
International caps	15 (2 goals)

Alvaro Arbeloa - Squad number 17

Positions	Right/Central Defence
Born	Salamanca, Spain
Age (at start of 07/08)	24
Birth date	17/01/83
Height	6ft 0ins
Other clubs	Real Madrid, Deportivo La Coruna
Honours	-
Liverpool debut	10/02/07 v Newcastle
Liverpool appearances	12 + 2 as substitute
Liverpool goals	1

31

Fabio Aurelio - Squad number 12

Position	Left Defence
Born	Sao Carlos, Brazil
Age (at start of 07/08)	27
Birth date	24/09/79
Height	5ft 8ins
Other clubs	Sao Paulo, Valencia
Honours	1998, 2000 Sao Paulo State C'ship, 2002, 2004 Spanish League, 2004 European Super Cup, 2006 FA Community Shield
Liverpool debut	13/08/06 v Chelsea
Liverpool appearances	14 + 11 as substitute
Liverpool goals	0

Jamie Carragher - Squad number 23

Position	Central Defence
Born	Bootle, Liverpool
Age (at start of 07/08)	29
Birth date	28/01/78
Height	6ft 1ins
Honours	2001, 2006 FA Cup, 2001, 2003 Lge Cup, 2001 UEFA Cup, 2001, 2005 European Super Cup, 2001, 2006 FA Community Shield, 2005 Champions Lge
Liverpool debut	08/01/97 v M'boro
Liverpool appearances	450 + 18 as substitute
Liverpool goals	4
International caps	34 (0 goals)

Stephen Darby - Squad number 39

Position	Right Defence
Born	Liverpool
Age (at start of 07/08)	18
Birth date	06/10/88
Height	5ft 8ins
Other clubs	-
Honours	FA Youth Cup 2006, 2007
Liverpool debut	-
Liverpool appearances	-
Liverpool goals	-

The Players 2007/08

Steve Finnan - Squad number 3

Position	Right Defence
Born	Limerick, Eire
Age (at start of 07/08)	31
Birth date	20/04/76
Height	6ft 0ins
Other clubs	Welling, Birmingham, Notts County, Fulham
Honours	2002 UEFA Intertoto Cup, 2005 Champions Lge, 2005 European Super Cup, 2006 FA Cup, 2006 FA Comm. Shield
Liverpool debut	17/08/03 v Chelsea
Liverpool appearances	169 + 13 as substitute
Liverpool goals	1
International caps	44 (1 goal)

Jack Hobbs - Squad number 46

Position	Central Defence
Born	Portsmouth
Age (at start of 07/08)	19
Birth date	18/08/88
Height	6ft 3ins
Other club	Lincoln City
Honours	2006 FA Youth Cup
Liverpool debut	-
Liverpool appearances	-
Liverpool goals	-

Sami Hyypia - Squad number 4

Position	Defence
Born	Porvoo, Finland
Age (at start of 07/08)	33
Birth date	07/10/73
Height	6ft 4ins
Other clubs	Pallo-Pelkot, Ku Mu, My Pa Anjalankoski, Willem II Tilburg
Honours	1992, 1995 Finnish Cup, 2001, 2006 FA Cup, 2001, 2003 Lge Cup, 2001 UEFA Cup, 2001, 2005 Euro Super Cup, 2001, 2006 FA Comm. Shield, 2005 Cham. Lge
Liverpool debut	07/08/99 at Sheff Wed
Liverpool appearances	400 + 1 as substitute
Liverpool goals	29
International caps	83 (5 goals)

Emiliano Insua - Squad number 48

Position	Left Defence
Born	Buenos Aires, Argentina
Age (at start of 07/08)	18
Birth date	07/01/89
Height	5ft 8ins
Other club	Boca Juniors
Honours	-
Liverpool debut	28/04/07 v Portsmouth
Liverpool appearances	2 + 0 as substitute
Liverpool goals	0

Miki Roque (on loan to Xerez)

Positions	Right/Central Defence
Born	Tremp, Catalonia, Spain
Age (at start of 07/08)	19
Birth date	08/07/88
Height	6ft 1ins
Other clubs	Lleida, Oldham Athletic
Honours	2006 FA Youth Cup
Liverpool debut	05/12/06 v Galatasaray
Liverpool appearances	0 + 1 as substitute
Liverpool goals	0

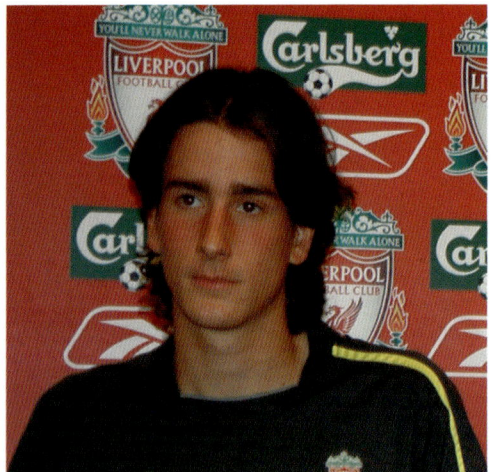

James Smith (on loan to Stockport County)

Positions	Left/Central Defence
Born	Liverpool
Age (at start of 07/08)	21
Birth date	17/10/85
Height	5ft 10ins
Other clubs	Ross County
Honours	-
Liverpool debut	25/10/06 v Reading
Liverpool appearances	0 + 1 as substitute
Liverpool goals	0

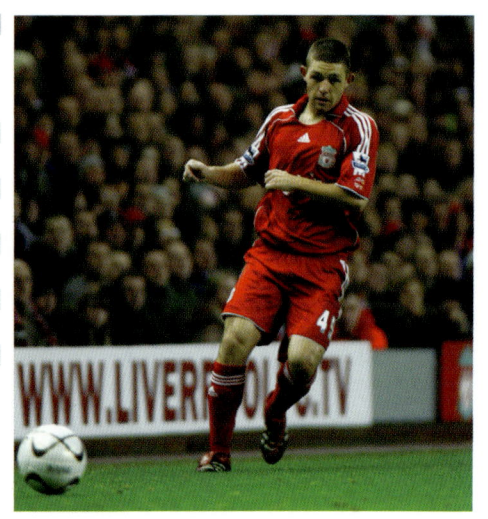

The Players 2007/08

Robbie Threlfall - Squad number 44

Position	Defence
Born	Liverpool
Age (at start of 07/08)	18
Birth date	25/11/88
Height	5ft 8ins
Other clubs	-
Honours	2006, 2007 FA Youth Cup
Liverpool debut	-
Liverpool appearances	-
Liverpool goals	-

Xabi Alonso - Squad number 14

Position	Central Midfield
Born	Tolosa, Spain
Age (at start of 07/08)	25
Birth date	25/11/81
Height	6ft 0ins
Other clubs	Eibar, Real Sociedad
Honours	2005 Champions League, 2005 European Super Cup, 2006 FA Cup, 2006 FA Community Shield
Liverpool debut	29/08/04 v Bolton W.
Liverpool appearances	117 + 19 as substitute
Liverpool goals	12
International caps	37 (1 goal)

Paul Anderson (on loan to Swansea City)

Position	Right Midfield
Born	Leicester
Age (at start of 07/08)	19
Birth date	23/07/88
Height	5ft 9ins
Other club	Hull City
Honours	2006 FA Youth Cup
Liverpool debut	-
Liverpool appearances	-
Liverpool goals	-

Yossi Benayoun - Squad number 11

Position	Right Midfield
Born	Dimona, Israel
Age (at start of 07/08)	27
Birth date	05/05/80
Height	5ft 8ins
Other clubs	Hapoel Be'er Sheva, Maccabi Haifa, Racing Santander, West Ham
Honours	2001, 2002 Israeli League
Liverpool debut	-
Liverpool appearances	-
Liverpool goals	-
International caps	58 (14 goals)

Ryan Flynn - Squad number 36

Position	Central Midfield
Born	Falkirk, Scotland
Age (at start of 07/08)	18
Birth date	04/09/88
Height	5ft 10ins
Other club	Falkirk
Honours	2006, 2007 FA Youth Cup
Liverpool debut	-
Liverpool appearances	-
Liverpool goals	-

Steven Gerrard MBE - Squad number 8

Positions	Central/Right Midfield
Born	Whiston, Merseyside
Age (at start of 07/08)	27
Birth date	30/05/80
Height	6ft 0ins
Honours	2001, 2006 FA Cup, 2001, 2003 Lge Cup, 2001 UEFA Cup, 2001 European Super Cup, 2001, 2006 FA Community Shield, 2005 Champions League
Liverpool debut	29/11/98 v Blackburn Rovers
Liverpool appearances	353 + 34 as substtute
Liverpool goals	75
International caps	57 (12 goals)

The Players 2007/08

Danny Guthrie (on loan to Bolton Wanderers)

Position	Central Midfield
Born	Shrewsbury
Age (at start of 07/08)	20
Birth date	18/04/87
Height	5ft 7ins
Other club	Southampton
Honours	-
Liverpool debut	25/10/06 v Reading
Liverpool appearances	2 + 5 as substitute
Liverpool goals	0

Adam Hammill (on loan to Southampton)

Position	Left Midfield
Born	Liverpool
Age (at start of 07/08)	19
Birth date	25/01/88
Height	5ft 8ins
Other club	Dunfermline Athletic
Honours	2006 FA Youth Cup
Liverpool debut	-
Liverpool appearances	-
Liverpool goals	-

Besian Idrizaj (on loan to Crystal Palace)

Position	Left Midfield
Born	Baden, Austria
Age (at start of 07/08)	19
Birth date	12/10/87
Height	6ft 2ins
Other clubs	Linzer ASK, Luton Town
Honours	-
Liverpool debut	-
Liverpool appearances	-
Liverpool goals	-

Harry Kewell – Squad number 7

Position	Left Midfield
Born	Smithfield, Sydney, Australia
Age (at start of 07/08)	28
Birth date	22/09/78
Height	5ft 11ins
Other club	Leeds United
Honours	2005 Champions League, 2006 FA Cup
Liverpool debut	17/08/03 v Chelsea
Liverpool appearances	100 + 24 as substitute
Liverpool goals	16
International caps	28 (9 goals)

Lucas Leiva – Squad number 21

Position	Central Midfield
Born	Dourados, Brazil
Age (at start of 07/08)	20
Birth date	09/01/87
Height	5ft 10ins
Other club	Gremio
Honours	2005 Brazilian Serie B, 2006, 2007 Rio Grande do Sul State Championship
Liverpool debut	-
Liverpool appearances	-
Liverpool goals	-

Sebastian Leto – Squad number 33

Position	Left Midfield
Born	Buenos Aires, Argentina
Age (at start of 07/08)	20
Birth date	30/08/86
Height	6ft 2ins
Other club	Club Atletico Lanus
Liverpool debut	-
Liverpool appearances	-
Liverpool goals	-

The Players 2007/08

Javier Mascherano - Squad number 20

Position	Central Midfield
Born	San Lorenzo, Argentina
Age (at start of 07/08)	23
Birth date	08/06/84
Height	5ft 9ins
Other clubs	River Plate, Corinthians, West Ham
Honours	2004 Argentine Lge (Closing C'ship), 2005 Brazilian Lge
Liverpool debut	24/02/07 v Sheff Utd
Liverpool appearances	11 + 0 as substitute
Liverpool goals	0
International caps	30 (2 goals)

Lee Peltier (on loan to Yeovil Town)

Position	Right Midfield
Born	Aigburth, Liverpool
Age (at start of 07/08)	20
Birth date	11/12/86
Height	5ft 10ins
Other club	Hull City
Honours	-
Liverpool debut	25/10/06 v Reading
Liverpool appearances	4
Liverpool goals	0

Jermaine Pennant - Squad number 16

Position	Right Midfield
Born	Nottingham
Age (at start of 07/08)	24
Birth date	15/01/83
Height	5ft 9ins
Other clubs	Notts County, Arsenal, Watford, Leeds United, Birmingham City
Honours	2004, 2006 FA Community Shield
Liverpool debut	09/08/06 v Macc. Haifa
Liverpool appearances	33 + 19 as substitute
Liverpool goals	1

Ray Putterill - Squad number 35

Position	Left Midfield
Born	Liverpool
Age (at start of 07/08)	18
Birth date	02/03/89
Height	5ft 8ins
Other clubs	-
Honours	2007 FA Youth Cup
Liverpool debut	-
Liverpool appearances	-
Liverpool goals	-

John Arne Riise - Squad number 6

Position	Left Midfield
Born	Molde, Norway
Age (at start of 07/08)	26
Birth date	24/09/80
Height	6ft 1ins
Other clubs	Aalesunds F.K., Monaco
Honours	2000 French League, 2001, 2005 European Super Cup, 2001, 2006 FA Comm. Shield, 2003 Lge Cup, 2005 Champs. Lge, 2006 FA Cup
Liverpool debut	12/08/01 v Man Utd
Liverpool appearances	265 + 39 as substitute
Liverpool goals	31
International caps	61 (6 goals)

Mohamed Sissoko - Squad number 22

Position	Central Midfield
Born	Mont-Saint-Aignan, France
Age (at start of 07/08)	22
Birth date	22/01/85
Height	6ft 2ins
Other clubs	Auxerre, Valencia
Honours	2004 Spanish League, 2004 UEFA Cup, 2004, 2005 European Super Cup, 2006 FA Cup, 2006 FA Comm. Shield
Liverpool debut	26/07/05 v FBK Kaunas
Liverpool appearances	62 + 11 as substitute
Liverpool goals	0
International caps (Mali)	10 (1 goal)

The Players 2007/08

Jay Spearing - Squad number 34

Position	Central Midfield
Born	Wirral
Age (at start of 07/08)	18
Birth date	25/11/88
Height	5ft 6ins
Other clubs	-
Honours	2006, 2007 FA Youth Cup
Liverpool debut	-
Liverpool appearances	-
Liverpool goals	-

Ryan Babel - Squad number 19

Position	Forward
Born	Amsterdam, Holland
Age (at start of 07/08)	20
Birth date	19/12/86
Height	6ft 0ins
Other club	Ajax
Honours	2005, 2006 Dutch Super Cup, 2006, 2007 Dutch Cup, 2007 UEFA U21 Championship
Liverpool debut	-
Liverpool appearances	-
Liverpool goals	-
International caps	14 (4 goals)

Peter Crouch - Squad number 15

Position	Centre Forward
Born	Macclesfield
Age (at start of 07/08)	26
Birth date	30/01/81
Height	6ft 7ins
Other clubs	Tottenham H, QPR, Portsmouth, Aston Villa, Norwich City, Southampton
Honours	2006 FA Cup, 2006 FA Community Shield
Liverpool debut	26/07/05 v FBK Kaunas
Liverpool appearances	72 + 26 as substitute
Liverpool goals	31
International caps	19 (12 goals)

Nabil El Zhar - Squad number 42

Position	Forward
Born	Ales, France
Age (at start of 07/08)	20
Birth date	27/08/86
Height	5ft 9ins
Other clubs (youth)	Olympique Ales, Nimes Olympique, AS Saint-Etienne
Honours	-
Liverpool debut	29/11/06 v Portsmouth
Liverpool appearances	0 + 3 as substitute
Liverpool goals	0

Dirk Kuyt - Squad number 18

Position	Centre Forward
Born	Katwijk, Holland
Age (at start of 07/08)	27
Birth date	22/07/80
Height	6ft 0ins
Other clubs	FC Utrecht, Feyenoord
Honours	2003 Dutch Cup
Liverpool debut	26/08/06 v West Ham
Liverpool appearances	38 + 10 as substitute
Liverpool goals	14
International caps	31 (5 goals)

Craig Lindfield - Squad number 38

Position	Centre Forward
Born	Wirral
Age (at start of 07/08)	18
Birth date	07/09/88
Height	6ft 0ins
Other clubs	-
Honours	2006, 2007 FA Youth Cup
Liverpool debut	-
Liverpool appearances	-
Liverpool goals	-

The Players 2007/08

Fernando Torres - Squad number 9

Position	Centre Forward
Born	Madrid, Spain
Age (at start of 07/08)	23
Birth date	20/03/84
Height	6ft 1ins
Other club	Atletico Madrid
Honours	2002 Spanish Second Division, 2002 UEFA U19 Championship
Liverpool debut	-
Liverpool appearances	-
Liverpool goals	-
International caps	42 (14 goals)

Andriy Voronin - Squad number 10

Position	Centre Forward
Born	Odessa, Ukraine
Age (at start of 07/08)	28
Birth date	21/07/79
Height	5ft 10ins
Other clubs	Borussia Moenchengladbach, Mainz, Cologne, Bayer Leverkusen
Honours	-
Liverpool debut	-
Liverpool appearances	-
Liverpool goals	-
International caps	45 (5 goals)

RESERVES

RESERVES LEAGUE NORTH TABLE 2006/07

		Pld	W	D	L	F	A	Pts
1	Bolton	18	10	3	5	21	16	33
2	Man Utd	18	9	4	5	24	17	31
3	Middlesboro	18	9	3	6	31	25	30
4	Man City	18	9	2	7	27	24	29
5	**Liverpool**	**18**	**8**	**2**	**8**	**24**	**19**	**26**
6	Blackburn R.	18	7	5	6	16	15	26
7	Sheff Utd	18	8	2	8	23	23	26
8	Newcastle U.	18	6	5	7	29	29	23
9	Everton	18	3	7	8	18	25	16
10	Wigan Ath.	18	2	5	11	8	28	11

Craig Lindfield - top scorer in 06/07

RESERVES LEAGUE RESULTS 2006/07

Date	Opponent	H/A	Result*
29.08.06	Manchester City	H	0-1
03.10.06	Newcastle United	H	1-4
10.10.06	Everton	A	1-2
19.10.06	Middlesbrough	H	2-3
01.11.06	Wigan Athletic	A	2-0
11.12.06	Blackburn Rovers	A	1-1
20.12.06	Bolton Wanderers	A	0-1
10.01.07	Sheffield United	H	1-0
01.02.07	Manchester United	A	0-0
22.02.07	Bolton Wanderers	H	1-0
06.03.07	Middlesbrough	A	0-1
13.03.07	Wigan Athletic	H	2-0
22.03.07	Blackburn Rovers	H	4-1
26.03.07	Newcastle United	A	3-0
02.04.07	Manchester City	A	1-3
10.04.07	Sheffield United	A	0-2
19.04.07	Manchester United	H	0-1
30.04.07	Everton	H	3-1

*Liverpool score shown first

RESERVES APPEARANCES & GOALS 2006/07

	Appearances	Goals
Paul Anderson	15	3
Godwin Antwi	7	0
Alvaro Arbeloa	1	0
Fabio Aurelio	3	0
Charlie Barnett	3	0
Jordy Brouwer	7	0
Michael Burns	2	0
Stephen Darby	12	0
Jerzy Dudek	3	0
Francisco Duran	2	0
Nabil El Zhar	14	3
Ryan Flynn	11	0
Robbie Fowler	2	2
Danny Guthrie	9	1
Adam Hammill	5	0
Jack Hobbs	11	1
Ronald Huth	7	0
Besian Idrizaj	8	4
Emiliano Insua	9	0
Harry Kewell	1	0
Craig Lindfield	14	5
David Martin	8	0
Javier Mascherano	1	0
Daniele Padelli	7	0
Gabriel Paletta	8	0
Lee Peltier	7	0
Jermaine Pennant	2	1
Ray Putterill	3	1
David Roberts	3	0
Miki Roque	9	0
Jimmy Ryan	1	0
Reneil Sappleton	1	1
James Smith	6	0
Jay Spearing	7	1
Robbie Threlfall	11	0
Bolo Zenden	4	1

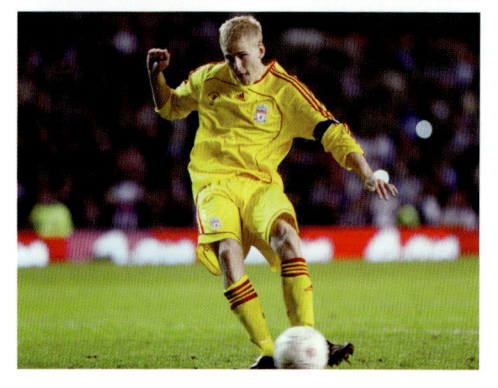

Robbie Threlfall - Gunning for the first team

FA PREMIER RESERVE LEAGUE NORTHERN SECTION FIXTURES 2007/08

SEPTEMBER

04 Middlesbrough (A)
19 Wigan Athletic (A) - 7.30pm KO

OCTOBER

02 Sunderland (H)
11 Manchester United (A)
25 Newcastle United (H)

NOVEMBER

06 Bolton Wanderers (H)
13 Blackburn Rovers (H)
27 Manchester City (A)

DECEMBER

04 Everton (H)

JANUARY

07 Blackburn Rovers (A)
22 Wigan Athletic (H)

FEBRUARY

13 Sunderland (A)
18 Newcastle United (A)
26 Manchester United (H)

MARCH

05 Bolton Wanderers (A)
11 Manchester City (H)
18 Middlesbrough (H)

APRIL

01 Everton (A)

All fixtures 7pm, subject to change.

Please note reserve play-off final is scheduled for Wednesday 5th May.

Copyright © and Database Right 2007 The FA Premier League Ltd. All rights reserved. Compiled in association with Atos Origin. All fixtures are subject to change. Home fixtures to be played at the Halliwell Jones Stadium, Warrington Wolves RLFC, subject to change. Please check on our website www.liverpoolfc.tv for up to date information on whether the match is still being played on the above scheduled date.

Nikolay Mihaylov (left) and Francisco Duran (right) - Overseas stars looking to catch the eye

THE ACADEMY

Despite the inconsistencies in league performance during the 2006/07 campaign, the U18s more than made up for it in the FA Youth Cup, as the young Reds became only the fifth club to retain the trophy courtesy of a penalty shoot-out triumph over Manchester United at Old Trafford.

Having been beaten 2-1 at Anfield having led through Craig Lindfield's strike, the Reds' youngsters edged the second leg 1-0 courtesy of a goal by Robbie Threlfall. After extra time failed to separate the sides (away goals do not count double in the competition), Liverpool converted all four of their spot-kicks to take the trophy 4-3 on penalties, David Martin saving one of the two United kicks missed.

Please note that home games are played at the Kirkby Academy (see fixtures on page 48).

FA PREMIER ACADEMY 2006/07 GROUP C

	P	W	D	L	F	A	Pts
1 Man City	28	21	3	4	63	28	66
2 Bolton	28	14	6	8	38	26	48
3 Blackburn	28	13	7	8	47	34	46
4 Man Utd	28	12	4	12	51	42	40
5 West Brom	28	12	2	14	44	45	38
6 Everton	28	6	13	9	38	38	31
7 Crewe	28	9	3	16	44	57	30
8 Liverpool	**28**	**7**	**8**	**13**	**29**	**37**	**29**
9 Wolves	28	6	7	15	30	52	25
7 Stoke	28	3	5	20	14	53	14

UNDER-18s' LEAGUE RESULTS 2006/07

Date	Opponent	H/A	Result*
19.08.06	Chelsea	H	0-1
26.08.06	Crystal Palace	A	1-3
02.09.06	Leeds United	H	1-1
09.09.06	Sunderland	A	1-3
16.09.06	Barnsley	H	0-1
23.09.06	Bolton Wanderers	A	1-1
30.09.06	Wolves	H	1-1
07.10.06	Everton	A	0-0
14.10.06	Crewe Alexandra	H	1-2
21.10.06	Manchester City	A	0-4
04.11.06	Manchester United	H	1-0
11.11.06	West Bromwich Albion	A	1-1
18.11.06	Blackburn Rovers	A	1-0
02.12.06	Stoke City	H	3-0
09.12.06	Crewe Alexandra	A	3-1
06.01.07	Manchester City	H	1-2
20.01.07	West Bromwich Albion	H	0-1
03.02.07	Blackburn Rovers	H	0-0
17.02.07	Bolton Wanderers	H	0-2
24.02.07	Wolves	A	3-0
03.03.07	Everton	H	1-1
15.03.07	Sheffield Wednesday	H	0-1
24.03.07	Middlesbrough	A	2-1
30.03.07	Manchester United	A	0-1
01.04.07	Sheffield United	A	0-1
21.04.07	Newcastle United	H	4-3
28.04.07	Stoke City	A	2-2
05.05.07	Huddersfield Town	A	1-3**

* Liverpool score shown first
** Played as U15 fixture

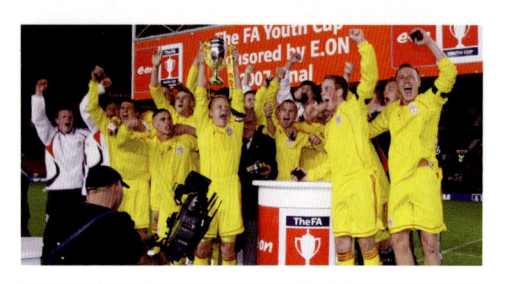

UNDER-18s APPEARANCES & GOALS 2006/07

	Appearances	Goals
Astrit Ajdarevic	4	0
Ali Asgari	1	0
Mattone Awang	13	1
Charlie Barnett	23	3
Paul Barratt	19	0
Michael Burns	19	0
Stephen Behan	20	0
Michael Collins	16	1
Stephen Darby	7	0
Nathan Eccleston	2	0
Morgan Evans	2	0
Ryan Flynn	8	4
Laurence Gaughan	19	0
Martin Hansen	6	0
Jack Hobbs	1	0
Steven Irwin	2	0
Sean Highdale	3	0
Martin Kelly	4	0
Joe Kennedy	1	0
Lawrence	1	0
Craig Lindfield	6	3
Josh Mimms	8	0
Shane O'Connor	13	0
Ben Parsonage	17	1
Jonathon Pringle	17	1
Ray Putterill	19	4
David Roberts	18	0
John Routledge	14	0
Jimmy Ryan	13	1
Michael Scott	11	2
Jay Spearing	23	1
Robbie Threlfall	9	1
Ryan Wignall	20	1
Lee Woodward	13	4

FA YOUTH CUP WINNERS 2007

Round 3: West Brom. 1-2 Liverpool (AET)
Liverpool goalscorers: Threlfall 1, Putterill 92

Round 4 Liverpool 2-0 Chelsea
Liverpool goalscorers: Ryan 30, Putterill 71

Round 5: Liverpool 1-0 Reading
Liverpool goalscorer: Ryan 22

Round 6: Sheffield United 1-3 Liverpool
Liverpool goalscorers: Flynn 34, Putterill 52, Darby 65

Semi-Final, 1st Leg: Newcastle United 2-4 Liverpool
Liverpool goalscorers: Barnett 24, Lindfield 40, Flynn 60, 68

Semi-Final, 2nd Leg: Liverpool 3-1 Newcastle United (Won 7-3 on agg.)
Liverpool goalscorers: Lindfield 48, 57, Ryan 83

Final, 1st Leg: Liverpool 1-2 Manchester United
Liverpool goalscorer: Lindfield 16

Teams:
Liverpool: Hansen, Darby, Burns, Spearing (captain,) Threlfall, Barnett, Ryan, Flynn, Lindfield, Woodward (Eccleston), Putterill.
Subs not used: Irwin, Roberts, Highdale, Parsonage.

Manchester United: Zieler, Eckersley, Evans, Strickland, Chester, Drinkwater (Bryan), Welbeck, Hewson, Brandy (James), Fagan, Galbraith.
Subs not used: McCormack, Woods, Moffatt.

Final, 2nd Leg: Manchester United 0-1 Liverpool (AET)
Liverpool goalscorer: Threlfall 55
(Liverpool won 4-3 on penalties after 2-2 on aggregate)

Penalties: (United took first kick)

United: Eikrem (saved); Fagan (scored); Chester (scored); Galbraith (scored); Hewson (missed).

Liverpool: Putterill (scored); Lindfield (scored); Flynn (scored); Threlfall (scored).

Teams:
Manchester United: Zieler, Eckersley, Evans (Moffatt), Strickland, Chester, Drinkwater (Bryan), Welbeck (Eikrem), Hewson, Brandy, Fagan, Galbraith.
Subs not used: McCormack, Woods.

Liverpool: Roberts, Darby, Burns, Spearing (captain,) Threlfall, Barnett, Ryan (Woodward), Flynn, Ajdarevic (Irwin), Lindfield, Putterill.
Subs not used: Mimms, Highdale, Parsonage.

FA PREMIER ACADEMY LEAGUE FIXTURES 2007/08

AUGUST
18 Aston Villa (A)
25 Sunderland (H)

SEPTEMBER
01 Huddersfield Town (H)
08 Nottingham Forest (A)
15 Sheffield Wednesday (H)
22 Middlesbrough (A)
29 Stoke City (A)

OCTOBER
06 Blackburn Rovers (H)
13 Wolverhampton W. (A)
20 Crewe Alexandra (H)
27 West Bromwich Albion (H)

NOVEMBER
03 Everton (H)
10 Bolton Wanderers (A)
17 Manchester City (H)

DECEMBER
01 Manchester United (A)
08 Crewe Alexandra (A)
15 West Bromwich Albion (H)

JANUARY
05 Bolton Wanderers (H)
12 Everton (A)
19 Manchester United (H)
26 Manchester City (A)

FEBRUARY
09 Stoke City (H)
16 Blackburn Rovers (A)

MARCH
01 Wolverhampton W. (H)
15 Barnsley (H)
29 Newcastle United (A)

APRIL
05 Derby County (H)
12 Leeds United (A)

All fixtures 11am, subject to change.

Dressing room celebrations following the young Reds' second successive FA Youth Cup success

LIVERPOOL LADIES

An impressive 2006/07 campaign saw Keith Cliffe's side gain promotion to the FA Women's Premier League after winning the Northern Division. At one stage the Reds trailed eventual runners-up Lincoln City by 12 points before storming back, taking the title by five points.

Cliffe decided to step down in the close season and was replaced by David Bradley, who will be aiming to consolidate in the top flight. On taking over, he declared: "No one is more obsessed with moving the club forward than me. I see the players as the most important part of the club."

Last season's top scorer, former England U19 international Chantelle Parry will be looking to be amongst the goals again, while the Reds have six internationals in their squad – all Welsh, namely Nicky Davies, Natalie Holt, Kelly Davies, Jade Thomas, Cheryl Foster and Jo Edwards.

A new season also sees a change in venue, with the club swapping Prescot's Valerie Park for the Ashley Travel Stadium in Skelmersdale.

SQUAD 2007/08

GOALKEEPERS

Nicky Davies, Kim Griffiths, Hannah Williams

DEFENDERS

Vicky Jones, Natalie Holt, Gayle Formston (captain), Jo Traynor, Betty Old, Louise Wright, Amie Fleming, Lisa Topping, Katie Nocton, Caroline Charlton

MIDFIELDERS

Tammy Byrne, Gill Hart, Kelly Jones, Micha Deane, Hannah Twig, Molly McCann, Emma Cantrell, Sophie Jones, Rachel Snellgrove, Natalie Sage, Lucy Osborne, Jeannie McGonagle

FORWARDS

Chantelle Parry, Cheryl Foster, Jo Edwards, Kelly Davies, Antonia Allen, Danielle Sheen, Jade Thomas, Shelley James

FA WOMEN'S PREMIER LEAGUE FIXTURES 2007/08

AUGUST
19 Bristol Academy (A)

SEPTEMBER
02 Cardiff City (A)
09 Watford (H)
16 Birmingham City (A)
23 Bristol Academy (H)
26 Everton (A)
30 Leeds United (FAPLC) (H)

OCTOBER
07 Chelsea (A)
10 Blackburn Rovers (H)
21 Arsenal (A)
28 Watford (A)
31 Everton (H)

NOVEMBER
11 Doncaster Rovers Belles (H)
14 Blackburn Rovers (A)
18 Charlton Athletic (A)
25 Cardiff City (H)

DECEMBER
02 Chelsea (H)
09 Leeds United (A)
16 Arsenal (H)

JANUARY
06 FA CUP ROUND 4
20 Leeds United (H)
27 Charlton Athletic/FAC 5 (H)

FEBRUARY
10 FA CUP ROUND 6

MARCH
09 FA CUP SEMI-FINAL

MAY
05 FA CUP FINAL

TBA
Doncaster Rovers Belles (A)
Birmingham City (H)

Fixtures subject to change. Home fixtures kick-off at 2pm subject to change.

16
arlsberg

SISSOKO
22
AGGER
5
12
orange.co.uk

avea
Carlsberg

The FA Com
The FA

TOP 10 MOMENTS 06/07

10

Perfect start

The Reds overcame Chelsea in the FA Community Shield in August, the 10th time the Reds have lifted the silverware. John Arne Riise and Peter Crouch were the scorers in Cardiff.

9

Xabi does it again

Having scored from 67 yards against Luton Town in the FA Cup in 2006, the Spanish star did it again from his own half, this time against Newcastle in the league.

Top 10 Moments 2006/07

8

Turkish delight

Peter Crouch would finish the season as Liverpool's top scorer in Europe, and his second in the 3-2 Group C victory over Galatasaray was the best of the lot. The striker produced a spectacular scissor kick from Steve Finnan's cross, right in front of The Kop.

7

Goal of the season

Daniel Agger's stunning 35-yard strike against West Ham back in August was named BBC *Match Of The Day*'s Goal of the Month and the club's Goal of the Season.

6 God leaves his mark

A routine 4-0 success over Sheffield United on February 24 will remain memorable in Anfield folklore as the day Robbie Fowler scored his final goals for the club, both penalties at The Kop End – fittingly his first there, and last, in his second spell.

5 Dutch delight

A tricky Champions League quarter-final, first leg at PSV Eindhoven appeared a strong test for the Reds – three goals later, and they had all but booked a berth in the last four.

Top 10 Moments 2006/07

4

Pennant first

There's rarely a bad time to score your first Liverpool goal, and so it proved for Jermaine Pennant, whose superb volley sealed a 2-0 triumph over Chelsea.

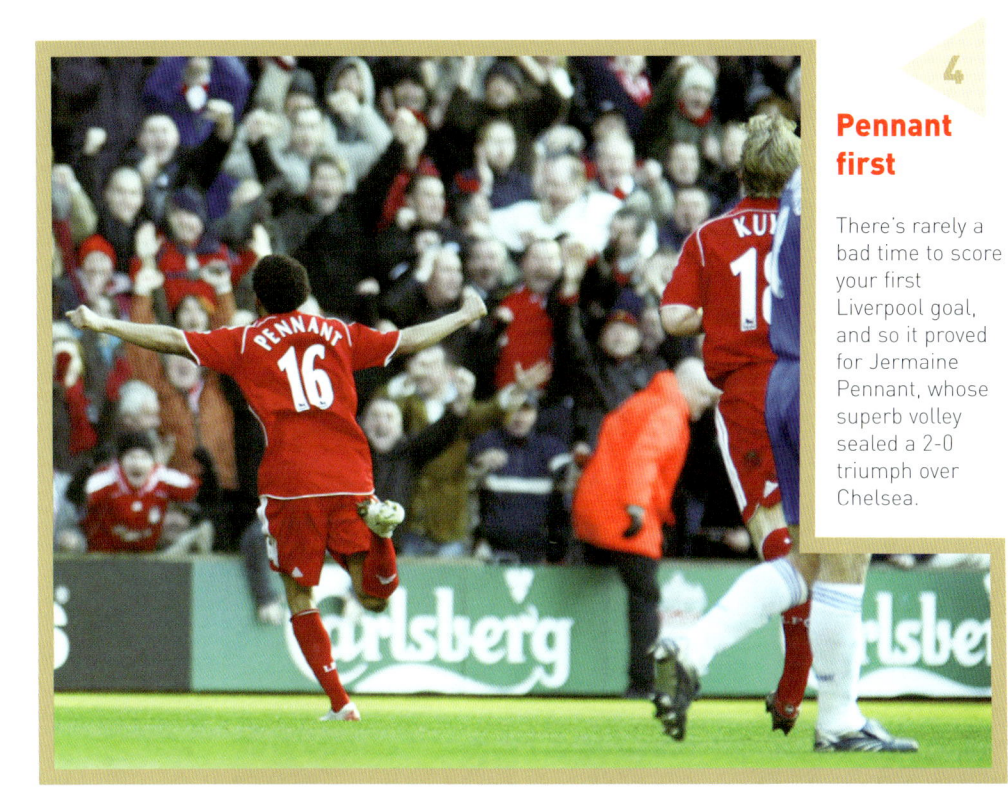

3

Crouch at the treble

The big Liverpool frontman netted his first hat-trick at club level to make Arsenal pay for the Reds' domestic cup disappointments, Rafa's men eventually running out 4-1 winners.

55

Liverpool FC : The Official Guide 2008

2

European champions stunned

The Reds came from behind to down favourites Barcelona 2-1 at the Nou Camp in the first leg of their Champions League last 16 tie.

1 Reina, penalty king

Although Athens ultimately proved a let down, the Champions League semi-final, at least provided another Anfield glory night. A 1-0 win levelled the aggregate scores, and then victory on penalties was secured thanks to Pepe Reina saving two Chelsea spot-kicks.

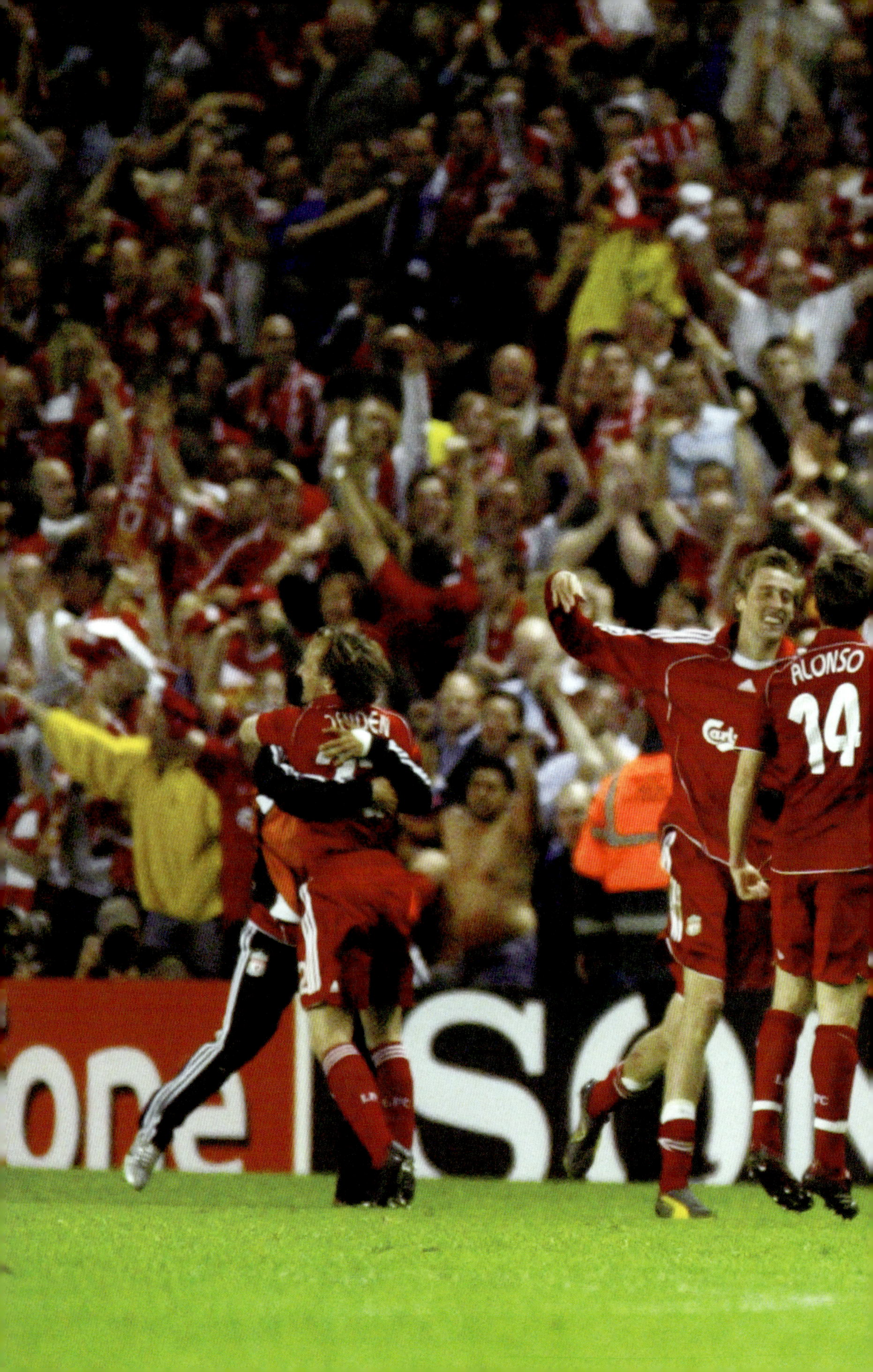
ALONSO
14

THE ROAD TO ATHENS

LIVERPOOL 2
MACCABI HAIFA 1

UEFA Champions League
Third Qualifying Round, 1st Leg
Wednesday August 9, 2005.
Attendance: 40,058

Goals: Boccoli (29), Bellamy (32), Gonzalez (87)
Booking: Sissoko (Liverpool), Magrashvili, Colautti (Maccabi Haifa)
Referee: Wolfgang Stark (Germany)

Team line-ups

Liverpool (4-4-1-1):

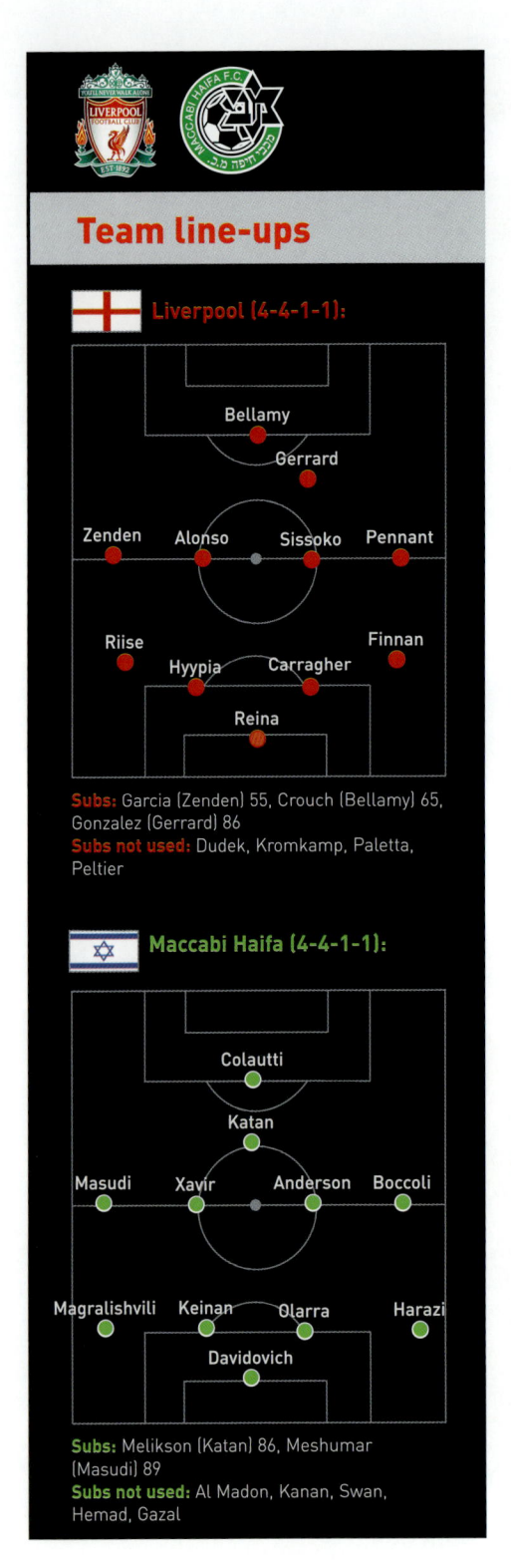

Bellamy
Gerrard
Zenden — Alonso — Sissoko — Pennant
Riise — Hyypia — Carragher — Finnan
Reina

Subs: Garcia (Zenden) 55, Crouch (Bellamy) 65, Gonzalez (Gerrard) 86
Subs not used: Dudek, Kromkamp, Paletta, Peltier

Maccabi Haifa (4-4-1-1):

Colautti
Katan
Masudi — Xavir — Anderson — Boccoli
Magralishvili — Keinan — Olarra — Harazi
Davidovich

Subs: Melikson (Katan) 86, Meshumar (Masudi) 89
Subs not used: Al Madon, Kanan, Swan, Hemad, Gazal

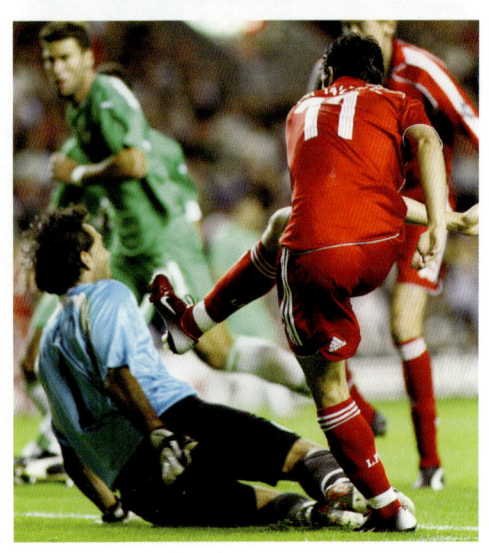

The Road To Athens

Team line-ups

Maccabi Haifa (4-4-1-1):

Colautti
Katan
Masudi — Xavir — Anderson — Boccoli
Magrashvili — Keinan — Olarra — Harazi
Davidovich

Subs: Meshumar (Keinan) 65, Melikson (Anderson) 71, Arbaitman (Masudi) 80
Subs not used: Al Madon, Kanan, Swan, Gazal

Liverpool (4-4-1-1):

Crouch
Garcia
Gonzalez — Alonso — Sissoko — Pennant
Warnock — Hyypia — Agger — Finnan
Reina

Subs: Aurelio (Warnock) 28, Gerrard (Sissoko) 67, Bellamy (Pennant) 86
Subs not used: Dudek, Kromkamp, Fowler, Zenden

MACCABI HAIFA 1
LIVERPOOL 1

UEFA Champions League
Third Qualifying Round, 2nd Leg
Tuesday August 22, 2006.
Attendance: 12,500
(Played at neutral venue: Valeri Lobanovski Stadium, Kiev)

Goals: Crouch (54), Colautti (63)
Bookings: Keinan, Anderson, Meshumar (Maccabi Haifa), Alonso, Hyypia (Liverpool)
Referee: Roberto Rosetti (Italy)

PSV EINDHOVEN 0
LIVERPOOL 0

**UEFA Champions League
Group C game 1**
Tuesday September 12, 2006.
Attendance: 35,000

Bookings: None
Referee: Massimo Busacca (Switzerland)

Team line-ups

PSV Eindhoven (4-4-2):

Kone, Farfan
Culina, Afellay, Mendez, Simons
Salcido, Alex, Reiziger, Kromkamp
Gomes

Subs: Aissati (Culina) 63, Vayrynen (Afellay) 74
Subs not used: Moens, Kluivert, Da Costa, Addo, Lamey

Liverpool (4-4-2):

Bellamy, Kuyt
Warnock, Zenden, Sissoko, Pennant
Aurelio, Agger, Carragher, Finnan
Reina

Subs: Alonso (Sissoko) 62, Gerrard (Bellamy) 72, Gonzalez (Aurelio) 81
Subs not used: Dudek, Hyypia, Garcia, Crouch

The Road To Athens

Team line-ups

Liverpool (4-4-2):

Crouch — Kuyt

Gonzalez — Alonso — Gerrard — Pennant

Riise — Agger — Carragher — Finnan

Reina

Subs: Zenden (Alonso) 21, Garica (Gonzalez) 36, Bellamy (Pennant) 79
Subs not used: Dudek, Hyypia, Fowler, Paletta

PSV Eindhoven (4-4-2):

Kone — Farfan

Afellay — Feher — Simons — Mendez

Salcido — Alex — Da Costa — Kromkamp

Gomes

Subs: Tardelli (Feher) 68, Beerens (Mendez) 81,
Subs not used: Moens, Reiziger, Cocu, Addo, Lamey

LIVERPOOL 2
PSV EINDHOVEN 0

**UEFA Champions League
Group C game 5**
Wednesday November 22, 2006.
Attendance: 41,948

Goals: Gerrard (65), Crouch (89)
Bookings: None
Referee: Domenico Messina (Italy)

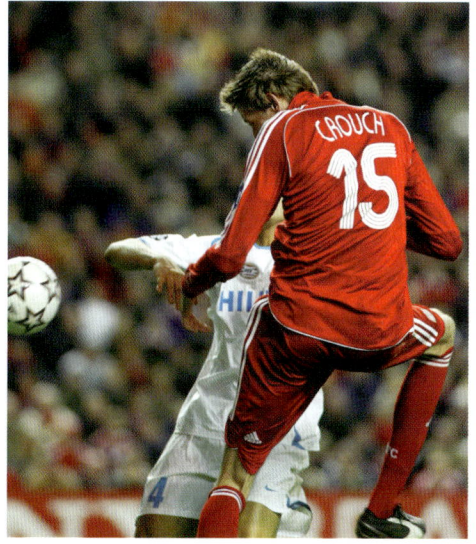

Team line-ups

Liverpool (4-4-2):

Kuyt, Crouch
Garcia, Alonso, Gerrard, Pennant
Aurelio, Agger, Carragher, Finnan
Reina

Subs: Gonzalez (Kuyt) 66, Sissoko (Pennant) 78, Bellamy (Crouch) 90
Subs not used: Dudek, Hyypia, Riise, Zenden

Galatasaray (4-4-2):

Sukur, Ilic
Turan, Akman, Topal, Sarioglu
Ak, Tomas, Song, Haspolatli
Mondragon

Subs: Karan (Haspolatli) 45, Sas (Topal) 45, Carrusca (Turan) 86
Subs not used: Elmas, Buruk, Asik, Kabze

LIVERPOOL 3
GALATASARAY 2

UEFA Champions League
Group C game 2
Wednesday September 27, 2006.
Attendance: 41,976

Goals: Crouch (9, 52), Garcia (14), Karan (59, 65)
Bookings: Alonso, Finnan (Liverpool), Akman, Sas (Galatasaray)
Referee: Luis Medina Cantalejo (Spain)

The Road To Athens

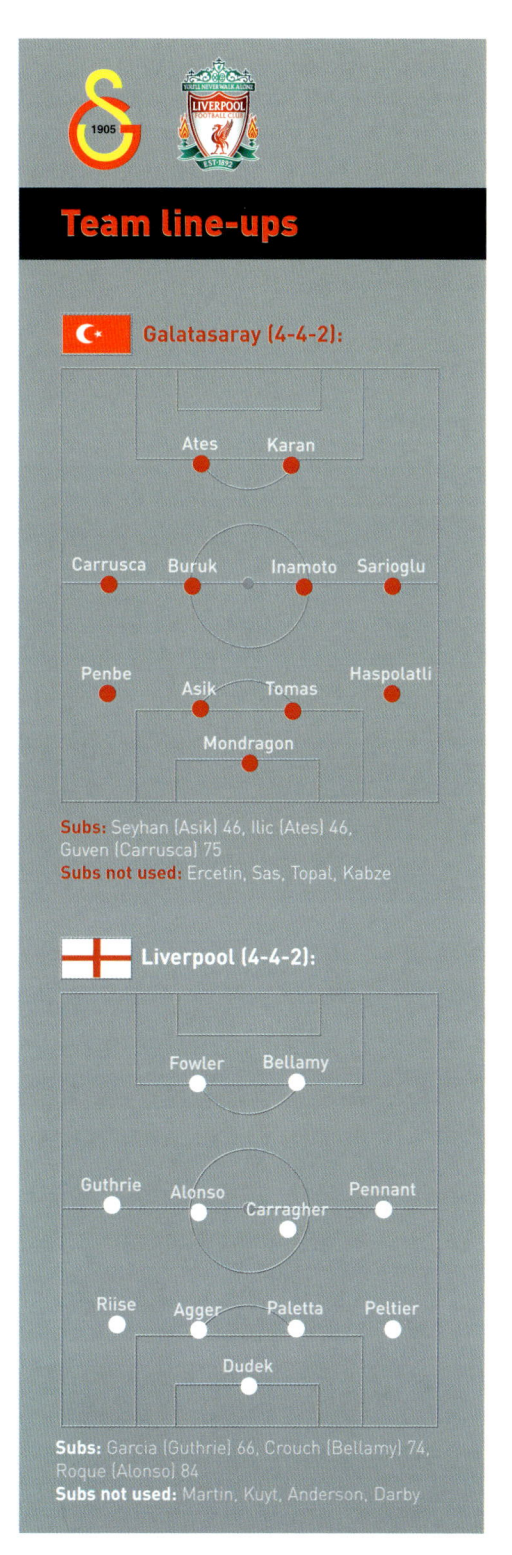

GALATASARAY 3
LIVERPOOL 2

**UEFA Champions League
Group C game 6**
Tuesday December 5, 2006.
Attendance: 23,000

Goals: Fowler (22), Ates (24), Buruk (28), Ilic (79), Fowler (90)
Bookings: Inamoto (Galatasaray), Pennant (Liverpool)
Referee: Olegario Benquerenca (Portugal)

Team line-ups

Galatasaray (4-4-2):

Ates, Karan
Carrusca, Buruk, Inamoto, Sarioglu
Penbe, Asik, Tomas, Haspolatli
Mondragon

Subs: Seyhan (Asik) 46, Ilic (Ates) 46, Guven (Carrusca) 75
Subs not used: Ercetin, Sas, Topal, Kabze

Liverpool (4-4-2):

Fowler, Bellamy
Guthrie, Alonso, Carragher, Pennant
Riise, Agger, Paletta, Peltier
Dudek

Subs: Garcia (Guthrie) 66, Crouch (Bellamy) 74, Roque (Alonso) 84
Subs not used: Martin, Kuyt, Anderson, Darby

Team line-ups

Bordeaux (4-4-2)

Laslandes, Darcheville

Micoud, Menegazzo, Mavuba, Alonso

Wendell, Jemmali, Henrique, Jurietti

Rame

Subs: Faubert (Alonso) 63, Chamakh (Laslandes) 63, Perea (Darcheville) 71
Subs not used: Valverde, Ducasse, Enakarhire, Marange

Liverpool (4-4-2)

Crouch, Bellamy

Gonzalez, Zenden, Alonso, Garcia

Riise, Hyypia, Carragher, Finnan

Reina

Subs: Kuyt (Crouch) 65, Sissoko (Gonzalez) 68, Warnock (Bellamy) 87
Subs not used: Dudek, Pennant, Paletta, Peltier

BORDEAUX 0
LIVERPOOL 1

UEFA Champions League Group C game 3
Wednesday October 18, 2006.
Attendance: 33,000

Goal: Crouch (58)
Bookings: Jurietti, Rame (Bordeaux), Zenden, Kuyt (Liverpool)
Referee: Tom Ovrebo (Norway)

The Road To Athens

Team line-ups

Liverpool (4-4-2):

Crouch, Kuyt
Garcia, Sissoko, Alonso, Gerrard
Riise, Hyypia, Carragher, Finnan
Reina

Subs: Zenden (Alonso) 57, Pennant (Crouch) 72, Fowler (Garcia) 78
Subs not used: Dudek, Agger, Aurelio, Warnock

Bordeaux (4-4-2):

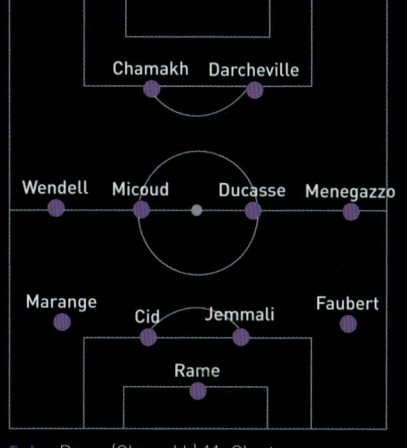

Chamakh, Darcheville
Wendell, Micoud, Ducasse, Menegazzo
Marange, Cid, Jemmali, Faubert
Rame

Subs: Perea (Chamakh) 11, Obertan (Darcheville) 59, Mavuba (Micoud) 74
Subs not used: Valverde, Henrique, Alonso, Francia

LIVERPOOL 3
BORDEAUX 0

UEFA Champions League
Group C game 4
Tuesday October 31, 2006.
Attendance: 41,978

Goals: Garcia (23, 76), Gerrard (71)
Booking: Sissoko (Liverpool)
Sending off: Menegazzo (Bordeaux)
Referee: Markus Merk (Germany)

BARCELONA 1
LIVERPOOL 2

UEFA Champions League
First knockout round, 1st Leg
Wednesday February 21, 2007.
Attendance: 88,000

Goals: Deco (14), Bellamy (43), Riise (74)
Bookings: Belletti, Zambrotta (Barcelona), Agger, Kuyt, Sissoko, Bellamy (Liverpool)
Referee: Kyros Vassaras (Greece)

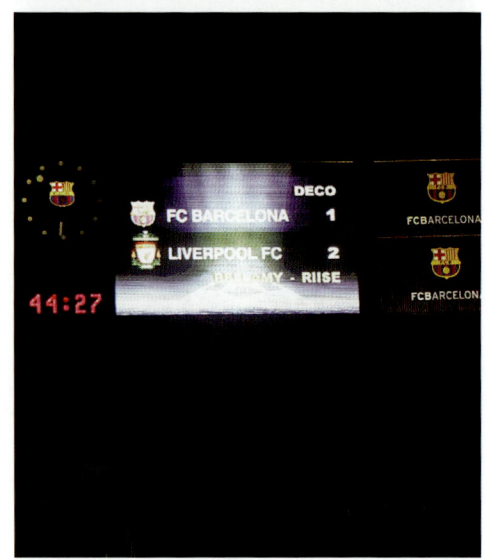

Team line-ups

Barcelona (4-3-3)

Saviola
Ronaldinho Messi
Motta Xavi Deco
Zambrotta Belletti
Puyol Marquez
Valdes

Subs: Iniesta (Motta) 54, Giuly (Xavi) 65, Gudjohnsen (Saviola) 82
Subs not used: Jorquera, Van Bronckhorst, Thuram, Oleguer

Liverpool (4-4-2)

Kuyt Bellamy
Riise Alonso Sissoko Gerrard
Arbeloa Agger Carragher Finnan
Reina

Subs: Pennant (Bellamy) 80, Zenden (Sissoko) 84, Crouch (Kuyt) 90
Subs not used: Dudek, Hyypia, Gonzalez, Mascherano

The Road To Athens

LIVERPOOL 0
BARCELONA 1

UEFA Champions League
First knockout round, 2nd Leg
Tuesday March 6, 2007.
Attendance: 42,579

Goal: Gudjohnsen (75)
Bookings: Arbeloa, Sissoko, Pennant, Reina (Liverpool), Thuram (Barcelona)
Referee: Herbert Fandel (Germany)

Team line-ups

Liverpool (4-4-2):

Bellamy
Kuyt
Riise — Alonso — Sissoko — Gerrard
Arbeloa — Agger — Carragher — Finnan
Reina

Subs: Pennant (Bellamy) 67, Aurelio (Riise) 77, Crouch (Kuyt) 89
Subs not used: Dudek, Hyypia, Mascherano, Zenden

Barcelona (4-3-3):

Eto'o
Ronaldinho — Messi
Iniesta — Xavi — Deco
Oleguer — Puyol — Marquez — Thuram
Valdes

Subs: Giuly (Eto'o) 61, Gudjohnsen (Thuram) 71
Subs not used: Jorquera, Zambrotta, Edmilson, Sylvinho, Saviola

PSV EINDHOVEN 0
LIVERPOOL 3

UEFA Champions League
Quarter-final, 1st Leg
Tuesday April 3, 2007.
Attendance: 36,500

Goals: Gerrard (27), Riise (49), Crouch (63)
Bookings: Kluivert, Feher (PSV Eindhoven), Mascherano, Kuyt (Liverpool)
Referee: Bertrand Layec (France)

Team line-ups

PSV Eindhoven (4-4-2)

Tardelli, Farfan
Culina, Cocu, Vayrynen, Mendez
Salcido, Simons, Da Costa, Kromkamp
Gomes

Subs: Sun (Farfan) 46, Kluivert (Mendez) 51, Feher (Kromkamp) 68
Subs not used: Moens, Addo, Marcellis

Liverpool (4-4-2)

Kuyt, Crouch
Aurelio, Alonso, Mascherano, Gerrard
Riise, Agger, Carragher, Finnan
Reina

Subs: Zenden (Riise) 65, Gonzalez (Aurelio) 75, Pennant (Crouch) 85
Subs not used: Dudek, Arbeloa, Hyypia, Bellamy

The Road To Athens

LIVERPOOL 1
PSV EINDHOVEN 0

**UEFA Champions League
Quarter-final, 2nd Leg**
Wednesday April 11, 2007.
Attendance: 41,447

Goal: Crouch (67)
Booking: Salcido (PSV Eindhoven)
Sending off: Marcellis (PSV Eindhoven)
Referee: Roberto Rosetti (Italy)

Team line-ups

Liverpool (4-4-2)

Crouch Bellamy
Zenden Alonso Sissoko Pennant
Riise Agger Hyypia Arbeloa
Reina

Subs: Fowler (Bellamy) 17, Gonzalez (Alonso) 72, Paletta (Agger) 78
Subs not used: Dudek, Gerrard, Mascherano, Carragher

PSV Eindhoven (4-4-2)

Kone Farfan
Culina Cocu Vayrynen Feher
Salcido Addo Simons Marcellis
Gomes

Subs: Sun (Feher) 62, Kluivert (Farfan) 62, Van Eijden (Kone) 71
Subs not used: Moens, Da Costa, Tardelli, Ter Horst

Liverpool FC : The Official Guide 2008

Team line-ups

Chelsea (4-1-3-2)

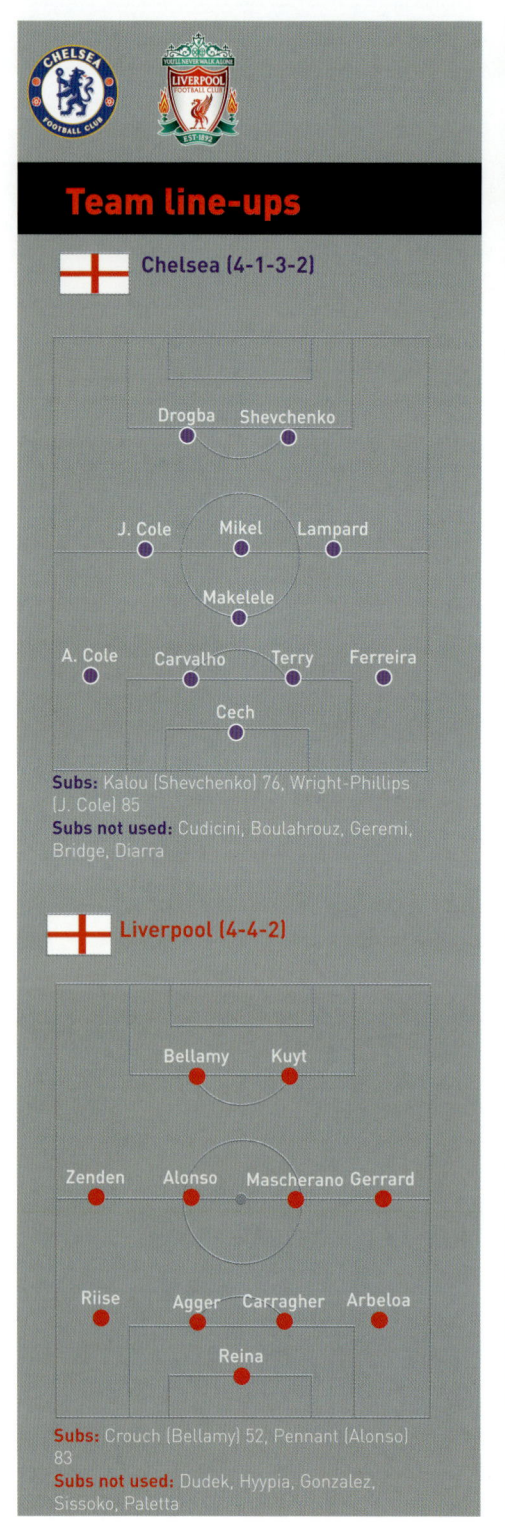

Drogba Shevchenko

J. Cole Mikel Lampard

Makelele

A. Cole Carvalho Terry Ferreira

Cech

Subs: Kalou (Shevchenko) 76, Wright-Phillips (J. Cole) 85
Subs not used: Cudicini, Boulahrouz, Geremi, Bridge, Diarra

Liverpool (4-4-2)

Bellamy Kuyt

Zenden Alonso Mascherano Gerrard

Riise Agger Carragher Arbeloa

Reina

Subs: Crouch (Bellamy) 52, Pennant (Alonso) 83
Subs not used: Dudek, Hyypia, Gonzalez, Sissoko, Paletta

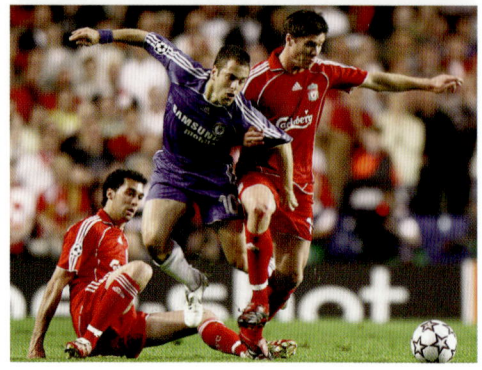

The Road To Athens

CHELSEA   **1**
LIVERPOOL   **0**

UEFA Champions League
Semi-final, 1st Leg
Wednesday April 25, 2007
Attendance: 39,483

Goal: J. Cole (29)
Booking: Mascherano (Liverpool)
Referee: Markus Merk (Germany)

LIVERPOOL 1
CHELSEA 0
(AET, Liverpool win 4-1 on penalties)

**UEFA Champions League
Semi-final, 2nd Leg**
Tuesday May 1, 2007
Attendance: 42,554

Goal: Agger (22)
Bookings: Agger, Zenden (Liverpool), A. Cole (Chelsea)
Referee: Manuel Enrique Mejuto Gonzalez (Spain)

The Road To Athens

Team line-ups

Liverpool (4-4-1-1)

```
            Crouch
             Kuyt
Zenden  Mascherano  Gerrard  Pennant
 Riise    Agger  Carragher  Finnan
             Reina
```

Subs: Alonso (Pennant) 78, Bellamy (Crouch) 106, Fowler (Mascherano) 118
Subs not used: Padelli, Arbeloa, Hyypia, Gonzalez

Chelsea (4-1-4-1)

```
            Drogba
Kalou  Lampard   Mikel   J. Cole
           Makelele
A. Cole  Essien  Terry  Ferreira
             Cech
```

Subs: Robben (J. Cole) 98, Wright-Phillips (Kalou) 107, Geremi (Makelele) 118
Subs not used: Cudicini, Boulahrouz, Bridge, Diarra

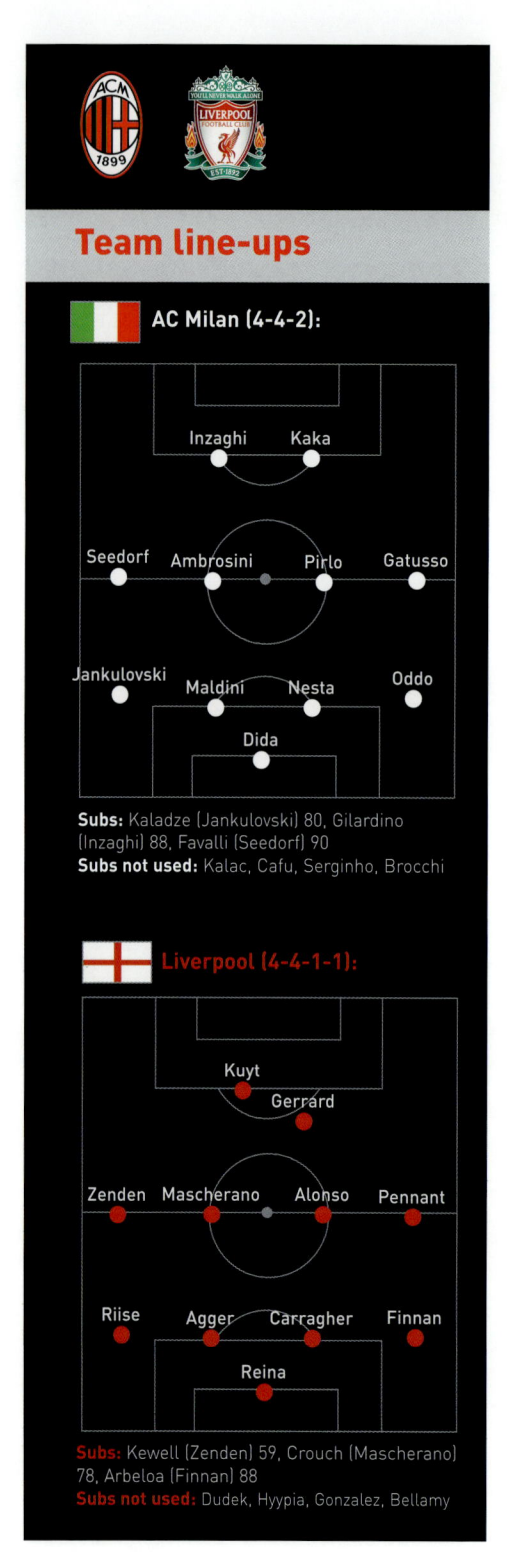

AC MILAN 2
LIVERPOOL 1

UEFA Champions League Final, Athens
Wednesday May 23, 2007
Attendance: 74,000

Goals: Inzaghi (45, 82), Kuyt (89)
Bookings: Gattuso, Jankulovski (AC Milan), Mascherano, Carragher (Liverpool)
Referee: Herbert Fandel (Germany)

Team line-ups

AC Milan (4-4-2):

Inzaghi, Kaka
Seedorf, Ambrosini, Pirlo, Gatusso
Jankulovski, Maldini, Nesta, Oddo
Dida

Subs: Kaladze (Jankulovski) 80, Gilardino (Inzaghi) 88, Favalli (Seedorf) 90
Subs not used: Kalac, Cafu, Serginho, Brocchi

Liverpool (4-4-1-1):

Kuyt
Gerrard
Zenden, Mascherano, Alonso, Pennant
Riise, Agger, Carragher, Finnan
Reina

Subs: Kewell (Zenden) 59, Crouch (Mascherano) 78, Arbeloa (Finnan) 88
Subs not used: Dudek, Hyypia, Gonzalez, Bellamy

The Road To Athens

EUROPEAN/WORLD ROLL OF HONOUR

EUROPEAN CHAMPIONS CUP/UEFA CHAMPIONS LEAGUE

WINNERS
1976/1977, 1977/1978, 1980/1981, 1983/1984, 2004/2005

RUNNERS-UP
1984/1985, 2006/2007

UEFA CUP

WINNERS
1972/1973, 1975/1976, 2000/2001

EUROPEAN CUP WINNERS' CUP

RUNNERS-UP
1965/1966

UEFA SUPER CUP

WINNERS
1977, 2001, 2005

RUNNERS-UP
1978, 1985

INTERCONTINENTAL CUP/FIFA CLUB WORLD CUP

RUNNERS-UP
1981, 1984, 2005

EUROPEAN RESULTS

Liverpool's impressive record in European competition was further extended in 2006/2007. Despite the ultimate disappointment in Athens, a seventh final appearance retains the club's proud record as having by far the best performances of any British team in the competition. Indeed, the five finals won is a proud honour bettered only by Real Madrid (nine wins in 12 finals) and AC Milan (seven successes out of 11). The Reds are also the joint record holders for the number of UEFA Cups won (three), while they are one of only five teams to have the right to wear the UEFA Badge of Honour, along with Real Madrid, AC Milan, Ajax and Bayern Munich.

The following pages document every Liverpool season in European competition, updated to take into account last season's statistics. Discounting the seasons when English clubs were barred from participating in European competition, from Liverpool's first season in competition (the European Champions Cup in 1964/1965), the club have failed to qualify for European football in only three campaigns.

The Road To Athens

LIVERPOOL'S FULL LIST OF RESULTS IN EUROPE

Season	Round	Venue	Opponents	Opponent Country	Score	Scorers	Att
1964-65	**EUROPEAN CUP**						
17th Aug	1 Leg 1	(a)	Reykjavik	Ice	W 5-0	Wallace 2, Hunt 2, Chisnall	10,000
14th Sept	1 Leg 2	(h)	Reykjavik	"	W 6-1	Byrne, St John 2, Hunt, Graham, Stevenson	32,957
25th Nov	2 Leg 1	(h)	Anderlecht	Bel	W 3-0	St John, Hunt, Yeats	44,516
16th Dec	2 Leg 2	(a)	Anderlecht	"	W 1-0	Hunt	60,000
10th Feb	3 Leg 1	(a)	FC Cologne	W.Ger	D 0-0		40,000
17th Mar	3 Leg 2	(h)	FC Cologne	"	D 0-0		48,432
24th Mar	Replay	Rotterdam	FC Cologne	"	D 2-2	St John, Hunt	45,000
			(Liverpool won on toss of a coin)				
4th May	SF Leg 1	(h)	Inter Milan	Ita	W 3-1	Hunt, Callaghan, St John	54,082
12th May	SF Leg 1	(a)	Inter Milan	"	L 0-3		90,000
1965-66	**EUROPEAN CUP WINNERS' CUP**						
29th Sept	Pr Leg 1	(a)	Juventus	Ita	L 0-1		12,000
13th Oct	Pr Leg 2	(h)	Juventus	"	W 2-0	Lawler, Strong	51,055
1st Dec	1 Leg 1	(h)	Standard Liege	Bel	W 3-1	Lawler 2, Thompson	46,112
15th Dec	1 Leg 2	(a)	Standard Liege	"	W 2-1	Hunt, St John	35,000
1st Mar	2 Leg 1	(a)	Honved	Hun	D 0-0		20,000
8th Mar	2 Leg 2	(h)	Honved	"	W 2-0	Lawler, St John	54,631
14th Apr	SF Leg 1	(a)	Celtic	Sco	L 0-1		80,000
19th Apr	SF Leg 2	(h)	Celtic	"	W 2-0	Smith, Strong	54,208
5th May	Final	Glasgow	B. Dortmund	W.Ger	L 1-2 aet	Hunt	41,657
1966-67	**EUROPEAN CUP**						
28th Sept	Pr Leg 1	(h)	Petrolul Ploesti	Rom	W 2-0	St John, Callaghan	44,463
12th Oct	Pr Leg 2	(a)	Petrolul Ploesti	"	L 1-3	Hunt	20,000
19th Oct	Replay	Brussels	Petrolul Ploesti	"	W 2-0	St John, Thompson	15,000
7th Dec	1 Leg 1	(a)	Ajax Amsterdam	Hol	L 1-5	Lawler	65,000
14th Dec	1 Leg 2	(h)	Ajax Amsterdam	"	D 2-2	Hunt 2	53,846
1967-68	**FAIRS CUP**						
19th Sept	1 Leg 1	(a)	Malmo	Swe	W 2-0	Hateley 2	14,314
4th Oct	1 Leg 2	(h)	Malmo	"	W 2-1	Yeats, Hunt	39,795
7th Nov	2 Leg 1	(h)	TSV Munich 1860	W.Ger	W 8-0	St John, Hateley, Smith (pen) Hunt 2, Thompson, Callaghan 2	44,812
14th Nov	2 Leg 2	(a)	TSV Munich 1860	"	L 1-2	Callaghan	10,000
28th Nov	3 Leg 1	(a)	Ferencvaros	Hun	L 0-1		30,000
9th Jan	3 Leg 2	(h)	Ferencvaros	"	L 0-1		46,892
1968-69	**FAIRS CUP**						
18th Sept	1 Leg 1	(a)	Athletic Bilbao	Spa	L 1-2	Hunt	35,000
2nd Oct	1 Leg 2	(h)	Athletic Bilbao	"	W 2-1 aet	Lawler, Hughes	49,567
			(Liverpool lost on toss of coin)				
1969-70	**FAIRS CUP**						
16th Sept	1 Leg 1	(h)	Dundalk	Rep. Ire	W 10-0	Evans 2, Lawler, Smith 2, Graham 2, Lindsay, Thompson, Callaghan	32,562
30th Sept	1 Leg 2	(a)	Dundalk	"	W 4-0	Thompson 2, Graham, Callaghan	6,000
12th Nov	2 Leg 1	(a)	Vitoria Setubal	Por	L 0-1		16,000
26th Nov	2 Leg 2	(h)	Vitoria Setubal	"	W 3-2	Smith (pen), Evans, Hunt	41,633

Season	Round	Venue	Opponents	Opponent Country	Score	Scorers	Att
1970-71	**FAIRS CUP**						
15th Sept	1 Leg 1	(h)	Ferencvaros	Hun	W 1-0	Graham	37,531
29th Sept	1 Leg 2	(a)	Ferencvaros	"	D 1-1	Hughes	25,000
21st Oct	2 Leg 1	(h)	D. Bucharest	Rom	W 3-0	Lindsay, Lawler, Hughes	36,525
4th Nov	2 Leg 2	(a)	D. Bucharest	"	D 1-1	Boersma	45,000
9th Dec	3 Leg 1	(a)	Hibernian	Sco	W 1-0	Toshack	30,296
22nd Dec	3 Leg 2	(h)	Hibernian	"	W 2-0	Heighway, Boersma	37,815
10th Mar	4 Leg 1	(h)	Bayern Munich	W.Ger	W 3-0	Evans 3	45,616
24th Mar	4 Leg 2	(a)	Bayern Munich	"	D 1-1	Ross	23,000
14th Apr	SF Leg 1	(h)	Leeds United	Eng	L 0-1		52,577
28th Apr	SF Leg 2	(a)	Leeds United	"	D 0-0		40,462
1971-72	**EUROPEAN CUP WINNERS' CUP**						
15th Sept	1 Leg 1	(a)	Servette Geneva	Swi	L 1-2	Lawler	16,000
29th Sept	1 Leg 2	(h)	Servette Geneva	"	W 2-0	Hughes, Heighway	38,591
20th Oct	2 Leg 1	(h)	Bayern Munich	W.Ger	D 0-0		42,949
3rd Nov	2 Leg 2	(a)	Bayern Munich	"	L 1-3	Evans	40,000
1972-73	**UEFA CUP**						
12th Sept	1 Leg 1	(h)	E. Frankfurt	W.Ger	W 2-0	Keegan, Hughes	33,380
26th Sept	1 Leg 2	(a)	E. Frankfurt	"	D 0-0		20,000
24th Oct	2 Leg 1	(h)	AEK Athens	Gre	W 3-0	Boersma, Cormack, Smith (pen)	31,906
7th Nov	2 Leg 2	(a)	AEK Athens	"	W 3-1	Hughes 2, Boersma	25,000
29th Nov	3 Leg 1	(a)	Dynamo Berlin	E.Ger	D 0-0		19,000
13th Dec	3 Leg 2	(h)	Dynamo Berlin	"	W 3-1	Boersma, Heighway, Toshack	34,140
7th Mar	4 Leg 1	(h)	Dynamo Dresden	E.Ger	W 2-0	Hall, Boersma	33,270
21st Mar	4 Leg 2	(a)	Dynamo Dresden	"	W 1-0	Keegan	35,000
10th Apr	SF Leg 1	(h)	Tottenham H.	Eng	W 1-0	Lindsay	42,174
25th Apr	SF Leg 2	(a)	Tottenham H.	"	L 1-2	Heighway	46,919
10th May	F Leg 1	(h)	B. Moench'bach	W.Ger	W 3-0	Keegan 2, Lloyd	41,169
23rd May	F Leg 2	(a)	B. Moench'bach	"	L 0-2		35,000
1973-74	**EUROPEAN CUP**						
19th Sept	1 Leg 1	(a)	Jeunesse D'Esch	Lux	D 1-1	Hall	5,000
3rd Oct	1 Leg 2	(h)	Jeunesse D'Esch	"	W 2-0	Mond o.g., Toshack	28,714
24th Oct	2 Leg 1	(a)	R.S. Belgrade	Yug	L 1-2	Lawler	40,000
6th Nov	2 Leg 2	(h)	R.S. Belgrade"		L 1-2	Lawler	41,774
1974-75	**EUROPEAN CUP WINNERS' CUP**						
17th Sept	1 Leg 1	(h)	Stromsgodset	Nor	W 11-0	Lindsay (pen), Boersma 2, Thompson 2, Heighway, Cormack, Hughes, Smith Callaghan, Kennedy	24,743
1st Oct	1 Leg 2	(a)	Stromsgodset	"	W 1-0	Kennedy	17,000
23rd Oct	2 Leg 1	(h)	Ferencvaros	Hun	D 1-1	Keegan	35,027
5th Nov	2 Leg 2	(a)	Ferencvaros	"	D 0-0		30,000
1975-76	**UEFA CUP**						
17th Sept	1 Leg 1	(a)	Hibernian	Sco	L 0-1		19,219
30th Sept	1 Leg 2	(h)	Hibernian	"	W 3-1	Toshack 3	29,963
22nd Oct	2 Leg 1	(a)	Real Sociedad	Spa	W 3-1	Heighway, Callaghan, Thompson	20,000
4th Nov	2 Leg 2	(h)	Real Sociedad	"	W 6-0	Toshack, Kennedy 2, Fairclough Heighway, Neal	23,796

The Road To Athens

Season	Round	Venue	Opponents	Opponent Country	Score	Scorers	Att
1975-76	**UEFA CUP (cont)**						
26th Nov	3 Leg 1	(a)	Slask Wroclaw	Pol	W 2-1	Kennedy, Toshack	46,000
10th Dec	3 Leg 2	(h)	Slask Wroclaw	"	W 3-0	Case 3	17,886
3rd Mar	4 Leg 1	(a)	Dynamo Dresden	E.Ger	D 0-0		33,000
17th Mar	4 Leg 2	(h)	Dynamo Dresden	"	W 2-1	Case, Keegan	39,300
30th Mar	SF Leg 1	(a)	Barcelona	Spa	W 1-0	Toshack	70,000
14th Apr	SF Leg 2	(h)	Barcelona	"	D 1-1	Thompson	55,104
28th Apr	F Leg 1	(h)	FC Bruges	Bel	W 3-2	Kennedy, Case, Keegan (pen)	49,981
19th May	F Leg 2	(a)	FC Bruges	"	D 1-1	Keegan	33,000
1976-77	**EUROPEAN CUP**						
14th Sept	1 Leg 1	(h)	Crusaders	N.Ire	W 2-0	Neal (pen), Toshack	22,442
28th Sept	1 Leg 2	(a)	Crusaders	"	W 5-0	Keegan, Johnson 2, McDermott Heighway	10,500
20th Oct	2 Leg 1	(a)	Trabzonspor	Tur	L 0-1		25,000
3rd Nov	2 Leg 2	(h)	Trabzonspor	"	W 3-0	Heighway, Johnson, Keegan	42,275
2nd Mar	3 Leg 1	(a)	St Etienne	Fra	L 0-1		38,000
16th Mar	3 Leg 2	(h)	St Etienne	"	W 3-1	Keegan, Kennedy, Fairclough	55,043
6th Apr	SF Leg 1	(a)	FC Zurich	Swi	W 3-1	Neal 2 (1 pen), Heighway	30,500
20th Apr	SF Leg 2	(h)	FC Zurich	"	W 3-0	Case 2, Keegan	50,611
25th May	Final	Rome	B. Moench'bach	W.Ger	W 3-1	McDermott, Smith, Neal (pen)	57,000
1977-78	**EUROPEAN CUP**						
19th Oct	2 Leg 1	(h)	Dynamo Dresden	E.Ger	W 5-1	Hansen, Case 2, Neal (pen) Kennedy	39,835
2nd Nov	2 Leg 2	(a)	Dynamo Dresden	"	L 1-2	Heighway	33,000
1st Mar	3 Leg 1	(a)	Benfica	Por	W 2-1	Case, Hughes	70,000
15th Mar	3 Leg 2	(h)	Benfica	"	W 4-1	Callaghan, Dalglish, McDermott, Neal	48,364
29th Mar	SF Leg 1	(a)	B. Moench'bach	W.Ger	L 1-2	Johnson	66,000
12th Apr	SF Leg 2	(h)	B. Moench'bach	"	W 3-0	Kennedy, Dalglish, Case	51,500
10th May	Final	Wembley	FC Bruges	Bel	W 1-0	Dalglish	92,000
1977-78	**EUROPEAN SUPER CUP**						
22nd Nov	Leg 1	(a)	SV Hamburg	W.Ger	D 1-1	Fairclough	16,000
6th Dec	Leg 2	(h)	SV Hamburg	"	W 6-0	Thompson, Mc Dermott 3, Fairclough, Dalglish	34,931
1978-79	**EUROPEAN CUP**						
13th Sept	1 Leg 1	(a)	Nottingham Forest	Eng	L 0-2		38,316
27th Sept	1 Leg 2	(h)	Nottingham Forest	"	D 0-0		51,679
1978-79	**EUROPEAN SUPER CUP**						
4th Dec	1 Leg 1	(a)	Anderlecht	Bel	L 1-3	Case	35,000
19th Dec	1 Leg 2	(h)	Anderlecht	"	W 2-1	Hughes, Fairclough	23,598
1979-80	**EUROPEAN CUP**						
19th Sept	1 Leg 1	(h)	Dynamo Tblisi	Rus	W 2-1	Johnson, Case	35,270
3rd Oct	1 Leg 2	(a)	Dynamo Tblisi	"	L 0-3		80,000

Liverpool FC : The Official Guide 2008

Season	Round	Venue	Opponents	Opponent Country	Score	Scorers	Att
1980-81	**EUROPEAN CUP**						
17th Sept	1 Leg 1	(a)	Oulu Palloseura	Fin	D 1-1	McDermott	14,000
1st Oct	1 Leg 2	(h)	Oulu Palloseura	"	W 10-1	Souness 3 (1pen), McDermott 3, Lee, R.Kennedy, Fairclough 2	21,013
22nd Oct	2 Leg 1	(a)	Aberdeen	Sco	W 1-0	McDermott	24,000
5th Nov	2 Leg 2	(h)	Aberdeen	"	W 4-0	Miller o.g., Neal, Dalglish, Hansen	36,182
4th Mar	3 Leg 1	(h)	CSKA Sofia	Bul	W 5-1	Souness 3, Lee, McDermott	37,255
18th Mar	3 Leg 2	(a)	CSKA Sofia	"	W 1-0	Johnson	65,000
8th Apr	SF Leg 1	(h)	Bayern Munich	W.Ger	D 0-0		44,543
22nd Apr	SF Leg 2	(a)	Bayern Munich	"	D 1-1	R.Kennedy	77,600
27th May	Final	Paris	Real Madrid	Spa	W 1-0	A.Kennedy	48,360
1981-82	**EUROPEAN CUP**						
16th Sept	1 Leg 1	(a)	Oulu Palloseura	Fin	W 1-0	Dalglish	8,400
30th Sept	1 Leg 2	(h)	Oulu Palloseura	"	W 7-0	Dalglish, McDermott 2, R.Kennedy, Johnson, Rush, Lawrenson	20,789
21st Oct	2 Leg 1	(a)	AZ '67 Alkmaar	Hol	D 2-2	Johnson, Lee	15,000
4th Nov	2 Leg 2	(h)	AZ '67 Alkmaar	"	W 3-2	McDermott (pen), Rush, Hansen	29,703
3rd Mar	3 Leg 1	(h)	CSKA Sofia	Bul	W 1-0	Whelan	27,388
17th Mar	3 Leg 2	(a)	CSKA Sofia	"	L 0-2 aet		60,000
1982-83	**EUROPEAN CUP**						
14th Sept	1 Leg 1	(a)	Dundalk	Rep. Ire	W 4-1	Whelan 2, Rush, Hodgson	16,500
28th Sept	1 Leg 2	(h)	Dundalk	"	W 1-0	Whelan	12,021
19th Oct	2 Leg 1	(a)	JK Helsinki	Fin	L 0-1		5,722
2nd Nov	2 Leg 2	(h)	JK Helsinki	"	W 5-0	Dalglish, Johnson, Neal, A.Kennedy 2	16,434
2nd Mar	3 Leg 1	(a)	Widzew Lodz	Pol	L 0-2		45,531
16th Mar	3 Leg 2	(h)	Widzew Lodz	"	W 3-2	Neal (pen), Rush, Hodgson	44,494
1983-84	**EUROPEAN CUP**						
14th Sept	1 Leg 1	(a)	BK Odense	Den	W 1-0	Dalglish	30,000
28th Sept	1 Leg 2	(h)	BK Odense	"	W 5-0	Robinson 2, Dalglish 2, Clausen o.g.	14,985
19th Oct	2 Leg 1	(h)	Athletic Bilbao	Spa	D 0-0		33,063
2nd Nov	2 Leg 2	(a)	Athletic Bilbao	"	W 1-0	Rush	47,500
7th Mar	3 Leg 1	(h)	Benfica	Por	W 1-0	Rush	39,096
21st Mar	3 Leg 2	(a)	Benfica	"	W 4-1	Whelan 2, Johnston, Rush	70,000
11th Apr	SF Leg 1	(h)	D. Bucharest	Rom	W 1-0	Lee	36,941
25th Apr	SF Leg 2	(a)	D. Bucharest	"	W 2-1	Rush 2	60,000
30th May	Final	Rome	AS Roma	Ita	W 1-1 aet	Neal	69,693
			(Liverpool won 4-2 on penalties)				
1984-85	**EUROPEAN CUP**						
19th Sept	1 Leg 1	(a)	Lech Poznan	Pol	W 1-0	Wark	35,000
3rd Oct	1 Leg 2	(h)	Lech Poznan	"	W 4-0	Wark 3, Walsh	22,143
24th Oct	2 Leg 1	(h)	Benfica	Por	W 3-1	Rush 3	27,733
7th Nov	2 Leg 2	(a)	Benfica	"	L 0-1		50,000
6th Mar	3 Leg 1	(a)	Austria Vienna	Aut	D 1-1	Nicol	21,000
20th Mar	3 Leg 2	(h)	Austria Vienna	"	W 4-1	Walsh 2, Nicol, Obermayer o.g.	32,761

The Road To Athens

Season	Round	Venue	Opponents	Opponent Country	Score	Scorers	Att
1984-85	**EUROPEAN CUP (cont)**						
10th Apr	SF Leg 1	(h)	Panathinaikos	Gre	W 4-0	Wark, Rush 2, Beglin	39,488
24th Apr	SF Leg 2	(a)	Panathinaikos	"	W 1-0	Lawrenson	60,000
29th May	Final	Brussels	Juventus	Ita	L 0-1		60,000
1984-85	**EUROPEAN SUPER CUP**						
16th Jan		(a)	Juventus	Ita	L 0-2		60,000
1991-92	**UEFA CUP**						
18th Sept	1 Leg 1	(h)	Kuusysi Lahti	Fin	W 6-1	Saunders 4, Houghton 2	17,131
2nd Oct	1 Leg 2	(a)	Kuusysi Lahti	"	L 0-1		8,435
23rd Oct	2 Leg 1	(a)	Auxerre	Fra	L 0-2		16,500
6th Nov	2 Leg 2	(h)	Auxerre	"	W 3-0	Molby (pen), Marsh, Walters	23,094
27th Nov	3 Leg 1	(a)	Swarovski Tirol	Aut	W 2-0	Saunders 2	12,500
11th Dec	3 Leg 2	(h)	Swarovski Tirol	"	W 4-0	Saunders 3, Venison	16,007
4th Mar	4 Leg 1	(a)	Genoa	Ita	L 0-2		40,000
18th Mar	4 Leg 2	(h)	Genoa	"	L 1-2	Rush	38,840
1992-93	**EUROPEAN CUP WINNERS' CUP**						
16th Sept	1 Leg 1	(h)	Apollon Limassol	Cyp	W 6-1	Stewart 2, Rush 4	12,769
29th Sept	1 Leg 2	(a)	Apollon Limassol	"	W 2-1	Rush, Hutchison	8,000
22nd Oct	2 Leg 1	(a)	Spartak Moscow	Rus	L 2-4	Wright, McManaman	60,000
4th Nov	2 Leg 2	(h)	Spartak Moscow	"	L 0-2		37,993
1995-96	**UEFA CUP**						
12th Sept	1 Leg 1	(a)	S. Vladikavkaz	Rus	W 2-1	McManaman, Redknapp	43,000
26th Sept	1 Leg 2	(h)	S. Vladikavkaz	"	D 0-0		35,042
17th Oct	2 Leg 1	(a)	Brondby	Den	D 0-0		37,648
31st Oct	2 Leg 2	(h)	Brondby	"	L 0-1		35,878
1996-97	**EUROPEAN CUP WINNERS' CUP**						
12th Sept	1 Leg 1	(a)	MyPa 47	Fin	W 1-0	Bjornebye	5,500
26th Sept	1 Leg 2	(h)	MyPa 47	"	W 3-1	Berger, Collymore, Barnes	39,013
17th Oct	2 Leg 1	(a)	Sion	Swi	W 2-1	Fowler, Barnes	16,500
31st Oct	2 Leg 2	(h)	Sion	"	W 6-3	McManaman, Bjornebye, Barnes, Fowler 2, Berger	38,514
6th Mar	3 Leg 1	(a)	Brann Bergen	Nor	D 1-1	Fowler	12,700
20th Mar	3 Leg 2	(h)	Brann Bergen	"	W 3-0	Fowler 2 (1 pen), Collymore	40,326
10th Apr	SF Leg 1	(a)	Paris St Germain	Fra	L 0-3		35,142
24th Apr	SF Leg 2	(h)	Paris St Germain	"	W 2-0	Fowler, Wright	38,984
1997-98	**UEFA CUP**						
16th Sept	1 Leg 1	(a)	Celtic	Sco	D 2-2	Owen, McManaman	48,526
30th Sept	1 Leg 2	(h)	Celtic	"	D 0-0		38,205
21st Oct	2 Leg 1	(a)	RC Strasbourg	Fra	L 0-3		18,813
4th Nov	2 Leg 2	(h)	RC Strasbourg	"	W 2-0	Fowler (pen), Riedle	32,426

Season	Round	Venue	Opponents	Opponent Country	Score	Scorers	Att
1998-99	**UEFA CUP**						
15th Sept	1 Leg 1	(a)	FC Kosice	Slovakia	W 3-0	Berger, Riedle, Owen	4,500
29th Sept	1 Leg 2	(h)	FC Kosice	"	W 5-0	Redknapp 2, Ince, Fowler 2	23,792
20th Oct	2 Leg 1	(h)	Valencia	Spa	D 0-0		36,004
3rd Nov	2 Leg 2	(a)	Valencia	"	D 2-2	McManaman, Berger	49,000
24th Nov	3 Leg 1	(a)	Celta Vigo	Spa	L 1-3	Owen	32,000
8th Dec	3 Leg 2	(h)	Celta Vigo	"	L 0-1		30,289
2000-01	**UEFA CUP**						
14th Sept	1 Leg 1	(a)	Rapid Bucharest	Rom	W 1-0	Barmby	12,000
28th Sept	1 Leg 2	(h)	Rapid Bucharest	"	D 0-0		37,954
26th Oct	2 Leg 1	(h)	Slovan Liberec	Cz Rep	W 1-0	Heskey	29,662
9th Nov	2 Leg 2	(a)	Slovan Liberec	"	W 3-2	Barmby, Heskey, Owen	6,808
23rd Nov	3 Leg 1	(a)	Olympiakos	Gre	D 2-2	Barmby, Gerrard	43,855
7th Dec	3 Leg 2	(h)	Olympiakos	"	W 2-0	Heskey, Barmby	35,484
15th Feb	4 Leg 1	(a)	AS Roma	Ita	W 2-0	Owen 2	59,718
22nd Feb	4 Leg 2	(h)	AS Roma	"	L 0-1		43,688
8th Mar	5 Leg 1	(a)	FC Porto	Por	D 0-0		21,150
15th Mar	5 Leg 2	(h)	FC Porto	"	W 2-0	Murphy, Owen	40,502
5th Apr	SF Leg 1	(a)	Barcelona	Spa	D 0-0		90,000
19th Apr	SF Leg 2	(h)	Barcelona	"	W 1-0	McAllister	44,203
16th May	Final	Dortmund	Alaves	Spa	W 5-4 aet	Babbel, Gerrard, McAllister (pen), Fowler, Geli o.g.	65,000
			(Liverpool won on golden goal)				
2001-02	**EUROPEAN CUP**						
8th Aug	Q. Leg 1	(a)	FC Haka	Fin	W 5-0	Heskey, Owen 3, Hyypia	33,217
21st Aug	Q. Leg 2	(h)	FC Haka	"	W 4-1	Fowler, Redknapp, Heskey, Wilson o.g.	31,602
			First Group Stage				
11th Sept	Group B	(h)	Boavista	Por	D 1-1	Owen	30,015
19th Sept	Group B	(a)	B. Dortmund	Ger	D 0-0		50,000
26th Sept	Group B	(h)	Dynamo Kiev	Ukr	W 1-0	Litmanen	33,513
16th Oct	Group B	(a)	Dynamo Kiev	"	W 2-1	Murphy, Gerrard	55,000
24th Oct	Group B	(a)	Boavista	Por	D 1-1	Murphy	6,000
30th Oct	Group B	(h)	B. Dortmund	Ger	W 2-0	Smicer, Wright	41,507
			Second Group Stage				
20th Nov	Group B	(h)	Barcelona	Spa	L 1-3	Owen	41,521
5th Dec	Group B	(a)	AS Roma	Ita	D 0-0		57,819
20th Feb	Group B	(h)	Galatasaray	Tur	D 0-0		41,605
26th Feb	Group B	(a)	Galatasaray	"	D 1-1	Heskey	22,100
13th Mar	Group B	(a)	Barcelona	Spa	D 0-0		75,362
19th Mar	Group B	(h)	AS Roma	Ita	W 2-0	Litmanen (pen), Heskey	41,794
3rd Apr	QF Leg 1	(h)	B. Leverkusen	Ger	W 1-0	Hyypia	42,454
9th Apr	QF Leg 2	(a)	B. Leverkusen	"	L 2-4	Xavier, Litmanen	22,500
2001-02	**EUROPEAN SUPER CUP**						
24th Aug		Monaco	Bayern Munich	Ger	W 3-2	Riise, Heskey, Owen	15,000

The Road To Athens

Season	Round	Venue	Opponents	Opponent Country	Score	Scorers	Att
2002-03	**EUROPEAN CUP**						
			First Group Stage				
17th Sept	Group B	(a)	Valencia	Spa	L 0-2		43,000
25th Sept	Group B	(h)	FC Basel	Swi	D 1-1	Baros	37,634
2nd Oct	Group B	(h)	Spartak Moscow	Rus	W 5-0	Heskey 2, Cheyrou, Hyypia, Diao	40,812
22nd Oct	Group B	(a)	Spartak Moscow	"	W 3-1	Owen 3	15,000
30th Oct	Group B	(h)	Valencia	Spa	L 0-1		41,831
12th Nov	Group B	(a)	FC Basel	Swi	D 3-3	Murphy, Smicer, Owen	35,000
2002-03	**UEFA CUP**						
28th Nov	3 Leg 1	(a)	Vitesse Arnhem	Hol	W 1-0	Owen	28,000
12th Dec	3 Leg 2	(h)	Vitesse Arnhem	"	W 1-0	Owen	23,576
20th Feb	4 Leg 1	(a)	Auxerre	Fra	W 1-0	Hyypia	20,452
27th Feb	4 Leg 2	(h)	Auxerre	"	W 2-0	Owen, Murphy	34,252
13th Mar	5 Leg 1	(a)	Celtic	Sco	D 1-1	Heskey	59,759
20th Mar	5 Leg 2	(h)	Celtic	"	L 0-2		44,238
2003-04	**UEFA CUP**						
24th Sept	1 Leg 1	(a)	Olimpija Ljubljana	Slovenia	D 1-1	Owen	10,000
15th Oct	1 Leg 2	(h)	Olimpija Ljubljana	"	W 3-0	LeTallec, Heskey, Kewell	42,880
6th Nov	2 Leg 1	(a)	Steaua Bucharest	Rom	D 1-1	Traore	25,000
27th Nov	2 Leg 2	(h)	Steaua Bucharest	"	W 1-0	Kewell	42,837
26th Feb	3 Leg 1	(h)	Levski Sofia	Bul	W 2-0	Gerrard, Kewell	39,149
3rd Mar	3 Leg 2	(a)	Levski Sofia	"	W 4-2	Gerrard, Owen, Hamann, Hyypia	40,281
11th Mar	4 Leg 1	(h)	O. Marseille	Fra	D 1-1	Baros	41,270
25th Mar	4 Leg 2	(a)	O. Marseille	"	L 1-2	Heskey	50,000
2004-05	**EUROPEAN CUP**						
10th Aug	Q. Leg 1	(a)	AK Graz	Aut	W 2-0	Gerrard 2	15,000
24th Aug	Q. Leg 2	(h)	AK Graz	"	L 0-1		42,950
			Group Stage				
15th Sept	Group A	(h)	AS Monaco	Fra	W 2-0	Cisse, Baros	33,517
28th Sept	Group A	(a)	Olympiakos	Gre	L 0-1		33,000
19th Oct	Group A	(h)	D. La Coruna	Spa	D 0-0		40,236
3rd Nov	Group A	(a)	D. La Coruna	"	W 1-0	Andrade o.g.	32,000
23rd Nov	Group A	(a)	AS Monaco	Fra	L 0-1		15,000
8th Dec	Group A	(h)	Olympiakos	Gre	W 3-1	Sinama-Pongolle, Mellor, Gerrard	42,045
22nd Feb	L. 16 L1	(h)	B. Leverkusen	Ger	W 3-1	Garcia, Riise, Hamann	40,942
9th Mar	L. 16 L2	(a)	B. Leverkusen	"	W 3-1	Garcia 2, Baros	23,000
5th Apr	QF Leg 1	(h)	Juventus	Ita	W 2-1	Hyypia, Garcia	41,216
13th Apr	QF Leg 1	(a)	Juventus	"	D 0-0		55,464
27th Apr	SF Leg 1	(a)	Chelsea	Eng	D 0-0		40,497
3rd May	SF Leg 1	(h)	Chelsea	"	W 1-0	Garcia	42,529
25th May	Final	Istanbul	AC Milan	Ita	W 3-3 aet	Gerrard, Smicer, Alonso	65,000
			(Liverpool won 3-2 on penalties)				

Season	Round	Venue	Opponents	Opponent Country	Score	Scorers	Att
2005-06	**EUROPEAN CUP**						
13th July	Q.1 Leg 1	(h)	TNS	Wal	W 3-0	Gerrard 3	44,760
19th July	Q.1 Leg 2	(a)	TNS	"	W 3-0	Cisse, Gerrard 2	8,009
26th July	Q.2 Leg 1	(a)	FBK Kaunas	Lith	W 3-1	Cisse, Carragher, Gerrard (pen)	8,300
2nd Aug	Q.2 Leg 2	(h)	FBK Kaunas	"	W 2-0	Gerrard, Cisse	43,717
10th Aug	Q.3 Leg 1	(a)	CSKA Sofia	Bul	W 3-1	Cisse, Morientes 2	16,512
23rd Aug	Q.3 Leg 2	(h)	CSKA Sofia	"	L 0-1		42,175
			Group Stage				
13th Sept	Group G	(a)	Real Betis	Spa	W 2-1	Sinama-Pongolle, Garcia	45,000
28th Sept	Group G	(h)	Chelsea	Eng	D 0-0		42,743
19th Oct	Group G	(a)	Anderlecht	Bel	W 1-0	Cisse	25,000
1st Nov	Group G	(h)	Anderlecht	Bel	W 3-0	Morientes, Garcia, Cisse	42,607
23rd Nov	Group G	(h)	Real Betis	Spa	D 0-0		42,077
6th Dec	Group G	(a)	Chelsea	Eng	D 0-0		41,598
21st Feb	L. 16 L1	(a)	Benfica	Por	L 0-1		65,000
8th Mar	L. 16 L2	(h)	Benfica	Por	L 0-2		42,745
2005-06	**EUROPEAN SUPER CUP**						
26th Aug		Monaco	CSKA Moscow	Rus	W 3-1 aet	Cisse 2, Garcia	18,000
2006-07	**EUROPEAN CUP**						
9th Aug	Q.3 Leg 1	(h)	Maccabi Haifa	Isr	W 2-1	Bellamy, Gonzalez	40,058
22nd Aug	Q.3 Leg 2	(a)	Maccabi Haifa	"	D 1-1	Crouch	12,500
			Group Stage				
12th Sept	Group C	(a)	PSV Eindhoven	Hol	D 0-0		35,000
27th Sept	Group C	(h)	Galatasaray	Tur	W 3-2	Crouch 2, Garcia	41,976
18th Oct	Group C	(a)	Bordeaux	Fra	W 1-0	Crouch	33,000
31st Oct	Group C	(h)	Bordeaux	Fra	W 3-0	Garcia 2, Gerrard	41,978
22nd Nov	Group C	(h)	PSV Eindhoven	Hol	W 2-0	Gerrard, Crouch	41,948
5th Dec	Group C	(a)	Galatasaray	Tur	L 2-3	Fowler 2	23,000
21st Feb	L. 16 L1	(a)	Barcelona	Spa	W 2-1	Bellamy, Riise	88,000
6th Mar	L. 16 L2	(h)	Barcelona	Spa	L 0-1		42,579
3rd Apr	QF L1	(a)	PSV Eindhoven	Hol	W 3-0	Gerrard, Riise, Crouch	36,500
11th Apr	QF L2	(h)	PSV Eindhoven	Hol	W 1-0	Crouch	41,447
25th Apr	SF L1	(a)	Chelsea	Eng	L 0-1		39,483
1st May	SF L2	(h)	Chelsea	Eng	W 1-0	Agger	42,554
			(Liverpool won 4-1 on penalties)				
23rd May	Final	Athens	AC Milan	Ita	L 1-2	Kuyt	74,000

The Road To Athens

Above: Tommy Smith and Ian Callaghan show off their European Cup winners' medals following Liverpool's first victory in the competition over Borrusia Moenchengladbach in 1977

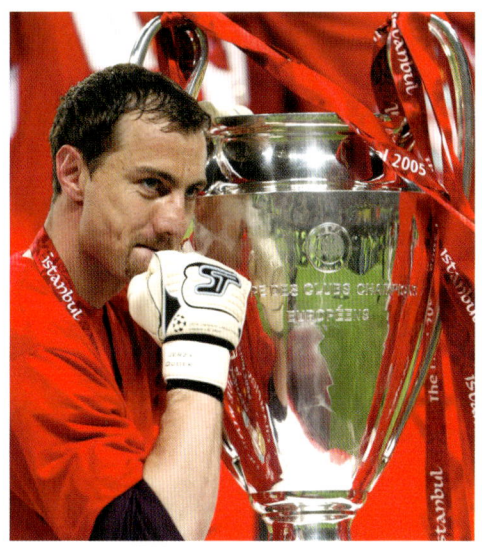

Above left: (L-to-R) Terry McDermott, matchwinner Kenny Dalglish and Alan Hansen celebrate European Cup success in 1978, while (above right) Jerzy Dudek revels in 2005 success

LIVERPOOL'S EUROPEAN OPPONENTS

Maccabi Haifa and PSV Eindhoven (twice in the season) became the newest additions to Liverpool's list of European opponents during the 2006/2007 season. The clash against the Israeli champions (the away leg being played in a neutral venue) meant that the list is down to 19 of countries the club has yet to face teams from, which runs as follows:

Albania, Andorra, Armenia, Azerbaijan, Belarus, Bosnia-Herzegovina, Croatia, Estonia, FYR Macedonia, Faroe Islands, Georgia, Kazakhstan, Latvia, Liechtenstein, Malta, Moldova, Montenegro, San Marino, Serbia.

Liverpool's opponents in the third qualifying round of the 2007/2008 UEFA Champions League are Toulouse, who are the 100th different European side to face the Reds while Spanish opposition remains the most frequent opposition, with the future addition of Toulouse taking the French tally to eight ahead of the former West Germany (seven) and Italy (five).

The countries, and the clubs who Liverpool have faced (up to and including the 2006-2007 season) are listed below and opposite:

AUSTRIA (3)
AK Graz, Austria Vienna, Swarovski Tirol.
BELGIUM (3)
FC Bruges, Anderlecht, Standard Liege.
BULGARIA (2)
CSKA Sofia, Levski Sofia.
CYPRUS (1)
Apollon Limassol.
CZECH REPUBLIC (1)
Slovan Liberec.
DENMARK (2)
Brondby, Odense.
ENGLAND (4)
Chelsea, Leeds United, Nottingham Forest, Tottenham Hotspur.
EAST GERMANY (2)
Dynamo Berlin, Dynamo Dresden.
FINLAND (5)
FC Haka , HJK Helsinki, Kuusysi Lahti, MyPa 47, Oulu Palloseura.
FRANCE (7)
Auxerre, Bordeaux, Olimpique Marseille, Monaco, Paris St Germain, RC Strasbourg, St Etienne.
GERMANY (2)
Bayer Leverkusen, Borussia Dortmund (2001).
GREECE (3)
AEK Athens, Olympiakos, Panathinaikos.
HOLLAND (3)
Ajax Amsterdam, AZ '67 Alkmaar, PSV Eindhoven, Vitesse Arnhem.
HUNGARY (2)
Ferencvaros, Honved.

ICELAND (1)
Reykjavik.
ISRAEL (1)
Maccabi Haifa.
ITALY (5)
AC Milan, Juventus, AS Roma, Genoa, Inter Milan.

LIVERPOOL'S EUROPEAN OPPONENTS

LITHUANIA (1)
FBK Kaunas.
LUXEMBOURG (1)
Jeunesse D'Esch.
NORTHERN IRELAND (1)
Crusaders.
NORWAY (2)
Brann Bergen, Stromsgodset.
POLAND (3)
Lech Poznan, Slask Wroclaw, Widzew Lodz.
PORTUGAL (4)
Benfica, Boavista, FC Porto, Vitoria Setubal.
REPUBLIC OF IRELAND (1)
Dundalk.
ROMANIA (4)
Dinamo Bucharest, Petrolul Ploesti,
Rapid Bucharest, Steaua Bucharest.
RUSSIA (4)
Dynamo Tblisi, Spartak Moscow,
Spartak Vladikavkaz, CSKA Moscow.
SCOTLAND (3)
Aberdeen, Celtic, Hibernian.
SLOVAKIA (1)
FC Kosice.
SLOVENIA (1)
Olimpija Ljubljana.
SPAIN (9)
Alaves, Atletico Bilbao, Barcelona, Celta Vigo,
Deportivo La Coruna, Real Betis, Real Madrid,
Real Sociedad, Valencia.
SWEDEN (1)
Malmo.
SWITZERLAND (4)
FC Basel, FC Sion, FC Zurich, Servette Geneva.
TURKEY (2)
Galatasaray, Trabzonspor.
WALES (1)
Total Network Solutions.
WEST GERMANY (7)
Bayern Munich, Borussia Moenchengladbach,
Borussia Dortmund (1966), FC Cologne,
Eintracht Frankfurt, Hamburg, 1860 Munich.
UKRAINE (1)
Dynamo Kiev.
YUGOSLAVIA (1)
Red Star Belgrade.

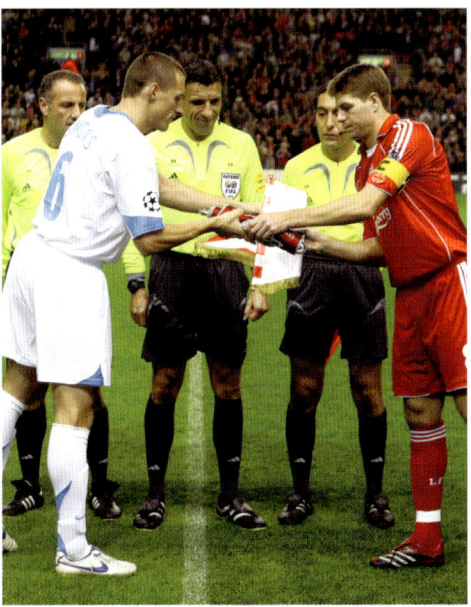

Liverpool in action for the first time in European competition against Maccabi Haifa and PSV Eindhoven in 2006/07

LIVERPOOL IN EUROPE: CLUB BY CLUB RECORD

Opposition	Played	Won	Drawn	Lost	For	Against
Aberdeen	2	2	0	0	5	0
AC Milan	2	1	0	1	4	5
AEK Athens	2	2	0	0	6	1
Ajax Amsterdam	2	0	1	1	3	7
Alaves	1	1	0	0	5	4
Anderlecht	6	5	0	1	11	4
Apollon Limassol	2	2	0	0	8	2
Athletic Bilbao	4	2	1	1	4	3
Austria Vienna	2	1	1	0	5	2
Auxerre	4	3	0	1	6	2
AZ '67 Alkmaar	2	1	1	0	5	4
Barcelona	8	3	3	2	6	6
Basel FC	2	0	2	0	4	4
Bayer Leverkusen	4	3	0	1	9	6
Bayern Munich	7	2	4	1	9	7
Benfica	8	5	0	3	14	8
Boavista	2	0	2	0	2	2
Bordeaux	2	2	0	0	4	0
Borussia Dortmund	3	1	1	1	3	2
B. Moenchengladbach	5	3	0	2	10	5
Brann Bergen	2	1	1	0	4	1
Brondby	2	0	1	1	0	1
Bruges	3	2	1	0	5	3
Celta Vigo	2	0	0	2	1	4
Celtic	6	1	3	2	5	6
Chelsea	6	2	3	1	2	1
Cologne	3	0	3	0	2	2
Crusaders	2	2	0	0	7	0
CSKA Moscow	1	1	0	0	3	1
CSKA Sofia	6	4	0	2	10	5
Deportivo La Coruna	2	1	1	0	1	0
Dinamo Bucharest	4	3	1	0	7	2
Dundalk	4	4	0	0	19	1
Dynamo Berlin	2	1	1	0	3	1
Dynamo Dresden	6	4	1	1	11	4
Dynamo Kiev	2	2	0	0	3	1
Dynamo Tblisi	2	1	0	1	2	4
Eintracht Frankfurt	2	1	1	0	2	0
Ferencvaros	6	1	3	2	3	4
Galatasaray	4	1	2	1	6	6
Genoa	2	0	0	2	1	4
Graz AK	2	1	0	1	2	1
Haka FC	2	2	0	0	9	1
Hamburg	2	1	1	0	7	1
Hibernian	4	3	0	1	6	2
HJK Helsinki	2	1	0	1	5	1
Honved	2	1	1	0	2	0
Inter Milan	2	1	0	1	3	4
Jeunesse D'Esch	2	1	1	0	3	1
Juventus	6	2	1	3	4	5
Kaunas FBK	2	2	0	0	5	1

LIVERPOOL IN EUROPE: CLUB BY CLUB RECORD

Opposition	Played	Won	Drawn	Lost	For	Against
Kosice FC	2	2	0	0	8	0
Kuusysi Lahti	2	1	0	1	6	2
Lech Poznan	2	2	0	0	5	0
Leeds United	2	0	1	1	0	1
Levski Sofia	2	2	0	0	6	2
Maccabi Haifa	2	1	1	0	3	2
Malmo	2	2	0	0	4	1
Monaco	2	1	0	1	2	1
Munich 1860	2	1	0	1	9	2
MyPa 47	2	2	0	0	4	1
Nottingham Forest	2	0	1	1	0	2
Odense	2	2	0	0	6	0
Olimpija Ljubljana	2	1	1	0	4	1
Olympiakos	4	2	1	1	7	4
Olympique Marseille	2	0	1	1	2	3
Oulu Palloseura	4	3	1	0	19	2
Panathinaikos	2	2	0	0	5	0
Paris St Germain	2	1	0	1	2	3
Petrolul Ploesti	3	2	0	1	5	3
Porto	2	1	1	0	2	0
PSV Eindhoven	4	3	1	0	6	0
Rapid Bucharest	2	1	1	0	1	0
Real Betis	2	1	1	0	2	1
Real Madrid	1	1	0	0	1	0
Real Sociedad	2	2	0	0	9	1
Red Star Belgrade	2	0	0	2	2	4
Reykjavik	2	2	0	0	11	1
Roma	5	3	1	1	5	2
St Etienne	2	1	0	1	3	2
Servette Geneva	2	1	0	1	3	2
Sion FC	2	2	0	0	8	4
Slask Wroclaw	2	2	0	0	5	1
Slovan Liberec	2	2	0	0	4	2
Spartak Moscow	4	2	0	2	10	7
Spartak Vladikavkaz	2	1	1	0	2	1
Standard Liege	2	2	0	0	5	2
Steaua Bucharest	2	1	1	0	2	1
Strasbourg RC	2	1	0	1	2	3
Stromsgodset	2	2	0	0	12	0
Swarowski Tirol	2	2	0	0	6	0
TNS	2	2	0	0	6	0
Tottenham Hotspur	2	1	0	1	2	2
Trabzonspor	2	1	0	1	3	1
Valencia	4	0	2	2	2	5
Vitesse Arnhem	2	2	0	0	2	0
Vitoria Setubal	2	1	0	1	3	3
Widzew Lodz	2	1	0	1	3	4
Zurich FC	2	2	0	0	6	1

Games decided on toss of coin (Petrolul) in a third game counted as a draw.
One-game ties decided on penalties count as wins or losses.
Statistics correct up to the end of 2006/2007 season.

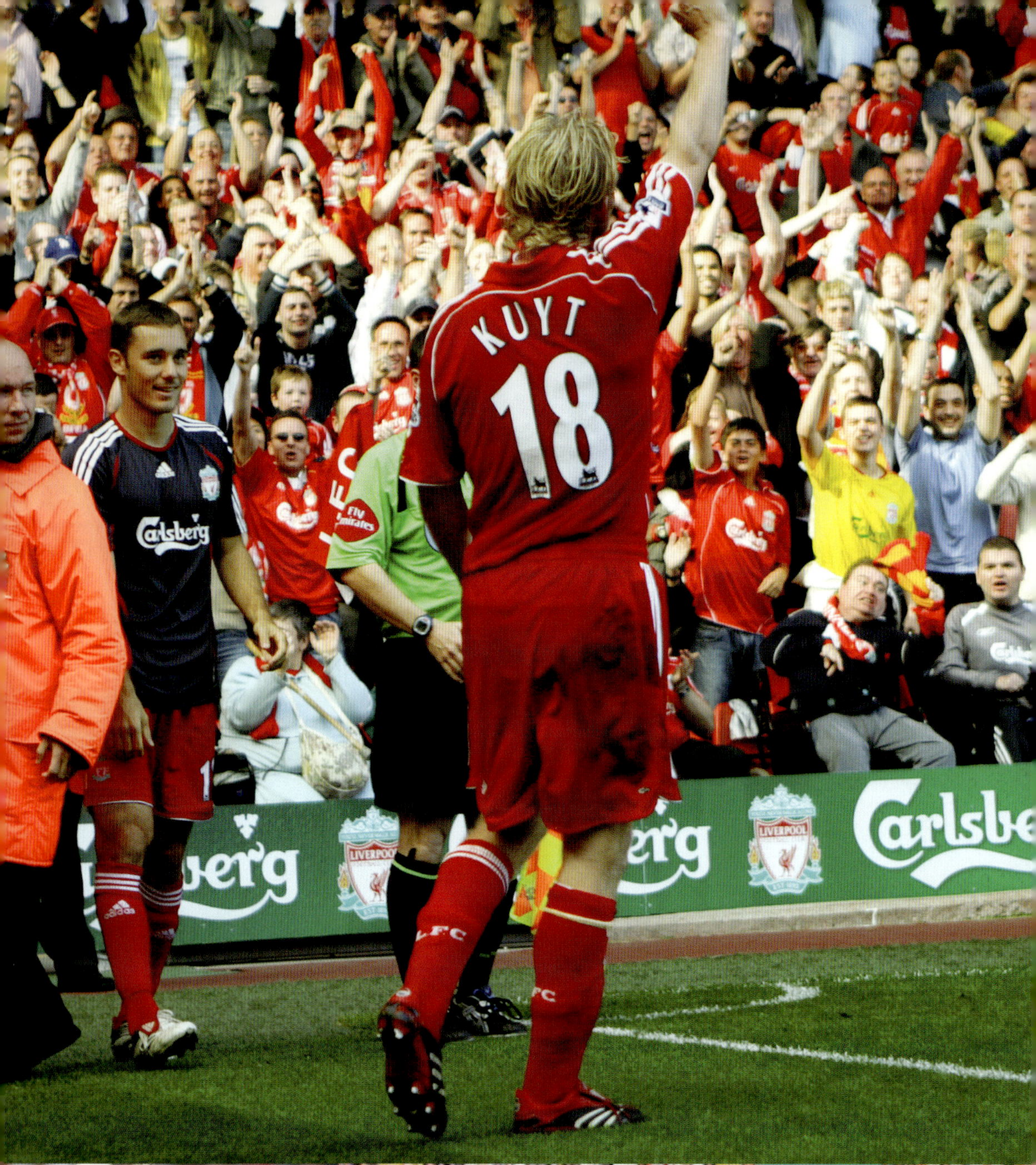
KUYT
18
Carlsberg
LIVERPOOL

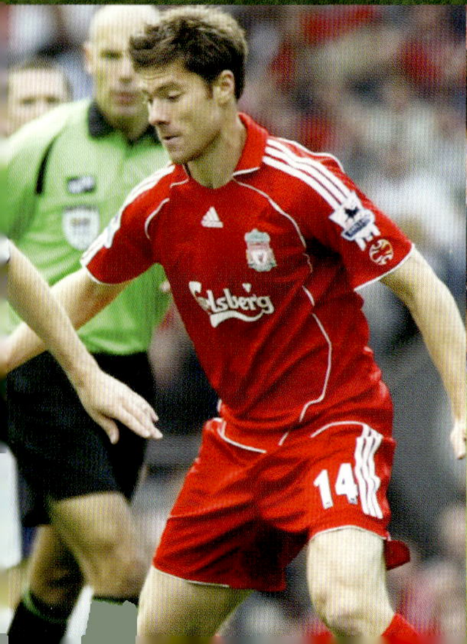
Carlsberg
14

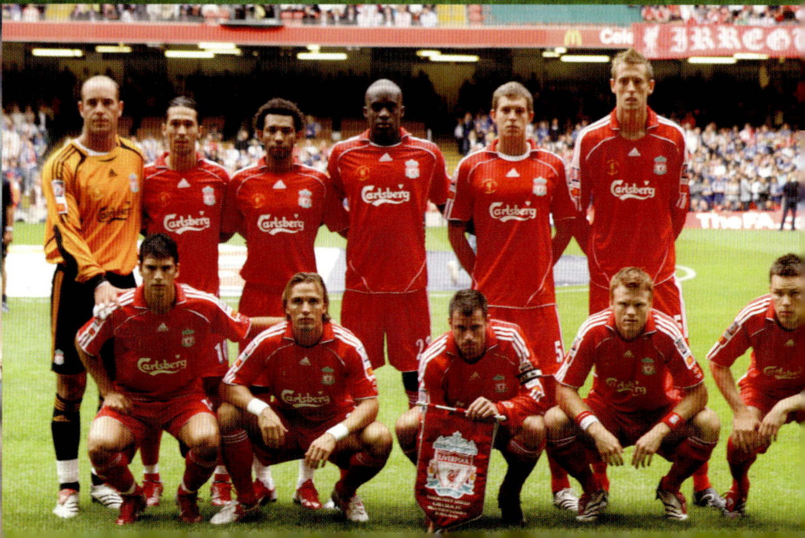
Carlsberg

THE 2006/07 SEASON

AND SO ANOTHER SEASON PASSES...

Where did it all go? We kept tabs on the goings on during 2006/07, and are sure we'll bring back some fond memories from Rafa Benitez's third season in charge.

August

Liverpool's World Cup stars Steven Gerrard, Jamie Carragher, Jose Reina and Jan Kromkamp return to action, although the Reds still go down 2-0 to Grasshoppers Zurich in a pre-season friendly. In the final game on their European tour a weakened Reds side concede five in the second half against MSV Mainz, the match having been goalless at the break before wholesale changes were made.

Steven Gerrard misses out on the England captaincy to John Terry, with the Anfield skipper being confirmed as vice-captain. Gerrard comes out on top in the FA Community Shield though, as goals from John Arne Riise and Peter Crouch earn a 2-1 win over Chelsea in Cardiff.

Dirk Kuyt completes his move from Feyenoord but not in time to make his debut at newly-promoted Sheffield United, where a Robbie Fowler penalty earns a point on the opening day of the Premiership season.

Liverpool overcome Maccabi Haifa 3-2 on aggregate to qualify for the Champions League, the away second leg being played in Ukraine due to the security situation in Israel. The resultant draw pairs the Reds alongside PSV Eindhoven, Bordeaux and Galatasaray.

Incoming:
Dirk Kuyt (Feyenoord), Nabil El Zhar (St. Etienne).

Outgoing:
Antonio Barragan (Deportivo La Coruna), Djimi Traore (Charlton Athletic), Danny O'Donnell (Crewe Alexandra, loan), Carl Medjani (Lorient), Scott Carson (Charlton Athletic, loan), Darren Potter (Wolves, loan), Anthony Le Tallec (Sochaux, loan), Robbie Foy (Scunthorpe United), Neil Mellor (Preston North End), Florent Sinama-Pongolle (Recreativo de Huelva, loan), Jan Kromkamp (PSV Eindhoven).

Injuries:
Jamie Carragher (ankle), John Arne Riise (ankle), Mohamed Sissoko (knee), Stephen Warnock (ankle).

Quotes of the month:
"Liverpool is the dream club I was looking for..there was nothing of the calibre of Liverpool, a brilliant club with an enormous reputation and fantastic, emphatic support and a fabulous history."
Dirk Kuyt, after signing for the Reds

"Our fans are the best in the world. We sold all our tickets and the way the fans got behind us was unbelievable."
John Arne Riise, on Liverpool fans at the FA Community Shield

"It was a special goal...but I'm not sure if it will become a regular thing."
Daniel Agger, following his goal against West Ham

AUGUST

THE GAMES

9	Maccabi Haifa	H	2-1	(Bellamy, Gonzalez)
13	Chelsea	N	2-1	(Riise, Crouch)
19	Sheff Utd	A	1-1	(Fowler pen)
22	Maccabi Haifa	A	1-1	(Crouch)
26	West Ham	H	2-1	(Agger, Crouch)

WHERE THEY STOOD

4	Everton
5	Chelsea
6	West Ham
7	**Liverpool**
8	Bolton Wanderers
9	Manchester City
10	Fulham

RAFA SAYS . . .

'It's not normal to see Liverpool conceding so many goals and that's why I'm not too worried.'

AND SO ANOTHER SEASON PASSES...

September
Peter Crouch scores twice against Andorra and notches the winner in Macedonia for England to take his tally to 11 in just 14 games for his country, while Steven Gerrard wins his 50th England cap in the latter match.

Liverpool City Council give the go-ahead for a new stadium on Stanley Park, with the club receiving £15m government funding assuming they can attract private investment to complete the £150m project. The end of the month also sees the Reds being awarded a £9m European grant towards building the new stadium – although they will have to spend the money before 2008, or they will have to give it back.

The Reds keep a first clean sheet of the season in their opening Champions League group match at PSV Eindhoven, while Xabi Alonso's 65-yard wonder goal seals a 2-0 victory over Newcastle United, Dirk Kuyt having scored the first, his first for the club. Former player Nigel Spackman is sacked as manager of Millwall while Peter Crouch hits two goals in his first start for five games in the 3-2 Champions League victory over Galatasaray.

Injuries:
John Arne Riise (ankle), Stephen Warnock (ankle).

Quotes of the month:
"It was funny at the time but I didn't want to carry on doing it until it became unfunny. I've stopped doing it for the time being but if I ever score a really big goal you never know."
Peter Crouch, on his robotic goal celebration

"He can play behind the defenders, on the wings and as a second striker. He can play well in all of these positions. Kuyt can do everything."
Rafael Benitez, impressed by his recent Dutch signing

"I came in too late. I didn't want to hurt him but I've seen it on TV and it doesn't look good. I wanted to say sorry to him."
Michael Ballack, in apologetic mood after being sent off for a stamp on Momo Sissoko

"I said last year, when nobody knew him, that he was a '20-20' player – 20 goals and 20 assists a season. In Europe there is maybe no-one else who is a '20-20' player. We came very close to signing him and everybody knows him now. He is the best character you can have. He works, he can head the ball, he can score goals – not like David Ginola or even Robbie Keane – but he is so functional in his way."
Martin Jol, another in praise of fellow countryman Dirk Kuyt

SEPTEMBER

THE GAMES

9	Everton	A	0-3	
12	PSV Eindhoven	A	0-0	
17	Chelsea	A	0-1	
20	Newcastle Utd	H	2-0	(Kuyt, Alonso)
23	Tottenham H.	H	3-0	(Gonzalez, Kuyt, Riise)
27	Galatasaray	H	3-2	(Crouch 2, Garcia)
30	Bolton W.	A	0-2	

WHERE THEY STOOD

6	Aston Villa
7	Arsenal
8	Reading
9	Liverpool
10	Blackburn Rovers
11	Manchester City
12	Fulham

RAFA SAYS . . .

'He can play behind the defenders, on the wings and as a second striker. Kuyt can do everything.'

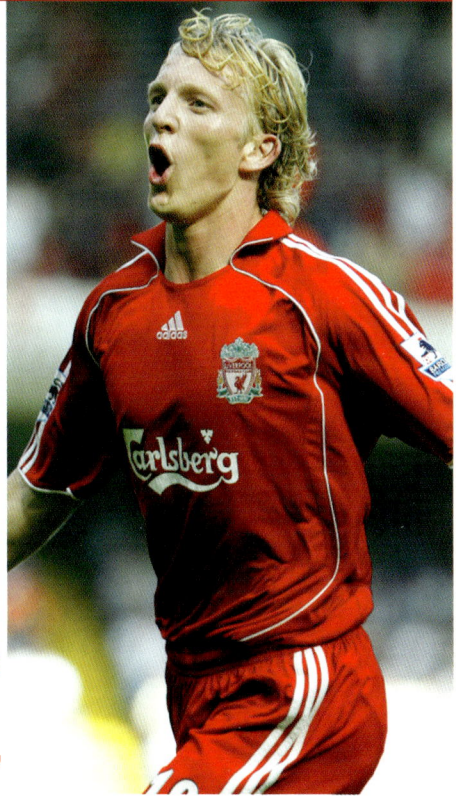

AND SO ANOTHER SEASON PASSES...

October

A shock 2-0 defeat at Bolton Wanderers derails the Reds' Premiership title ambitions, with Rafa Benitez unhappy with the Trotters' first goal, a free-kick given when Jose Reina was wrongly adjudged to have handled the ball outside the area. It is revealed that Peter Crouch and Daniel Agger were both burgled in unrelated incidents while playing against Galatasaray. Jermaine Pennant fails to land an England call-up, while Steven Gerrard takes time out to promote Liverpool's museums.

Craig Bellamy is named as Wales skipper in the absence of Ryan Giggs – although his first game as captain ends in a 5-1 home defeat to Slovakia, while it is confirmed that young Moroccan prospect Nabil El Zahr has signed a four-year contract with the Reds.

Daniel Agger's impressive start to the campaign is rewarded with the PFA Fans' Player of the Month award for September. Liverpool's Legends draw 2-2 with their Celtic counterparts in Glasgow, a game played in aid of the Marina Dalglish Appeal and Celtic's own charity.

Blackburn Rovers defender Lucas Neill reveals his interest in joining the Reds, while five former stars, including first goalscorer Ian Rush, feature in a Legends side who defeat the Celebs 2-0 in Sky One's *The Match*.

Jerzy Dudek is sent off in Liverpool reserves' 2-1 defeat to Everton's second string, while Craig Bellamy and Sami Hyypia are on target for Wales and Finland respectively in Euro 2008 qualifiers. Steven Gerrard is nominated for the FIFA World Player of the Year and European Player of the Year (Ballon d'Or) awards while Craig Bellamy breaks his Premiership duck for the Reds – although they are held by the Welsh striker's previous club Blackburn Rovers at Anfield – the Reds' first Saturday 3pm kick-off of the season. It was also the 95th game in succession that Rafa Benitez has fielded a different team.

Progress is made in the cup competitions though. Back-to-back Champions League group wins over Bordeaux seal the Reds' place in the last 16 with two matches still to go (the 3-0 win at Anfield being the first time in 100 games where an unchanged XI was selected), while Reading are beaten in the Carling Cup. Chris Kirkland signs a permanent deal with Wigan Athletic, where he has been on loan. Dirk Kuyt is amongst the goals to the delight of his father, who is in the crowd as the Reds inflict Aston Villa's first defeat of the season.

Outgoing:
Salif Diao (Stoke City, loan), Chris Kirkland (Wigan Athletic).

Injuries:
Dirk Kuyt (ankle), Daniel Agger (wrist), Steven Gerrard (hamstring), Craig Bellamy (calf), Luis Garcia (hamstring).

Quotes of the month:

"No player would not want the opportunity to go to a club like that, with so much history and prestige. I didn't have a say and I didn't move on (in August, when a swap deal involving Stephen Warnock fell through). But now I'm hopefully in just as good a position when those opportunities present themselves again in January, or if not then, I'll get a free transfer in June."

Lucas Neill, planning for the future

"Peter Crouch is fantastic. That goal Crouch scored was magic. If Fowler had scored it, it would have been all over the newspapers. If Thierry Henry had scored it, it would be goal of the season."

Teddy Sheringham, on Crouch's goal against Galatasaray

OCTOBER

THE GAMES

14	Blackburn R.	H	1-1	(Bellamy)
18	**Bordeaux**	**A**	**1-0**	(Crouch)
22	Man Utd	A	0-2	
25	Reading	H	4-3	(Fowler, Riise, Paletta, Crouch)
28	Aston Villa	H	3-1	(Kuyt, Crouch, Garcia)
31	**Bordeaux**	**H**	**3-0**	(Garcia 2, Gerrard)

WHERE THEY STOOD

5 Arsenal
6 Everton
7 Aston Villa
8 Liverpool
9 Fulham
10 Reading
11 Blackburn Rovers

RAFA SAYS . . .

'Two wins in a row will put us back in a challenging position. I do not accept that rotation is the problem.'

AND SO ANOTHER SEASON PASSES...

November

Noel White resigns from the Liverpool board following his admittance that he was the 'anonymous' director who criticised Rafael Benitez in the media. The reserves beat their Wigan counterparts 2-0 to record their first league win of the season – while the U18s do likewise, 1-0 against Manchester United.

Jamie Carragher makes his 300th Premiership appearance in the victory over Reading, while Sami Hyypia is voted the Finnish Player of the Year for the sixth time in eight years.

The Reds reached the quarter-finals of the Carling Cup, although they had to settle for only the one goal at Birmingham City. Unfortunately Momo Sissoko suffers a dislocated shoulder in the match, keeping him out of action until the New Year.

Steve Finnan makes his 100th league appearance for the club in the 0-0 draw at Middlesbrough. The result at the Riverside creates an unwanted landmark – although ending a run of five successive away defeats in the league, the result means the Reds have failed to score in six successive away games, their worst run since 1991/92. However, the Reds secure top spot in Group C of the Champions League following the 2-0 defeat of PSV Eindhoven.

Steven Gerrard's strike in the match means he has now equalled Ian Rush's European Cup goals record of 14. The 0-0 draw with Portsmouth takes the club's run of clean sheets to seven in eight matches, and creates a new record for Jose Reina. The Spanish stopper has beaten Ray Clemence's best for most clean sheets in the first 50 league games for the Reds.

Outgoing:
David Mannix (Accrington Stanley, loan).

Injuries:
Momo Sissoko (shoulder), Xabi Alonso (hip), Mark Gonzalez (hamstring),
Jermanine Pennant (hamstring), Luis Garcia (hamstring), Bolo Zenden (knee ligament).

Quotes of the month:
"Jamie has matured into a world-class defender and deserves every accolade thrown his way. He may have enjoyed some fantastic successes on the pitch but he has never forgotten where he has come from. And it is so refreshing that people like him still exist."

John Aldridge salutes the Reds' vice-captain

"If you're fighting Muhammad Ali in his prime, you don't just go in there and trade blows with him."

Steve Coppell, on the prospect of facing the Reds

"I suffered too much pressure, that is why I head-butted him. I didn't want to attack him. We have had a discussion and I just wanted to intimidate him with a head-to-head, but he moved at the last moment so it became a blow. In future, I will try to remain more lucid and try to contain my envy."

Fernando Menegazzo – Bordeaux man reveals his reasons for head-butting John Arne Riise

"We fear no one in the competition, and we want to go all the way to Athens. I'm sure other teams, at home and in Europe, fear playing us more than we fear them."

Pepe Reina foresees Liverpool's Champions League progress

NOVEMBER

THE GAMES

4	Reading	H	2-0	(Kuyt 2)
8	Birmingham C.	A	1-0	(Agger)
12	Arsenal	A	0-3	
18	Middlesbrough	A	0-0	
22	PSV Eindhoven	H	2-0	(Gerrard, Crouch)
25	Man City	H	1-0	(Gerrard)
29	Portsmouth	H	0-0	

WHERE THEY STOOD

4 Bolton Wanderers
5 Aston Villa
6 Arsenal
7 **Liverpool**
8 Reading
9 Everton
10 Fulham

RAFA SAYS . . .

'I don't know a lot of right-wingers better than Pennant in the Premiership.'

AND SO ANOTHER SEASON PASSES . . .

December
Liverpool end their Premiership away hoodoo in style, four first-half goals including a Craig Bellamy double at Wigan Athletic proving too much for the home side. The club also confirm takeover talks have been held with Dubai International Capital.
The 4-0 defeat of Fulham is Rafael Benitez's 50th league success in only 93 games, quicker than it took Bob Paisley to achieve. The match also sees Jamie Carragher hit the target – his first goal of the 21st century!
Steven Gerrard is awarded the freedom of Huyton by Knowsley Council, while the Reds are paired with holders Barcelona in the Champions League. The 3-0 win at Charlton Athletic means that the Reds have now scored 11 goals without reply in three games – with Jose Reina keeping six successive clean sheets.
The Carling Cup tie against Arsenal at Anfield is postponed due to fog just an hour before kick-off. Blackburn Rovers end Liverpool's eight-match unbeaten run in the league on Boxing Day, although they are soon back to winning ways at Tottenham Hotspur.
Steven Gerrard is awarded the MBE for services to football.

Quotes of the month:
"As far as Liverpool is concerned, I only ever want them to lose two games, and those are the ones against us. So I'm not going into the dugout with a red and white scarf. It will be blue and white – and that's not Everton!"
Paul Jewell, the then Wigan Athletic manager, highlighting his allegiance

"I like the people here when I walk around the city. When I came here everyone was so nice and wanted to help. Maybe the only bad thing is the weather. It seems to be raining all the time."
Daniel Agger, on settling in

"Liverpool have a very shrewd manager in Rafa Benitez...I'm a big fan of Steven Gerrard. I like committed and passionate players. He's a tremendous player and would warrant a place in any side throughout Europe."
Ronaldinho, in praise of the Reds' manager and captain

"Four games is a lot of games and if you want to keep the tradition, maybe play two games, it would be enough. We want to play Boxing Day and we want to play New Year's Day – I feel that is enough."
Rafael Benitez, feeling the strain of the festive season

DECEMBER

THE GAMES

2	Wigan Ath.	A	4-0	(Bellamy 2, Kuyt, McCulloch o.g.)
5	Galatasaray	A	2-3	(Fowler 2)
9	Fulham	H	4-0	(Gerrard, Carragher, Garcia, Gonzalez)
16	Charlton A.	A	3-0	(Alonso pen, Bellamy, Gerrard)
23	Watford	H	2-0	(Bellamy, Alonso)
26	Blackburn R.	A	0-1	
30	Tottenham H.	A	1-0	(Garcia)

WHERE THEY STOOD

1. Manchester United
2. Chelsea
3. Bolton Wanderers
4. Liverpool
5. Arsenal
6. Portsmouth
7. Everton

RAFA SAYS . . .

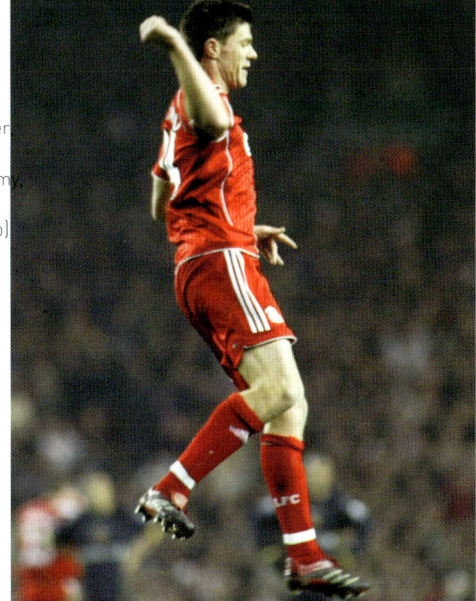

'Four games is a lot and if you want to keep tradition, maybe play two games...we want to play Boxing Day and New Year's Day.'

AND SO ANOTHER SEASON PASSES...

January

Liverpool retained their place in third spot in the Premiership courtesy of a 3-0 demolition of Bolton Wanderers on New Year's Day, taking the club's recent run to only one defeat in 10 – with one conceded, that in the 1-0 defeat at Blackburn Rovers.

Liverpool plan to petition FIFA in a bid to sign West Ham United's on-loan Argentine international Javier Mascherano. The midfielder will need special dispensation to play for the Reds this season after already playing for two clubs since July 1st. FIFA rules state that a player cannot player for three clubs in one year, although this can apparently be wavered if a player's career is at stake – a case that could be accepted as Mascherano has only played six minutes for the Hammers since October.

The Kop do their part against Arsenal in the FA Cup, spelling out a mosaic spelling the words 'The Truth' in response to the injustice following the Hillsborough Disaster and recent comments made by Kelvin McKenzie, the then editor of *The Sun*. However, in the end they can not inspire events on the pitch, as the holders bow out 3-1.

Jamie Carrager is offered a testimonial having played in the first team for 10 years, while a weakened Reds side are beaten 6-3 by Arsenal in the Carling Cup quarter-final, Julio Baptista scoring four times. Danny Guthrie, who made his first-team debut against Reading in the Carling Cup earlier this season, agrees a new contract with the club keeping him at Anfield until at least 2009. Lucas Neill insists his move to West Ham ahead of the Reds is not about the money, while Liverpool step up their bid for second place following the 2-0 victory over champions Chelsea.

Dubai International Capital withdraw their takeover of the club after news emerges that George Gillett, billionaire owner of the Montreal Canadians ice hockey club, is prepared to offer £5,000 per share, giving the club a value of £172m.

Markus Babbel, now back in his homeland with VFB Stuttgart, confirms that he plans to retire at the end of the season.

Incoming:

Emiliano Insua (Boca Juniors, loan), Daniele Padelli (Sampdoria, loan), Jordy Brouwer (Ajax), Astrit Ajdarevic (Falkenburg), Alvaro Arbeloa (Deportivo La Coruna), Francisco Manuel Duran (Malaga), Ronald Huth (Tacuary FC).

Outgoing:

James Smith (Ross County, loan), Adam Hammill (Dunfermline Athletic, loan), Stephen Warnock (Blackburn Rovers), Salif Diao (Stoke City), David Mannix (unattached), Darren Potter (Wolves).

Injuries:

Mark Gonzalez (shin), Luis Garcia (knee).

Quote of the month:

"I think if I had signed a three or four-year contract with Liverpool I would still be there now because I would have renewed it. It was the club I really got a kick out of. The players and supporters made me feel very welcome. I was at a club which really suited me. Why didn't I stay? I don't know. You would have to ask Gerard Houllier."

Nicolas Anelka - any regrets?

"It's always an advantage for us playing at home because of the crowd, we've got the best fans in the world. I love playing at home – it gives us a big advantage and we're going to use it. We just feel like when we go into a game, we're not going to concede a goal and we're going to win. That's a feeling any team would like to have."

John Arne Riise hails the fans

The 2006/07 Season

JANUARY

THE GAMES

1	Bolton W.	H	3-0	(Crouch, Gerrard, Kuyt)
6	Arsenal	H	1-3	(Kuyt)
9	Arsenal	H	3-6	(Fowler, Gerrard, Hyypia)
13	Watford	A	3-0	(Bellamy, Crouch 2)
20	Chelsea	H	2-0	(Kuyt, Pennant)
30	West Ham	A	2-1	(Kuyt, Crouch)

WHERE THEY STOOD

1. Manchester United
2. Chelsea
3. **Liverpool**
4. Arsenal
5. Bolton Wanderers
6. Portsmouth
7. Reading

RAFA SAYS . . .

'When you look at the bigger picture you can see how much progress has been made.'

AND SO ANOTHER SEASON PASSES...

February

Just a week after the collapse of the takeover of the club by D.I.C., American tycoons George Gillett and Tom Hicks reach an agreement to take over on February 6. The offer, worth £5,000 per share, values the club at £174.1m, and along with the club's £44.8m debt it values Liverpool FC at £218.9m.

Steven Gerrard skippers England in the absence of John Terry, in the 1-0 friendly defeat to Spain at Old Trafford. Rafael Benitez is named Manager of the Month for January, after picking up four league wins from four – with only one goal conceded.

Jamie Carragher and Steven Gerrard are named in Marcello Lippi's European squad for a friendly against Manchester United on March 13 while the youth team progress to the semi-finals of the FA Youth Cup after defeating Sheffield United 3-1.

Craig Bellamy and John Arne Riise hit back for Liverpool as the Reds claim an impressive 2-1 win at Barcelona in the Champions League last 16 first-leg tie.

The club confirm that Ukraine striker Andriy Voronin will join in the summer, after agreeing a Bosman move from Bayer Leverkusen while Javier Mascherano is finally cleared to play for Liverpool, making his debut in the 4-0 stroll over Sheffield United. However, it's not such a good day for Peter Crouch, who was forced off in the first half with a broken nose.

Outgoing:
David Martin (Accrington Stanley, loan).

Injuries:
Peter Crouch (broken nose).

Quotes of the month:

"This is great for Liverpool, our supporters and the shareholders – it is the beginning of a new era. They are bringing to the table tremendous and relevant experience, a passion for sport, real resources and a strong commitment to the traditions of Liverpool."

Rick Parry, keen on the Reds' takeover

"We believe in the future of the club, the future of the league, the new TV contracts are outstanding and we are proud to be a part of it. This is truly the largest sport in the world, the most important sport in the world, and this is the most important club in the most important sport in the world. What a privilege we have to be associated with it and we hope that with the good graces of Rick (Parry) and his team that we will have on-the-pitch success and economic success."

George Gillett, impressed with the club

"I look at it (the takeover) as a supporter as much as a player, and the main thing is to have a great team competing for honours every year in a brilliant new stadium. That's a legacy which will serve the club for the next 100 years. (The new owners) told me and Stevie (Gerrard)...they had the interests of the club at heart and want to bring success. That's all you want to hear. It was a privilege. We're just players, so for them to feel they should come and speak to us was great."

Jamie Carragher, relishing a new era

"I love Steven Gerrard. He is an emblem of Liverpool. I saw a replay of the Champions League final...it was so emotional to watch Gerrard...Gerrard was the heart of the team. When he went to celebrate with the supporters after the match and to speak to them, I felt very emotional. The other player who is difficult for us to play against is Peter Crouch. He came to Barcelona on a visit and asked to see us play. Someone at the club thought he was a basketball player, but I told them: 'No, he is a Liverpool player'. We know Crouch is also a good finisher with his feet."

Joan Laporta, Barcelona president

FEBRUARY

THE GAMES

3	Everton	H	0-0	
10	Newcastle U.	A	1-2	(Bellamy)
21	**Barcelona**	A	**2-1**	(Bellamy, Riise)
24	Sheff Utd	H	4-0	(Fowler 2 pens, Hyypia, Gerrard)

WHERE THEY STOOD

1. Manchester United
2. Chelsea
3. **Liverpool**
4. Arsenal
5. Bolton Wanderers
6. Reading
7. Everton

RAFA SAYS . . .

'If we could have Bellamy running at defenders... then turning into Fowler with the goal in sight, it would be perfect.'

AND SO ANOTHER SEASON PASSES...

March

Rick Parry believes there are exciting times ahead after returning from a trip to Dallas to meet new owners George Gillett and Tom Hicks – while the Reds' chief executive confirms plans for a new Kop at the new stadium. Steve Finnan makes his 400th league appearance in the defeat to Manchester United, while Rafael Benitez and Jamie Carragher give their backing to a campaign to posthumously award a knighthood to Bob Paisley. An urgent rethink is made by the club's American owners as they consider the possibility of expanding the planned 60,000 capacity new stadium, eventually to 80,000.

Aston Villa hold the Reds to a 0-0 draw although the point edges the club closer to a guaranteed top-four spot. Academy director Steve Heighway hails the youth team as they reach a second successive FA Youth Cup final courtesy of a 3-1 win at Anfield, 7-3 on aggregate over their Newcastle United counterparts. Rafa Benitez insists clubs should be allowed to enter reserve teams in the Football League, and confirms he will be staying as manager after being given assurances from the new owners.

Steven Gerrard receives his MBE from the Queen – while his autobiography is also named Sports Book of the Year. It is confirmed that George Gillett and Tom Hicks have had their takeover rubber-stamped by the Stock Exchange, while Steven Gerrard scores twice in England's 3-0 Euro 2008 qualifying win in Andorra. Peter Crouch scores a hat-trick as the Reds gain revenge over Arsenal, 4-1 at Anfield. Craig Bellamy donates some of his club fine to cash-strapped Wrexham FC, allowing the League Two strugglers to bring in three players on loan.

Incoming:
Gary Mackay Steven (Ross County).

Outgoing:
Danny Guthrie (Southampton, loan), Godwin Antwi (Accrington Stanley, loan), Lee Peltier (Hull City, loan), Besian Idrizaj (Luton Town, loan), Miki Roque (Oldham Athletic, loan), David Martin (Accrington Stanley, loan).

Injuries:
David Martin (ankle), Francisco Duran (cruciate ligament).

Quotes of the month:

"I would have trouble explaining how we lost that in Spanish – in English I find it almost impossible."

Rafael Benitez, stunned by the Manchester United result

"My wife and I have just had our first child and she's a Scouser. Maybe next time I'll have a son and he can play for Spain or England!"

Pepe Reina, enjoying life in the north west

"With the squad Liverpool have, and if they get their away form right immediately, they can win the title. I'd don't think Liverpool are as far away from winning the Premiership as some might mention."

Martin O'Neill, tips the Reds for a future title push

"I had a conversation with the Queen – it was mostly about football. She wished me all the best for the forthcoming internationals and just told me to keep doing what I've been doing."

Steven Gerrard meets the Queen

The 2006/07 Season

MARCH

THE GAMES

3	Man Utd	H	0-1	
6	**Barcelona**	**H**	**0-1**	
18	Aston Villa	A	0-0	
31	Arsenal	H	4-1	(Crouch 3, Agger)

WHERE THEY STOOD

1. Manchester United
2. Chelsea
3. **Liverpool**
4. Arsenal
5. Bolton Wanderers
6. Everton
7. Tottenham Hotspur

RAFA SAYS . . .

'He (Jamie Carragher) reminds me of a hunting dog, when I want something specific done in defence he is very willing to learn.'

AND SO ANOTHER SEASON PASSES...

April
Liverpool ease into the Champions League semi-finals 4-0 on aggregate, the 3-0 first-leg demolition of PSV Eindhoven in Holland proving key. Steven Gerrard, who opened the scoring, becomes the club's record goalscorer in the European Cup, one ahead of Ian Rush. The same game also sees Jamie Carragher make his 58th in the competition – another club record. Alvaro Arbeloa's goal in the 2-1 win at Reading means that it is the first time since squad numbers were introduced in 1993/94 that a player wearing the No. 2 shirt had scored for the Reds.

The club reveal plans to launch a TV channel, while Steven Gerrard is nominated for the PFA Player Of The Year award. The Reds' youth team lose 2-1 at Anfield in the FA Youth Cup final first leg against Manchester United, Craig Lindfield having put John Owens' side in front.

Fixture congestion forces the club reserve side to withdraw from the Liverpool Senior Cup, ahead of a semi-final against Everton. Rafael Benitez insists he is happy to stay with the club, after revealing that he was offered more money to take over at Real Madrid.

John Arne Riise (300 appearances) and Jose Reina (100) mark Liverpool landmarks in the 2-0 defeat of Wigan Athletic, a result which confirms a top-four place. The Spanish goalkeeper also claims a new club record in the process, keeping more clean sheets in his first 100 Liverpool games than any other previous Reds goalkeeper. His new mark is 55, with Ray Clemence on 51, Bruce Grobbelaar 50 and Jerzy Dudek 45.

Steven Gerrard is the only Liverpool player named in the PFA Team of the Year. The Champions League semi-final, first leg at Chelsea sees Jamie Carragher equal Ian Callaghan's club European appearance record.

Liverpool's youngsters retain the FA Youth Cup with a penalty shoot-out triumph over Manchester United, after winning the second leg 1-0. The triumph also comes as an ideal parting gift for academy director Steve Heighway, who will be leaving his role at the end of the season.

There is also derby victory for the reserves (for whom Harry Kewell makes a second-half appearance, his first run-out since the 2006 FA Cup final), who defeat Everton's second string 3-1.

Injuries:
Fabio Aurelio (Achilles tendon), Craig Bellamy (knee).

Quotes of the month:
"Crouch was superb. Fortunately it's not every day we meet someone of a basketball player's size. I don't mean that to be disrespectful, because he has the size of a basketball player but the skill of a real footballer. If it had merely been a basketball player Kolo and Gallas would have had no problem handling him."
Arsene Wenger salutes the big man

"I'm a bit embarrassed to be honest. He is someone I've watched as a kid and I never dreamt I'd break one of his records. I don't think I'll be breaking any of his other ones."
Steven Gerrard, on breaking Ian Rush's European Cup scoring record for the Reds

"Maybe he has had to win me over but Gerard Houllier told me he was a very good player, even though he is not the sort of player people talk too much about. He has quality and understands the game. I have seen that all in these last few years."
Rafael Benitez, in praise of Steve Finnan

The 2006/07 Season

APRIL

THE GAMES

3	PSV Eindhoven	A	3-0	(Gerrard, Riise, Crouch)
7	Reading	A	2-1	(Arbeloa, Kuyt)
11	PSV Eindhoven	H	1-0	(Crouch)
14	Man City	A	0-0	
18	Middlesboro	H	2-0	(Gerrard 2, 1 pen)
21	Wigan Ath.	H	2-0	(Kuyt 2)
25	Chelsea	A	0-1	
28	Portsmouth	A	1-2	(Hyypia)

WHERE THEY STOOD

1. Manchester United
2. Chelsea
3. **Liverpool**
4. Arsenal
5. Bolton Wanderers
6. Everton
7. Portsmouth

RAFA SAYS . . .

'If you want to earn 85-90 points each year in the league, then you need players who are motivated for every game.'

AND SO ANOTHER SEASON PASSES...

May

Liverpool reach their second Champions League final in three years after overcoming Chelsea 4-1 on penalties, having won 1-0 in the second leg at Anfield courtesy of Daniel Agger's first-half strike. Pepe Reina is the shoot-out hero, saving from Arjen Robben and Geremi. The match also saw Jamie Carragher make a record 90th European appearance, one more than the legendary Ian Callaghan. The final will also be a repeat of 2005, after AC Milan overcome Manchester United 3-0 at the San Siro, 5-3 on aggregate.

Former midfielder and coach Sammy Lee is confirmed as the new manager of Bolton Wanderers while it is revealed that Robbie Fowler will leave the club at the end of the season. Brazilian U20 skipper Lucas Leiva will join the club in the summer, the midfielder being brought in from Gremio. Robbie Fowler captains the side as the final Premiership game ends in a 2-2 draw against Charlton Athletic at Anfield. Fowler is substituted late on and receives a standing ovation, and ironically misses out on a possible final goal in front of The Kop as the Reds are awarded a penalty soon after, converted by Harry Kewell. A final position of third is a repeat of 2005/06.

Alas there is no repeat of 2005's Istanbul heroics, as AC Milan gain revenge in the Champions League final. Two goals from Pipo Inzaghi ensure victory for the Italians, with Dirk Kuyt's late goal failing to inspire a comeback. Incidentally, the final sees Pepe Reina and his dad Miguel Reina become only the third father and son pairing to play in a European Cup final.

It is confirmed that Mark Gonzalez will leave the club, with a deal agreed with Real Betis.

On-loan Adam Hammill suffers defeat in the Scottish Cup final as his Dunfermline Athletic side are beaten 1-0 by SPL champions Celtic.

Steven Gerrard, Jamie Carragher, Peter Crouch and Scott Carson (who is also named in the U21 squad for the European Championships) are named in the England squad for the games against Brazil and Estonia, while Craig Bellamy scores twice for Wales against New Zealand.

Incoming:
Krisztian Nemeth, Andras Simon (MTK Hungaria).

Injuries:
Pepe Reina (shoulder), Mark Gonzalez (ankle), Alvaro Arbeloa (ankle), Xabi Alonso (nose). Momo Sissoko (knee).

Quotes of the month:

"Our supporters – they are the special ones. At Stamford Bridge we won in the stands. The other supporters were with their flags, but our supporters were with their hearts."
Rafael Benitez hails the Red support ahead of the Champions League semi-final, second leg

"I am hugely impressed by the way myself and my family have been received here, it is truly wonderful, that is why I wanted to share the moment with the fans. They are amazing."
George Gillett hails the fans in the wake of Chelsea

"The manager has been great and I can't thank him enough for giving me a chance by bringing me back to Liverpool."
Robbie Fowler, grateful to Rafa

"With investment in the summer and the squad here staying together, we can promise to push Chelsea and United all the way next year."
Steven Gerrard outlines plans for 2007-08

"If Rafa said he wanted to buy 'Snoogy Doogy' we would back him."
George Gillett, happy to fund the manager

The 2006/07 Season

MAY

THE GAMES

1	Chelsea	H	1-0*aet	(Agger)
			*Liverpool win 4-1 on penalties	
5	Fulham	A	0-1	
13	Charlton Ath.	H	2-2	(Alonso, Kewell pen)
23	AC Milan	N	1-2	(Kuyt)

WHERE THEY FINISHED

1. Manchester United
2. Chelsea
3. **Liverpool**
4. Arsenal
5. Tottenham Hotspur
6. Everton
7. Bolton Wanderers

RAFA SAYS . . .

'We wanted to pay tribute to Robbie (Fowler) and the supporters were fantastic as always.'

113

Liverpool FC : The Official Guide 2008

2006/07

- ● Game played
- ○ Substituted player
- ● Unused sub
- ● Goal scored
- ○ Used Sub
- ● Substituted sub

Players (1–25): Jerzy Dudek, Alvaro Arbeloa, Steve Finnan, Sami Hyypia, Daniel Agger, John Arne Riise, Harry Kewell, Steven Gerrard, Robbie Fowler, Luis Garcia, Mark Gonzalez, Fabio Aurelio, Xabi Alonso, Peter Crouch, Jermaine Pennant, Craig Bellamy, Dirk Kuyt, Javier Mascherano, Mohamed Sissoko, Jamie Carragher, Florent Sinama-Pongolle, Jose Reina

DATE	OPPONENTS		RES	ATT
August				
9	Maccabi Haifa (CLQ3 1st)	H	2-1	40,058
13	Chelsea (Com Shield)	N	2-1	56,275
19	Sheff Utd	H	1-1	31,726
22	Maccabi Haifa (CLQ3 2nd)	A^	1-1	12,500
26	West Ham	H	2-1	43,965
September				
9	Everton	A	0-3	40,004
12	PSV (CL Group 1)	A	0-0	35,000
17	Chelsea	A	0-1	41,882
20	Newcastle	H	2-0	43,754
23	Spurs	H	3-0	44,330
27	Galatasaray (CL Group 2)	H	3-2	41,976
30	Bolton	A	0-2	25,061
October				
14	Blackburn	H	1-1	44,206
18	Bordeaux (CL Group 3)	A	1-0	33,000
22	Man Utd	A	0-2	75,828
25	Reading (Carling Cup 3rd)	H	4-3	42,445
28	Aston Villa	H	3-1	44,117
31	Bordeaux (CL Group 4)	H	3-0	41,978
November				
4	Reading	H	2-0	43,741
8	Birmingham (Carling Cup 4th)	A	1-0	23,061
12	Arsenal	A	0-3	60,110
18	Middlesbrough	A	0-0	31,424
22	PSV (CL Group 5)	H	2-0	41,948
25	Man City	H	1-0	44,081
29	Portsmouth	H	0-0	42,467
December				
2	Wigan	A	4-0*	22,089
5	Galatasaray (CL Group 6)	A	2-3	23,000
9	Fulham	H	4-0	44,189
16	Charlton	A	3-0	27,111
23	Watford	H	2-0	42,807
26	Blackburn	A	0-1	29,342
30	Spurs	A	1-0	36,170
January				
1	Bolton	H	3-0	41,370
6	Arsenal (FA Cup 3rd)	H	1-3	43,619
9	Arsenal (Carling Cup 5th)	H	3-6	42,614
13	Watford	A	3-0	19,746
20	Chelsea	H	2-0	44,245
30	West Ham	A	2-1	34,966
February				
3	Everton	H	0-0	44,234
10	Newcastle	A	1-2	52,305
21	Barcelona (CL last 16 1st)	A	2-1	88,000
24	Sheff Utd	H	4-0	44,198
March				
3	Man Utd	H	0-1	44,403
6	Barcelona (CL last 16 2nd)	H	0-1	42,579
18	Aston Villa	A	0-0	42,551
31	Arsenal	H	4-1	43,958
April				
3	PSV (CL quarter-final 1st)	A	3-0	36,500
7	Reading	H	2-1	24,121
11	PSV (CL quarter-final 2nd)	H	1-0	41,447
14	Man City	A	0-0	45,883
18	Middlesbrough	H	2-0	41,458
21	Wigan	H	2-0	43,003
25	Chelsea (CL semi-final 1st)	A	0-1	39,483
28	Portsmouth	A	1-2	20,201
May				
1	Chelsea (CL semi-final 2nd)	H	1-0•	42,554
5	Fulham	A	0-1	24,554
13	Charlton	H	2-2	43,134
23	AC Milan (CL Final)	N	1-2	74,000

^ match played in Kiev, Ukraine
* own goal v Wigan (McCulloch)
• AET, Liverpool won 4-1 on penalties

114

The 2006/07 Season

FINAL TABLE

BARCLAYS PREMIERSHIP TABLE 2006/07

			HOME					AWAY					
Team	Pd	W	D	L	F	A	W	D	L	F	A	Pts	GD
1. Manchester Utd	38	15	2	2	46	12	13	3	3	37	15	89	+56
2. Chelsea	38	12	7	0	37	11	12	4	3	27	13	83	+40
3. Liverpool	38	14	4	1	39	7	6	4	9	18	20	68	+30
4. Arsenal	38	12	6	1	43	16	7	5	7	20	19	68	+28
5. Tottenham Hotspur	38	12	3	4	34	22	5	6	8	23	32	60	+3
6. Everton	38	11	4	4	33	17	4	9	6	19	19	58	+16
7. Bolton Wanderers	38	9	5	5	26	20	7	3	9	21	32	56	-5
8. Reading	38	11	2	6	29	20	5	5	9	23	27	55	+5
9. Portsmouth	38	11	5	3	28	15	3	7	9	17	27	54	+3
10. Blackburn Rovers	38	9	3	7	31	25	6	4	9	21	29	52	-2
11. Aston Villa	38	7	8	4	20	14	4	9	6	23	27	50	+2
12. Middlesbrough	38	10	3	6	31	24	2	7	10	13	25	46	-5
13. Newcastle United	38	7	7	5	23	20	4	3	12	15	27	43	-9
14. Manchester City	38	5	6	8	10	16	6	3	10	19	28	42	-15
15. West Ham United	38	8	2	9	24	26	4	3	12	11	33	41	-24
16. Fulham	38	7	7	5	18	18	1	8	10	20	42	39	-22
17. Wigan Athletic	38	5	4	10	18	30	5	4	10	19	29	38	-22
18. Sheffield United	38	7	6	6	24	21	3	2	14	8	34	38	-23
19. Charlton Athletic	38	7	5	7	19	20	1	5	13	15	40	34	-26
20. Watford	38	3	9	7	19	25	2	4	13	10	34	28	-30

115

MINUTES ON PITCH 2006/2007

	LEAGUE	FA CUP	LEAGUE CUP	CHAMP. LEAGUE	FA COM. SHIELD	TOTAL
DUDEK	180	90	180	90	0	540
KROMKAMP	90	0	0	0	0	90
ARBELOA	705	0	0	362	0	1067
FINNAN	2889	90	0	1108	90	4177
HYYPIA	2033	0	90	450	0	2573
AGGER	2165	90	180	1098	90	3623
RIISE	2569	60	79	1072	90	3870
KEWELL	46	0	0	31	0	77
GERRARD	3080	90	90	967	30	4257
FOWLER	605	0	252	177	0	1034
GARCIA	999	90	65	461	66	1681
GONZALEZ	1216	0	100	265	56	1637
AURELIO	1014	30	90	322	34	1490
ALONSO	2659	90	95	1106	30	3980
CROUCH	1509	90	90	780	89	2558
PENNANT	1969	90	180	834	60	3133
BELLAMY	1918	0	179	545	24	2666
KUYT	2582	90	29	929	0	3630
MASCHERANO	616	0	0	376	0	992
SISSOKO	1228	0	89	606	90	2013
CARRAGHER	2980	90	15	1200	90	4375
SINAMA-PONGOLLE	0	0	0	0	1	1
REINA	3150	0	90	1290	90	4620
WARNOCK	54	0	238	121	0	413
PALETTA	209	0	270	102	0	581
PADELLI	90	0	0	0	0	90
ZENDEN	810	0	180	728	60	1778
ROQUE	0	0	0	6	0	6
GUTHRIE	32	0	119	66	0	217
PELTIER	0	0	254	90	0	344
SMITH	0	0	16	0	0	16
EL ZHAR	51	0	0	0	0	51
INSUA	165	0	0	0	0	165

PLAYER GOALS 2006/2007 SEASON

ALL COMPETITIONS			
	1ST HALF	**2ND HALF**	**TOTAL**
CROUCH	6	12	18
KUYT	6	8	14
GERRARD	1	10	11
BELLAMY	6	3	9
FOWLER	5	2	7
GARCIA	4	2	6
RIISE	2	3	5
AGGER	3	1	4
ALONSO	1	3	4
GONZALEZ	0	3	3
HYYPIA	0	3	3
ARBELOA	1	0	1
CARRAGHER	0	1	1
KEWELL	0	1	1
PALETTA	0	1	1
PENNANT	1	0	1
OWN GOAL	1	0	1
TOTAL	**37**	**53**	**90**

Celebrations as Jermaine Pennant's super strike helps down Chelsea at Anfield

APPEARANCES & GOALS FOR LIVERPOOL

AT END OF 2006/07 SEASON - CURRENT SQUAD ONLY

L'POOL	LGE GMS	LGE GLS	FA GMS	FA GLS	L. CUP GMS	L. CUP GLS	EURO GMS (inc Spr Cup)	EURO GLS	OTHER GMS (inc C. Shield & C. World)	OTHER GLS	L'POOL GMS	GLS
ARBELOA	9	1	0	0	0	0	5	0	0	0	14	1
FINNAN	121	1	10	0	5	0	44	0	2	0	182	1
HYYPIA	275	20	24	1	17	2	81	6	4	0	401	29
AGGER	31	2	1	0	2	1	12	1	1	0	47	4
RIISE	205	21	13	3	12	2	69	4	5	1	304	31
KEWELL	83	12	9	0	4	1	27	3	1	0	124	16
GERRARD	268	44	20	5	17	6	78	19	4	1	387	75
AURELIO	17	0	1	0	1	0	5	0	1	0	25	0
ALONSO	91	9	6	2	2	0	34	1	3	0	136	12
CROUCH	64	17	7	3	2	1	22	7	3	3	98	31
PENNANT	34	1	1	0	2	0	14	0	1	0	52	1
KUYT	34	12	1	1	2	0	11	1	0	0	48	14
MASCHERANO	7	0	0	0	0	0	4	0	0	0	11	0
SISSOKO	42	0	6	0	2	0	20	0	3	0	73	0
CARRAGHER	325	3	25	0	23	0	91	1	4	0	468	4
REINA	68	0	5	0	1	0	27	0	3	0	104	0
ROQUE	0	0	0	0	0	0	1	0	0	0	1	0
GUTHRIE	3	0	0	0	3	0	1	0	0	0	7	0
PELTIER	0	0	0	0	3	0	1	0	0	0	4	0
EL ZHAR	3	0	0	0	0	0	0	0	0	0	3	0
INSUA	2	0	0	0	0	0	0	0	0	0	2	0
SMITH	0	0	0	0	1	0	0	0	0	0	1	0
LE TALLEC	17	0	4	0	2	0	9	1	0	0	32	1
CARSON	4	0	1	0	1	0	3	0	0	0	9	0

MAN OF THE SEASON

For the first time, readers of the official *LFC Magazine* were given a say in who would secure the publication's Player of the Year award. There were four outstanding candidates, but it was Jamie Carragher who prevailed, taking 30.8% of the vote. His closest rival was skipper Steven Gerrard, who picked up 27.5% while the top four was made up of Daniel Agger (23.1%) and Steve Finnan (18.7%).

10 YEARS OF CARRA

Liverpool's man of the season was granted a testimonial during the 2006/07 and in tribute to Jamie Carrragher, we list his playing statistics throughout his career at Anfield.

Carra has won a clutch of domestic and European winners' medals since making his debut as a substitute in place of Rob Jones against Middlesbrough in the League Cup in January 1997.

As well as this, Liverpool's run to the UEFA Champions League final in 2006/07 enabled him to pass Ian Callaghan as the Reds player who has represented the club most times in Europe (91 appearances at the end of 2006/07).

JAMIE CARRAGHER LIVERPOOL STATISTICS

SEASON (APPS/GOALS)	LEAGUE A	G	FA CUP A	G	LGE CUP A	G	EUROPE A	G	WRLD CC A	G	CH. SH. A	G	TOTAL A	G
1996/97	1 + (1)	1	0	0	0 + (1)	0	0	0	0	0	0	0	1 + (2)	1
1997/98	17 + (3)	0	0	0	2	0	1	0	0	0	0	0	20 + (3)	0
1998/99	34	1	2	0	2	0	6	0	0	0	0	0	44	1
1999/00	33 + (3)	0	2	0	2	0	0	0	0	0	0	0	37 + (3)	0
2000/01	30 + (4)	0	6	0	6	0	12	0	0	0	0	0	54 + (4)	0
2001/02	33	0	2	0	1	0	16	0	0	0	0 + (1)	0	52 + (1)	0
2002/03	34 + (1)	0	3	0	3 + (2)	0	11	0	0	0	0	0	51 + (3)	0
2003/04	22	0	3	0	0	0	4	0	0	0	0	0	29	0
2004/05	38	0	0	0	3	0	15	0	0	0	0	0	56	0
2005/06	36	0	6	0	0	0	13	1	2	0	0	0	57	1
2006/07	34 + (1)	1	1	0	0 + (1)	0	13	0	0	0	1	0	49 + (2)	1
TOTAL	312 + (13)	3	25	0	19 + (4)	0	91	1	2	0	1 + (1)	0	450 + (18)	4

OVERALL 468 APPEARANCES, 4 GOALS

(Appearances are listed as starts with substitute appearances in brackets)

JAMIE CARRAGHER'S EUROPEAN APPEARANCES AND GOALS

	GAMES	GOALS
EUROPEAN CUP	61	1
EUROPEAN CUP WINNERS' CUP	0	0
UEFA CUP	28	0
UEFA SUPER CUP	2	0
TOTAL	**91**	**1**

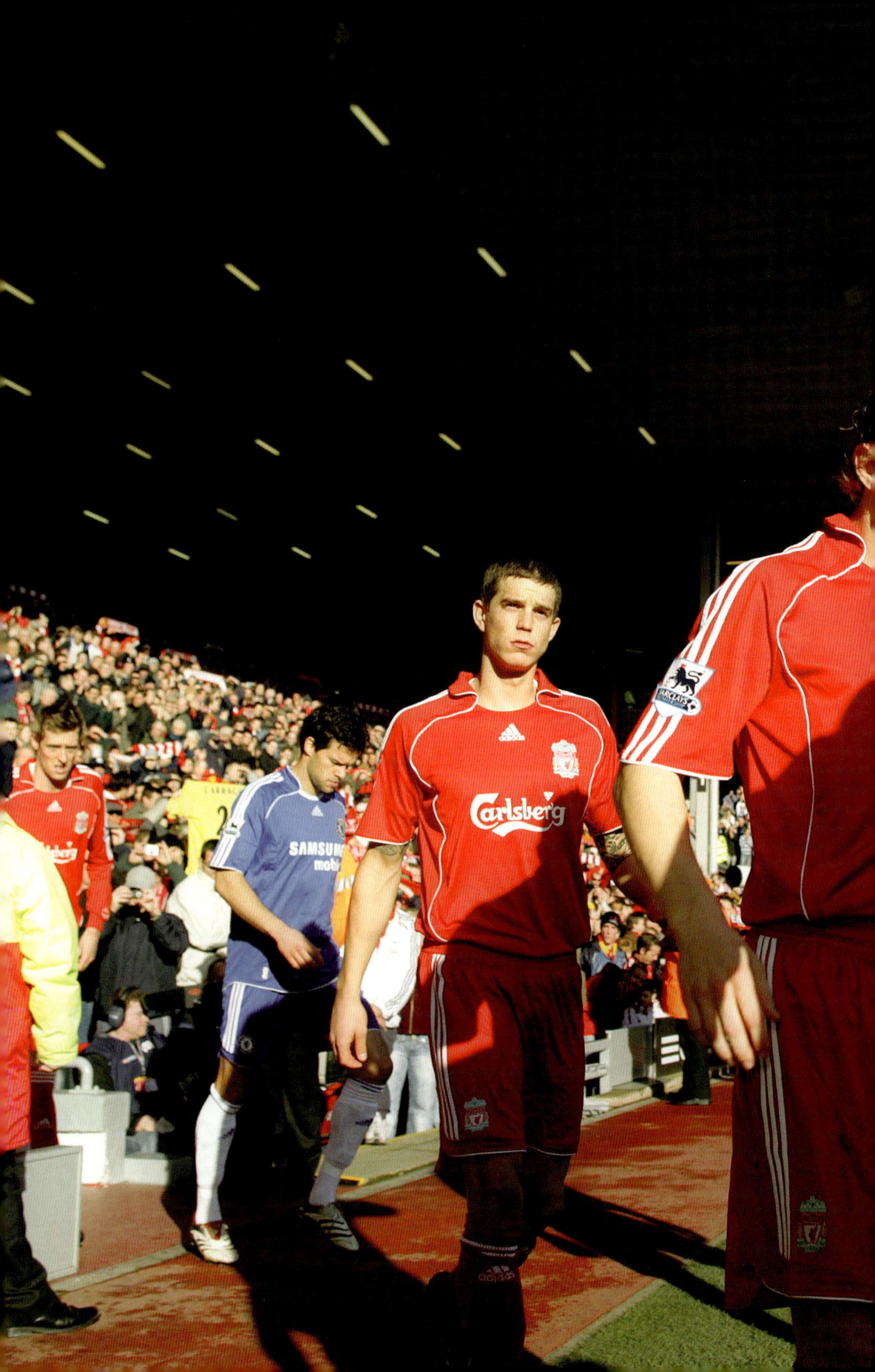
Carlsberg

THE TOP FLIGHT

MOST POINTS WON BY TEAMS IN PREMIER LEAGUE HISTORY

		POINTS	HIGHEST POS	SEASONS IN PREMIERSHIP
1	MANCHESTER UNITED	1232	1st (9 times)	15
2	ARSENAL	1081	1st (3 times)	15
3	CHELSEA	1013	1st (2 times)	15
4	LIVERPOOL	999	2nd (2001/2002)	15
5	NEWCASTLE UNITED	829	2nd (2 times)	14
6	ASTON VILLA	817	2nd (1992/1993)	15
7	TOTTENHAM HOTSPUR	788	5th (2 times)	15
8	BLACKBURN ROVERS	747	1st (1994/1995)	13
9	EVERTON	735	4th (2004/2005)	15
10	LEEDS UNITED	692	3rd (1999/2000)	12
11	WEST HAM UNITED	596	5th (1998/1999)	12
12	SOUTHAMPTON	587	8th (2002/2003)	13
13	MIDDLESBROUGH	559	7th (2004/2005)	12
14	MANCHESTER CITY	452	8th (2004/2005)	10
15	COVENTRY CITY	409	11th (2 times)	9
16	SHEFFIELD WEDNESDAY	392	7th (3 times)	8
17	WIMBLEDON (MK DONS)	391	6th (1993/1994)	8
18	BOLTON WANDERERS	376	6th (2004/2005)	8
19	CHARLTON ATHLETIC	361	7th (2003/2004)	8
20	LEICESTER CITY	342	8th (1999/2000)	8
21	FULHAM	275	9th (2003/2004)	6
22	DERBY COUNTY	263	8th (1998/1999)	6
23	NOTTINGHAM FOREST	239	3rd (1994/1995)	5
24	SUNDERLAND	229	7th (2 times)	6
25	IPSWICH TOWN	224	5th (2000/2001)	5
26	QUEENS PARK RANGERS	216	5th (1992/1993)	4
27	NORWICH CITY	201	3rd (1992/1993)	4
28	BIRMINGHAM CITY	177	10th (2003/2004)	4
29	PORTSMOUTH	176	9th (2006/2007)	4
30	CRYSTAL PALACE	160	18th (2004/2005)	4
31	SHEFFIELD UNITED	132	14th (1992/1993)	3
32	WEST BROMWICH ALB.	90	17th (2004/2005)	3
33	OLDHAM ATHLETIC	89	19th (1992/1993)	2
=	WIGAN ATHLETIC	89	10th (2005/2006)	2
35	BRADFORD CITY	62	17th (1999/2000)	2
36	READING	55	8th (2006/2007)	1
37	WATFORD	52	20th (1999/2000)	2
38	BARNSLEY	35	19th (1997/1998)	1
39	WOLVERHAMPTON W.	33	20th (2003/2004)	1
40	SWINDON TOWN	30	22nd (1994/1995)	1

THE LEAGUE FINISHES

DIVISION ONE/PREMIERSHIP - 92 SEASONS

Number of times

First	18
Second	11
Third	7
Fourth	7
Fifth	9
Sixth	2
Seventh	4
Eighth	4
Ninth	4
Tenth	2
Eleventh	5
Twelfth	4
Thirteenth	2
Fourteenth	1
Fifteenth	1
Sixteenth	4
Seventeenth	3
Eighteenth	2
Nineteenth	1
Twentieth	0
Twenty-first	0
Twenty-second	1

DIVISION TWO - 11 SEASONS

Number of times

First	4
Third	4
Fourth	2
Eleventh	1

LEAGUE SEQUENCE RECORDS

12	MOST LEAGUE WINS IN SUCCESSION (21st April 1990 - 6th October 1990)
6	MOST LEAGUE DRAWS IN SUCCESSION (12th February - 19th March 1975)
9	MOST LEAGUE DEFEATS IN SUCCESSION (29th April 1899 - 14th October 1899)
21	MOST HOME LEAGUE WINS IN SUCCESSION (29th January 1972 - 30th December 1972)
6	MOST HOME LEAGUE DRAWS IN SUCCESSION (10th November 1951 - 5th January 1952)
4	MOST HOME LEAGUE DEFEATS IN SUCCESSION (24th November 1923 - 25th December 1923)
6	MOST AWAY LEAGUE WINS IN SUCCESSION (4 occasions, most recent 22nd January 2002 - 13th April 2002)
6	MOST AWAY LEAGUE DRAWS IN SUCCESSION (24th October 1967 - 26th December 1967)
20	MOST AWAY LEAGUE DEFEATS IN SUCCESSION (7th March 1953 - 16th January 1954)

Nigel Clough (top) and Stan Collymore (bottom) celebrate goals against Manchester United in 1994 and Newcastle United in 1996, two of the club's most memorable Premier League games

PREMIER LEAGUE: CLUB-BY-CLUB

LIVERPOOL'S LEAGUE RECORD - CLUB-BY-CLUB
(Only teams in Premier League in 2006-07 included)

	PLAYED	WON	DREW	LOST	FOR	AGAINST
ARSENAL	166	68	40	58	236	210
ASTON VILLA	164	77	36	51	289	241
BLACKBURN ROVERS	118	48	36	34	208	163
BOLTON WANDERERS	108	44	29	35	167	134
CHARLTON ATHLETIC	56	29	8	19	93	70
CHELSEA	128	58	26	44	202	182
EVERTON	176	65	55	56	238	212
FULHAM	40	22	11	7	78	41
MANCHESTER CITY	142	72	33	37	258	188
MANCHESTER UNITED	148	49	43	56	192	205
MIDDLESBROUGH	130	55	38	37	223	164
NEWCASTLE UNITED	144	67	37	40	245	183
PORTSMOUTH	54	21	14	19	94	84
READING	2	2	0	0	4	1
SHEFFIELD UNITED	118	55	27	36	192	153
TOTTENHAM HOTSPUR	128	60	33	35	203	143
WATFORD	16	12	1	3	37	16
WEST HAM UNITED	100	52	28	20	162	92
WIGAN ATHLETIC	4	4	0	0	10	0

LIVERPOOL GOALS v PREMIER LEAGUE OPPONENTS

	GAMES PLAYED	GOALS IN FIXTURE	AVE. PER GAME	LIVERPOOL GOALS	AVE. PER GAME
ARSENAL	30	70	2.33	41	1.37
ASTON VILLA	30	77	2.57	48	1.6
BARNSLEY	2	6	3.00	3	1.50
BIRMINGHAM CITY	8	23	2.88	12	1.50
BLACKBURN ROVERS	26	70	2.69	39	1.5
BOLTON WANDERERS	16	45	2.81	28	1.75
BRADFORD CITY	4	8	2.00	6	1.50
CHARLTON ATHLETIC	16	43	2.69	27	1.69
CHELSEA	30	75	2.5	34	1.13
COVENTRY CITY	18	44	2.44	27	1.50
CRYSTAL PALACE	8	26	3.25	20	2.50
DERBY COUNTY	12	30	2.50	22	1.83
EVERTON	30	66	2.2	35	1.17
FULHAM	12	35	2.92	24	2.00
IPSWICH TOWN	10	27	2.70	20	2.00
LEEDS UNITED	24	71	2.96	48	2.00
LEICESTER CITY	16	33	2.06	19	1.19
MANCHESTER CITY	20	51	2.55	33	1.65
MANCHESTER UNITED	30	75	2.5	31	1.03
MIDDLESBROUGH	24	52	2.17	34	1.42
NEWCASTLE UNITED	28	86	3.07	52	1.86
NORWICH CITY	8	24	3.00	17	2.13
NOTTINGHAM FOREST	10	29	2.90	18	1.80
OLDHAM ATHLETIC	4	12	3.00	8	2.00
PORTSMOUTH	8	19	2.38	13	1.63
QUEENS PARK RANGERS	8	20	2.50	13	1.62
READING	2	5	2.50	4	2.00
SHEFFIELD UNITED	6	13	2.17	8	1.33
SHEFFIELD WEDNESDAY	16	43	2.69	27	1.69
SOUTHAMPTON	26	78	3.00	45	1.73
SUNDERLAND	12	19	1.58	13	1.08
SWINDON TOWN	2	9	4.50	7	3.50
TOTTENHAM HOTSPUR	30	82	2.73	50	1.67
WATFORD	4	11	2.75	8	2.00
WEST BROMWICH ALBION	6	19	3.17	19	3.17
WEST HAM UNITED	24	56	2.33	38	1.58
WIGAN ATHLETIC	4	10	2.50	10	2.50
WIMBLEDON	16	39	2.44	22	1.37
WOLVERHAMPTON WANDERERS	2	3	1.50	2	1.00

FULL LEAGUE RECORD - CLUB-BY-CLUB

	PLAYED	WON	DREW	LOST	FOR	AGAINST
ARSENAL	166	68	40	58	236	210
ASTON VILLA	164	77	36	51	289	241
BARNSLEY	12	7	2	3	23	15
BIRMINGHAM CITY	94	46	20	28	157	132
BLACKBURN ROVERS	118	48	36	34	208	163
BLACKPOOL	40	18	9	13	72	62
BOLTON WANDERERS	108	44	29	35	167	134
BRADFORD CITY	26	18	2	6	45	22
BRADFORD PARK AVENUE	6	3	1	2	10	8
BRENTFORD	10	4	3	3	16	16
BRIGHTON & HOVE ALB.	16	8	6	2	36	20
BRISTOL CITY	30	16	3	11	52	39
BRISTOL ROVERS	16	10	1	5	32	21
BURNLEY	74	29	19	26	117	95
BURTON SWIFTS	4	3	1	0	17	3
BURTON UNITED	2	1	0	1	3	2
BURTON WANDERERS	2	1	0	1	5	3
BURY	48	26	14	8	92	53
CARDIFF CITY	26	8	2	16	35	51
CARLISLE UNITED	2	2	0	0	3	0
CHARLTON ATHLETIC	56	29	8	19	93	70
CHELSEA	128	58	26	44	202	182
CHESTERFIELD	2	1	1	0	7	2
COVENTRY CITY	68	39	16	13	113	45
CREWE ALEXANDRA	4	4	0	0	20	1
CRYSTAL PALACE	26	15	6	5	57	17
DARWEN	2	1	1	0	4	0
DERBY COUNTY	124	64	28	32	240	155
DONCASTER ROVERS	10	5	2	3	19	13
EVERTON	176	65	55	56	238	212
FULHAM	40	22	11	7	78	41
GAINSBOROUGH TRINITY	2	2	0	0	8	2
GLOSSOP	4	3	1	0	11	5
GRIMSBY TOWN	36	18	10	8	87	47
HUDDERSFIELD TOWN	68	25	17	26	113	113
HULL CITY	6	5	1	0	15	7
IPSWICH TOWN	60	28	19	13	110	59
LEEDS UNITED	100	51	25	24	164	101
LEICESTER CITY	88	36	19	33	143	121
LEYTON ORIENT	14	9	2	3	37	15
LINCOLN CITY	20	11	4	5	42	28
LOUGHBOROUGH T.	2	2	0	0	5	2
LUTON TOWN	28	13	9	6	52	33
MANCHESTER CITY	142	72	33	37	258	188
MANCHESTER UNITED	148	49	43	56	192	205
MIDDLESBROUGH	130	55	38	37	223	164
MIDDLESBROUGH IRON.	2	2	0	0	8	0
MILLWALL	4	3	1	0	6	3
NEWCASTLE UNITED	144	67	37	40	245	183
NORTHAMPTON TOWN	2	1	1	0	5	0
NORTHWICH VICTORIA	2	2	0	0	7	2
NORWICH CITY	46	24	11	11	84	47
NOTTINGHAM FOREST	100	50	24	26	167	99
NOTTS COUNTY	60	34	12	14	110	63
OLDHAM ATHLETIC	24	14	4	6	39	30
OXFORD UNITED	6	5	1	0	20	3
PLYMOUTH ARGYLE	10	5	3	2	22	15
PORTSMOUTH	54	21	14	19	94	84
PORT VALE	12	7	3	2	38	20
PRESTON NORTH END	64	26	17	21	114	99
QUEENS PARK RANGERS	40	28	6	6	68	34

FULL LEAGUE RECORD - CLUB-BY-CLUB

	PLAYED	WON	DREW	LOST	FOR	AGAINST
READING	2	2	0	0	4	1
ROTHERHAM UNITED	20	14	3	3	57	21
SCUNTHORPE UNITED	8	6	2	0	17	8
SHEFFIELD UNITED	118	55	27	36	192	153
SHEFFIELD WEDNESDAY	116	54	26	36	197	165
SOUTHAMPTON	74	35	18	21	112	86
STOKE CITY	106	53	27	26	176	113
SUNDERLAND	140	60	31	49	234	210
SWANSEA CITY	20	10	4	6	51	27
SWINDON TOWN	2	1	1	0	7	2
TOTTENHAM HOTSPUR	128	60	33	35	203	143
WALSALL	4	2	2	0	11	3
WATFORD	16	12	1	3	37	16
WEST BROMWICH ALBION	114	53	33	28	176	127
WEST HAM UNITED	100	52	28	20	162	92
WIGAN ATHLETIC	4	4	0	0	10	0
WIMBLEDON	28	11	10	7	41	31
WOLVERHAMPTON WANDERERS	88	43	16	29	136	106

UNBEATEN HOME LEAGUE RECORD

LIVERPOOL'S LONGEST RUNS UNBEATEN AT HOME (LEAGUE)

NO. OF GAMES	FIRST GAME OF RUN	DAY BEFORE RUN ENDED	DATE OF DEFEAT	VISITING WINNERS
63	25.02.1978	30.01.1981	31.01.1981	Leicester City
34	24.03.1970	31.12.1971	01.01.1972	Leeds United
31	27.03.1976	04.11.1977	05.11.1977	Aston Villa
30	15.10.2005	02.03.2007	03.03.2007	Manchester United
29	21.01.1961	17.08.1962	18.08.1962	Blackpool
27	01.01.1966	21.04.1967	22.04.1967	West Bromwich A.
27	24.02.1973	23.04.1974	24.04.1974	Arsenal
26	20.03.1982	22.04.1983	23.04.1983	Norwich City
26	26.11.1989	02.03.1991	03.03.1991	Arsenal
25	18.04.1987	30.09.1988	01.10.1988	Newcastle United
23	13.02.1904	08.09.1905	09.09.1905	Blackburn Rovers
22	29.01.1972	09.02.1973	10.02.1973	Arsenal
22	23.11.1974	28.11.1975	29.11.1975	Norwich City

LONGEST RUNS UNBEATEN AT HOME (LEAGUE - 20 OR MORE, CHRONOLOGICALLY)

23	13.02.1904	08.09.1905	09.09.1905	Blackburn Rovers
29	21.01.1961	17.08.1962	18.08.1962	Blackpool
27	01.01.1966	21.04.1967	22.04.1967	West Bromwich Albion
34	24.03.1970	31.12.1971	01.01.1972	Leeds United
22	29.01.1972	09.02.1973	10.02.1973	Arsenal
27	24.02.1973	23.04.1974	24.04.1974	Arsenal
22	23.11.1974	28.11.1975	29.11.1975	Norwich City
31	27.03.1976	04.11.1977	05.11.1977	Aston Villa
63	25.02.1978	30.01.1981	31.01.1981	Leicester City
26	20.03.1982	22.04.1983	23.04.1983	Norwich City
25	18.04.1987	30.09.1988	01.10.1988	Newcastle United
26	26.11.1989	02.03.1991	03.03.1991	Arsenal
30	15.10.2005	02.03.2007	03.03.2007	Manchester United

PREMIER LEAGUE NUMBERS GAME

SQUAD NUMBERS

Number Players (with Premiership appearances in brackets)

1	Grobbelaar (29),	James (171),	Westerveld (75),	Dudek (92)	
2	R.Jones (125),	Henchoz (135)	Kromkamp (14)	Arbeloa (9)	
3	Burrows (4),	Dicks (24),	Scales (3),	Kvarme (45),	Ziege (16),
	Xavier (14),	Finnan (121)			
4	Nicol (35),	McAteer (100),	Song (34),	Hyypia (202)	
5	M.Wright (104),	Staunton (44),	Baros (68)	Agger (31)	
6	Hutchison (11),	Babb (128),	Babbel (42),	Riise (102)	
7	Clough (39),	McManaman (101),	Smicer (91),	Kewell (83)	
8	Stewart (8),	Collymore (61),	Leonhardsen (37),	Heskey (150),	Gerrard (98)
9	Rush (98),	Fowler (144),	Anelka (20),	Diouf (55),	Cisse (49),
10	Barnes (135),	Owen (178),	Garcia (77)		
11	Walters (35),	Redknapp (103),	Smicer (30)	Fowler (14)	Gonzalez (25)
12	Whelan (23),	Scales (62),	Harkness (38),	Hyypia (73),	Dudek (35),
	P.Jones (2),	Pellegrino (12)	Aurelio (17)		
13	James (14),	Riedle (60),	Murphy (130),	Le Tallec (4)	
14	Molby (25),	Ruddock (19),	Heggem (54),	Alonso (91)	
15	Redknapp (99),	Berger (148),	Diao (11)	Crouch (64)	
16	Thomas (99),	Dundee (3),	Hamann (191),	Pennant (34)	
17	McManaman (108),	Ince (65),	Gerrard (129),	Josemi (21)	Bellamy (27)
18	Rosenthal (3),	Owen (38),	Ferri (2),	Meijer (24),	Riise (103),
	Nunez (18)	Kuyt (34)			
19	Piechnik (1),	Kennedy (16),	Friedel (14),	Arphexad (2),	Morientes (41)
20	Bjornebye (128),	Barmby (32),	Le Tallec (13),	Carson (4),	Mascherano (7)
21	Marsh (2),	Matteo (127),	McAllister (55),	Diao (26),	Traore (48)
22	Harkness (43),	Camara (33),	Kirkland (25),	Sissoko (42)	
23	Fowler (108),	Carragher (325)			
24	L.Jones (3),	Murphy (40),	Diomede (2),	S-Pongolle (38),	
25	Ruddock (96),	Thompson (48),	Biscan (72),	Reina (68)	
27	Vignal (11)				
28	Gerrard (41),	Cheyrou (31),	Warnock (40)		
29	Friedel (11),	S.Wright (14),	Luzi (1),	Paletta (3)	
30	Traore (40),	Zenden (7),	Padelli (1)		
31	Raven (1)				
32	Newby (1),	Welsh (4)	Zenden (16)		
33	Mellor (12)				
34	Potter (2)				
35	Guthrie (3)				
36	Otsemobor (4)				
37	Litmanen (26)				
42	El Zhar (3)				
48	Insua (2)				

MOST APPEARANCES IN PREMIER LEAGUE

Top 20 total appearances in Premier League

Jamie Carragher	**325**
Sami Hyypia	**275**
Steven Gerrard	**268**
Robbie Fowler	266
Steve McManaman	240
Jamie Redknapp	231
Michael Owen	216
David James	214
John Arne Riise	**205**
Dietmar Hamann	191

Top 20 total appearances in Premier League

Danny Murphy	170
John Barnes	162
Rob Jones	155
Emile Heskey	150
Patrik Berger	148
Stig Inge Bjornebye	139
Mark Wright	137
Stephane Henchoz	135
Ian Rush	130

PREMIER LEAGUE CAPTAINS

LIVERPOOL CAPTAINS IN PREMIER LEAGUE GAMES (MOST SUCCESSFUL FIRST)

CAPTAIN	PLD	W	D	L	PTS	WIN %	AVE PTS. PER GAME
Steve Nicol	9	6	2	1	20	66.67	2.22
Jamie Carragher	11	7	2	2	23	63.64	2.09
Steve McManaman	8	5	1	2	16	62.50	2.00
Robbie Fowler	22	12	4	6	40	54.55	1.82
Sami Hyypia	128	67	31	30	232	52.34	1.81
Steven Gerrard	123	63	30	30	219	51.22	1.78
John Barnes	87	43	25	19	154	49.43	1.77
Ian Rush	87	40	20	27	140	45.98	1.61
Jamie Redknapp	22	10	5	7	35	45.45	1.59
Paul Ince	65	28	18	19	102	43.08	1.57
Neil Ruddock	2	0	2	0	2	0.00	1.00
Mark Wright	17	4	4	9	16	23.53	0.94
Phil Babb	1	0	0	1	0	0.00	0.00
TOTAL	**582**	**285**	**144**	**153**	**999**	**48.97**	**1.72**

Steve Nicol - Top skipper

MOST GOALS IN PREMIER LEAGUE

Top 20 goalscorers in Premier League

Robbie Fowler	128
Michael Owen	118
Ian Rush	45
Steven Gerrard	**44**
Steve McManaman	41
Emile Heskey	39
Jamie Redknapp	29
Patrik Berger	28
Stan Collymore	26
Danny Murphy	25

Top 20 goalscorers in Premier League

Own Goals	25
John Barnes	22
John Arne Riise	**21**
Sami Hyypia	20
Milan Baros	19
Luis Garcia	18
Peter Crouch	**17**
Paul Ince	14
Djibril Cisse	13
Harry Kewell/Dirk Kuyt	**12**

Liverpool FC : The Official Guide 2008

Jamie Carragher hails his goal in Liverpool's record 7-1 Premier League triumph, against Southampton (top), while Milan Baros (above), scored two in the 6-0 demolition of West Brom

PREMIER LEAGUE FACTS & FIGURES

PREMIER LEAGUE RECORD

Season	P	W	D	L	F	A	Pts	Pos
1992-1993	42	16	11	15	62	55	59	6
1993-1994	42	17	9	16	59	55	60	8
1994-1995	42	21	11	10	65	37	74	4
1995-1996	38	20	11	7	70	34	71	3
1996-1997	38	19	11	8	62	37	68	4
1997-1998	38	18	11	9	68	42	65	3
1998-1999	38	15	9	14	68	49	54	7
1999-2000	38	19	10	9	51	30	67	4
2000-2001	38	20	9	9	71	39	69	3
2001-2002	38	24	8	6	67	30	80	2
2002-2003	38	18	10	10	61	41	64	5
2003-2004	38	16	12	10	55	37	60	4
2004-2005	38	17	7	14	52	41	58	5
2005-2006	38	25	7	6	57	25	82	3
2006-2007	38	20	8	10	57	27	68	3

BIGGEST PREMIER LEAGUE WINS (TOP FIVE)

Date	Opponents	Venue	Score	Scorers	Attendance
16th Jan 1999	Southampton	Home	Won 7-1	Fowler 3, Matteo, Carragher, Owen, Thompson	44,011
26th Apr 2003	West Brom	Away	Won 6-0	Owen 4, Baros 2	27,128
9th Feb 2002	Ipswich Town	Away	Won 6-0	Abel Xavier, Heskey 2, Hyypia, Owen 2	25,608
28th Oct 1995	Manchester City	Home	Won 6-0	Rush 2, Redknapp, Fowler 2, Ruddock	39,267
20th Aug 1994	Crystal Palace	Away	Won 6-1	Fowler, McManaman 2, Molby (pen), Rush 2	18,084

BIGGEST PREMIER LEAGUE DEFEATS (TOP SIX)

Date	Opponents	Venue	Score	Scorer	Attendance
19th Dec 1992	Coventry City	Away	Lost 5-1	Redknapp	19,779
5th Apr 2003	Manchester United	Away	Lost 4-0		67,639
2nd Oct 2005	Chelsea	Home	Lost 4-1	Gerrard	44,235
16th Dec 2001	Chelsea	Away	Lost 4-0		41,174
25th Apr 1998	Chelsea	Away	Lost 4-1	Riedle	34,639
3rd Apr 1992	Blackburn Rovers	Away	Lost 4-1	Rush	15,032

AVERAGE ATTENDANCES

Season	High	Low	Average
1992-1993	44,619	29,574	37,009
1993-1994	44,601	24,561	38,503
1994-1995	40,014	27,183	34,175
1995-1996	40,820	34,063	39,552
1996-1997	40,892	36,126	39,776
1997-1998	44,532	34,705	40,628
1998-1999	44,852	36,019	43,321
1999-2000	44,929	40,483	44,074
2000-2001	44,806	38,474	43,698
2001-2002	44,371	37,153	43,389
2002-2003	44,250	41,462	43,243
2003-2004	44,374	34,663	42,677
2004-2005	44,224	35,064	42,587
2005-2006	44,983	42,293	44,236
2006-2007	44,403	41,370	43,561

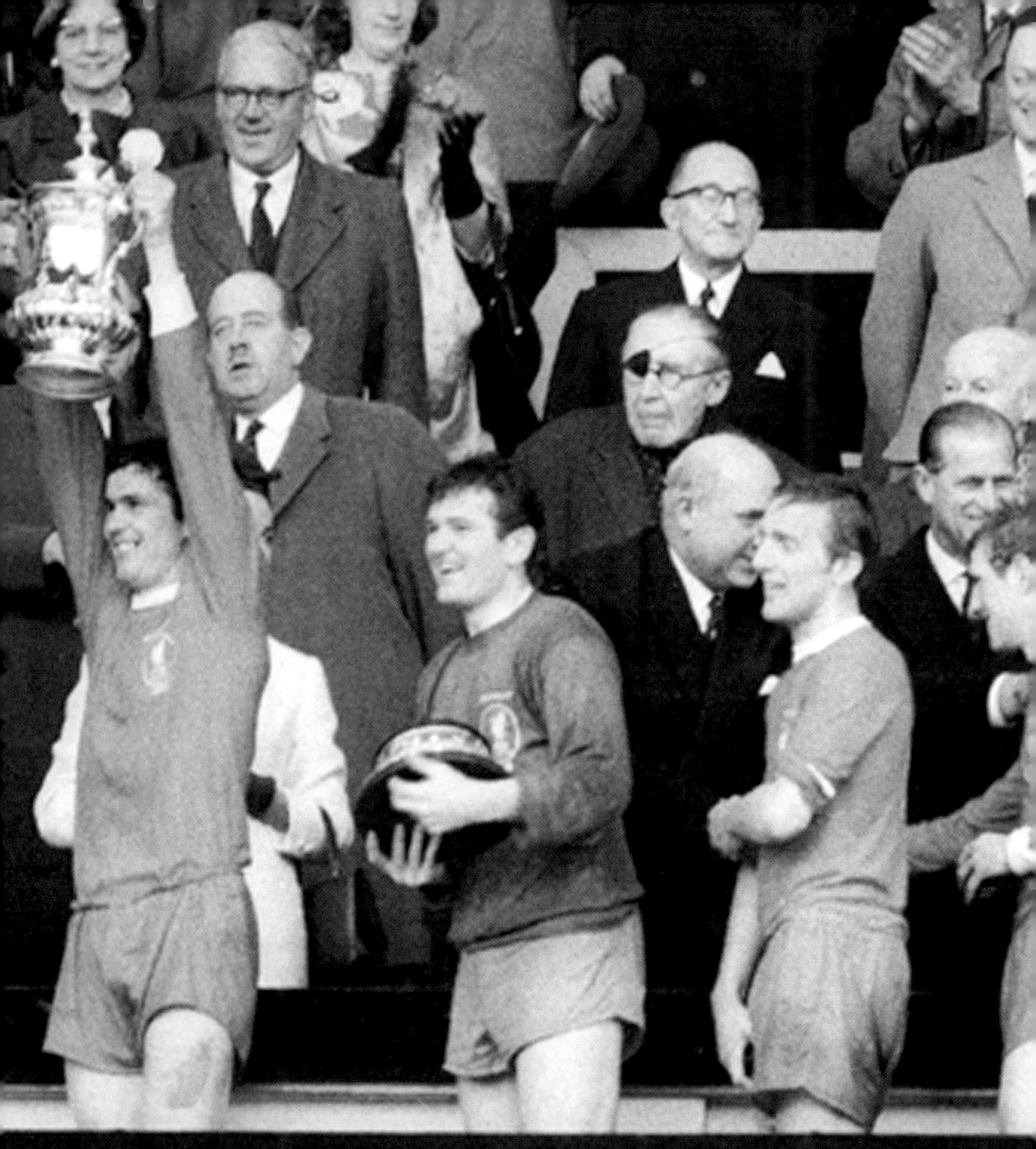

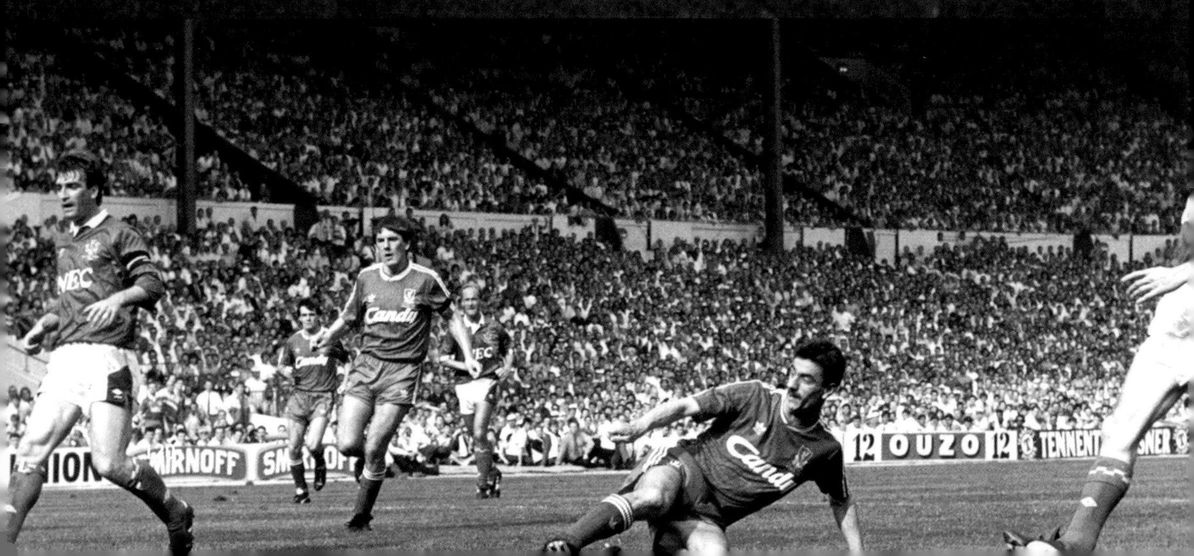
12 OUZO 12
Candy

THE CUPS

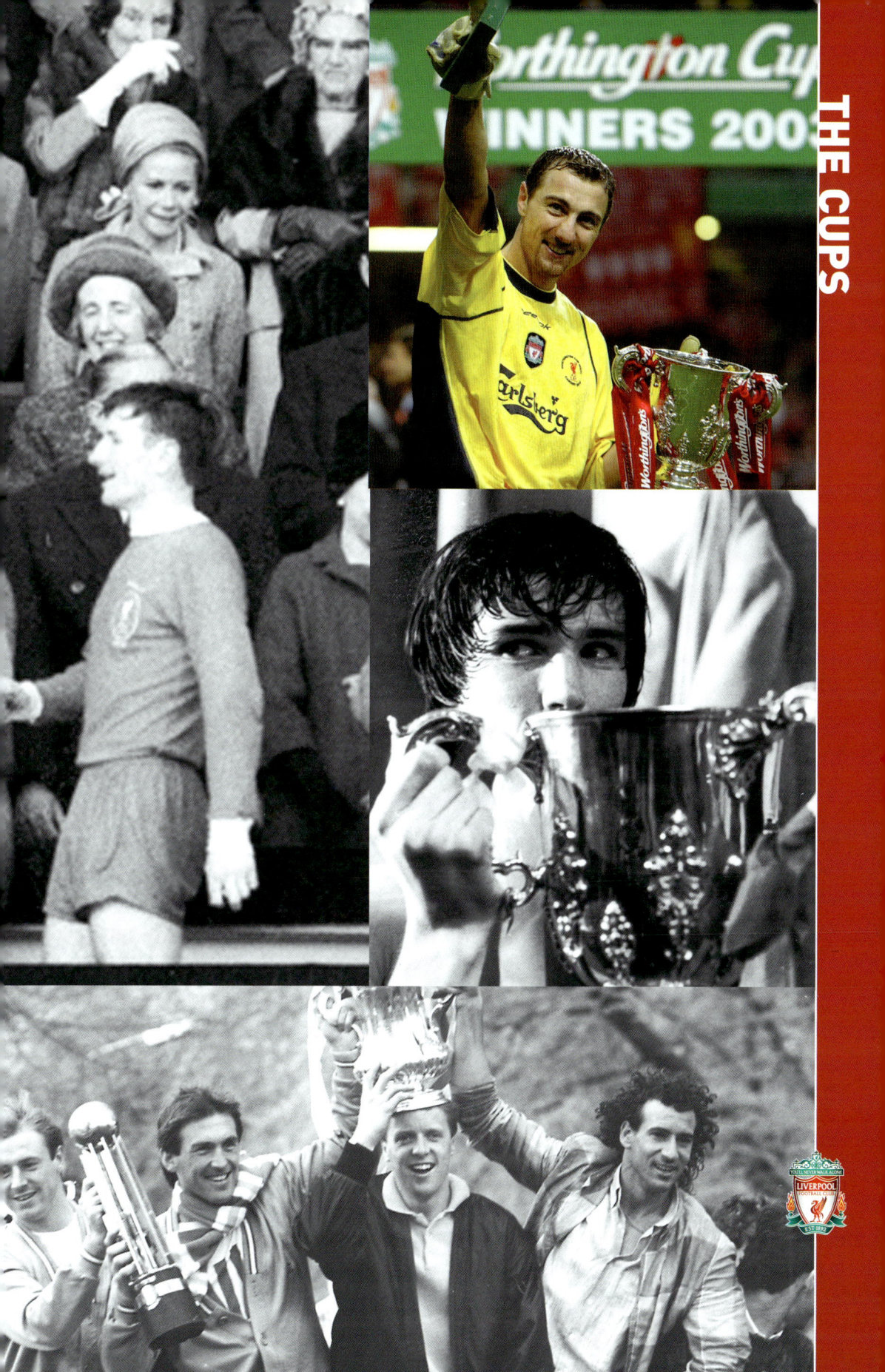

THE FA CUP RECORD

Date	Round	Venue	Opponents	Opponent Division	Score	Scorers	Att
1892-93							
15th Oct	1st Qual	(a)	Nantwich	Non Lge	W 4-0	Miller 3, Wyllie	700
29th Oct	2nd Qual	(h)	Newtown	Non Lge	W 9-0	Wyllie 3, McVean 2, McCartney H.McQueen, Cameron, Townsend o.g.	4,000
19th Nov	3rd Qual	(a)	Northwich Victoria	Non Lge	L 1-2	Wyllie	1,000
1893-94							
27th Jan	1	(h)	Grimsby Town	2	W 3-0	Bradshaw (2), McQue	8,000
10th Feb	2	(h)	Preston North End	1	W 3-2	Henderson (2), McVean	18,000
24th Feb	3	(a)	Bolton Wanderers	1	L 0-3		20,000
1894-95							
2nd Feb	1	(a)	Barnsley St Peters	Non Lge	*D 2-1	Mc Vean, Ross	4,000
11th Feb	1 Rep.	(h)	Barnsley St Peters	Non Lge	W 4-0	Bradshaw, Drummond, McVean, H.McQueen	4,000
16th Feb	2	(h)	Nottingham Forest	1	L 0-2		5,000
1895-96							
1st Feb	1	(h)	Millwall	Non Lge	W 4-1	Ross, Becton, Allan, Bradshaw	10,000
15th Feb	2	(a)	Wolverhampton W.	1	L 0-2		15,000
1896-97							
30th Jan	1	(h)	Burton Swifts	2	W 4-3	Hannah, Allan, Cleghorn, Ross	4,000
13th Feb	2	(a)	West Bromwich Alb.	1	W 2-1	McVean, Neill	16,000
27th Feb	3	(h)	Nottingham Forest	1	D 1-1	Becton	15,000
3rd Mar	3 Rep.	(a)	Nottingham Forest	1	W 1-0	Allan	10,000
20th Mar	S.F.	Bramall La.	Aston Villa	1	L 0-3		30,000
1897-98							
29th Jan	1	(h)	Hucknall St John's	Non Lge	W 2-0	Becton, McQue	8,000
12th Feb	2	(a)	Newton Heath	2	D 0-0		12,000
16th Feb	2 Rep	(h)	Newton Heath	2	W 2-1	Wilkie, Cunliffe	6,000
25th Feb	3	(a)	Derby County	1	D 1-1	Bradshaw	20,000
2nd Mar	3 Rep	(h)	Derby County	1	L 1-5	Becton (pen)	15,000
1898-99							
28th Jan	1	(h)	Blackburn Rovers	1	W 2-0	Cox, Allan	14,000
11th Feb	2	(h)	Newcastle United	1	W 3-1	Morgan, Raisbeck, Higgins o.g.	7,000
25th Feb	3	(a)	West Bromwich Alb.	1	W 2-0	Morgan, Robertson	17,124
18th Mar	S.F.	Nottingham	Sheffield United	1	D 2-2	Allan, Morgan	35,000
23rd Mar	S.F. Rep	Bolton	Sheffield United	1	D 4-4	Walker, Allan, Boyle o.g., Cox	20,000
30th Mar	S.F.Rep (2)	Derby	Sheffield United	1	L 0-1		20,000
1899-1900							
27th Jan	1	(a)	Stoke City.	1	D 0-0		8,000
1st Feb	1 Rep	(h)	Stoke City	1	W 1-0	Hunter	10,000
17th Feb	2	(h)	West Bromwich Alb.	1	D 1-1	Cox	15,000
21st Feb	2 Rep	(a)	West Bromwich Alb.	1	L 1-2	Robertson	13,000
1900-01							
5th Jan	Qual	(a)	West Ham United	Non Lge	W 1-0	Raybould	6,000
9th Feb	1	(a)	Notts County	1	L 0-2		15,000

* (Match counted as a draw after Barnsley protest)

The Cups

Date	Round	Venue	Opponents	Opponent Division	Score	Scorers	Att
1901-02							
25th Jan	1	(h)	Everton	1	D 2-2	T.Robertson (pen), Hunter	25,000
30th Jan	1 Rep	(a)	Everton	1	W 2-0	Raisbeck, Hunter	20,000
8th Feb	2	(a)	Southampton	Non Lge	L 1-4	Fleming	20,000
1902-03							
7th Feb	1	(a)	Manchester United	2	L 1-2	Raybould	15,000
1903-04							
6th Feb	1	(a)	Blackburn Rovers	1	L 1-3	Raybould	10,000
1904-05							
4th Feb	1	(h)	Everton	1	D 1-1	Parkinson	28,000
8th Feb	1 Rep	(a)	Everton	1	L 1-2	Goddard	40,000
1905-06							
13th Jan	1	(h)	Leicester Fosse	2	W 2-1	Raybould, Goddard	12,000
3rd Feb	2	(h)	Barnsley	2	W 1-0	West	10,000
24th Feb	3	(h)	Brentford	Non Lge	W 2-0	Hewitt, Goddard	20,000
10th Mar	4	(h)	Southampton	Non Lge	W 3-0	Raybould 3	20,000
31st Mar	S.F.	Villa Park	Everton	1	L 0-2		37,000
1906-07							
12th Jan	1	(h)	Birmingham City	1	W 2-1	Raybould 2	20,000
2nd Feb	2	(a)	Oldham Athletic	Non Lge	W 1-0	McPherson	21,500
23rd Feb	3	(h)	Bradford City	2	W 1-0	Cox	18,000
9th Mar	4	(a)	Sheffield Wed.	1	L 0-1		30,000
1907-08							
11th Jan	1	(h)	Derby County	2	W 4-2	Cox, Gorman, Bradley, Parkinson	15,000
1st Feb	2	(h)	Brighton	Non Lge	D 1-1	Cox	36,000
5th Feb	2 Rep	(a)	Brighton	Non Lge	W 3-0	Bradley 2, Cox	10,000
22nd Feb	3	(a)	Newcastle United	1	L 1-3	Saul	45,987
1908-09							
16th Jan	1	(h)	Lincoln City	Non Lge	W 5-1	Orr 3, Hewitt, Parkinson	8,000
6th Feb	2	(h)	Norwich City	Non Lge	L 2-3	Cox, Robinson	25,000
1909-10							
15th Jan	1	(a)	Bristol City	1	L 0-2		10,000
1910-11							
14th Jan	1	(h)	Gainsborough Trin.	2	W 3-2	Bowyer 2, Goddard	15,000
4th Feb	2	(a)	Everton	1	L 1-2	Parkinson	50,000
1911-12							
13th Jan	1	(h)	Leyton	Non Lge	W 1-0	Parkinson	33,000
3rd Feb	2	(a)	Fulham	2	L 0-3		30,000

Date	Round	Venue	Opponents	Opponent Division	Score	Scorers	Att
1912-13							
15th Jan	1	(h)	Bristol City	2	W 3-0	Goddard (pen), Peake, Lacey	15,000
1st Feb	2	(a)	Arsenal	1	W 4-1	Metcalf 3, Lacey	8,653
22nd Feb	3	(h)	Newcastle United	1	D 1-1	Lacey	37,903
26th Feb	3 Rep	(a)	Newcastle United	1	L 0-1		45,000
1913-14							
10th Jan	1	(h)	Barnsley	2	D 1-1	Lacey	33,000
15th Jan	1 Rep	(a)	Barnsley	2	W 1-0	Lacey	23,999
31st Jan	2	(h)	Gillingham	Non Lge	W 2-0	Lacey, Ferguson	42,045
21st Feb	3	(a)	West Ham United	Non Lge	D 1-1	Miller	15,000
25th Feb	3 Rep	(h)	West Ham United	Non Lge	W 5-1	Lacey 2, Miller 2, Metcalf	43,729
7th Mar	4	(h)	QPR	Non Lge	W 2-1	Sheldon, Miller	43,000
28th Mar	S.F.	Tottenham	Aston Villa	1	W 2-0	Nicholl 2	27,474
25th Apr	Final	Crystal Pal.	Burnley	1	L 0-1		72,778
1914-15							
9th Jan	1	(h)	Stockport County	2	W 3-0	Pagnam 2, Metcalf	10,000
30th Jan	2	(a)	Sheffield United	1	L 0-1		25,000
1919-20							
10th Jan	1	(a)	South Shields	2	D 1-1	Lewis	10,000
14th Jan	1 Rep	(h)	South Shields	2	W 2-0	Lewis, Sheldon	40,000
31st Jan	2	(a)	Luton Town	Non Lge	W 2-0	Lacey 2	12,640
23rd Feb	3	(h)	Birmingham City	2	W 2-0	Sheldon, T.Miller	50,000
6th Mar	4	(a)	Huddersfield Town	2	L 1-2	T.Miller	44,248
1920-21							
8th Jan	1	(h)	Manchester United	1	D 1-1	Chambers	36,000
12th Jan	1 Rep	(a)	Manchester United	1	W 2-1	Lacey, Chambers	29,189
29th Jan	2	(a)	Newcastle United	1	L 0-1		61,400
1921-22							
7th Jan	1	(a)	Sunderland	1	D 1-1	Forshaw	30,000
11th Jan	1 Rep	(h)	Sunderland	1	W 5-0	Forshaw 2, Chambers 2, W.Wadsworth	46,000
28th Jan	2	(h)	West Bromwich Alb.	1	L 0-1		50,000
1922-23							
13th Jan	1	(h)	Arsenal	1	D 0-0		37,000
17th Jan	1 Rep	(a)	Arsenal	1	W 4-1	Chambers 2, Johnson, McKinlay (pen)	40,000
3rd Feb	2	(a)	Wolverhampton W.	2	W 2-0	Johnson, Forshaw	40,079
24th Feb	3	(h)	Sheffield United	1	L 1-2	Chambers	51,859
1923-24							
12th Jan	1	(h)	Bradford City	2	W 2-1	Chambers 2	25,000
2nd Feb	2	(a)	Bolton Wanderers	1	W 4-1	Walsh 3, Chambers	51,596
23rd Feb	3	(a)	Southampton	2	D 0-0		18,671
27th Feb	3 Rep	(h)	Southampton	2	W 2-0	Chambers, Forshaw	49,000
8th Mar	4	(a)	Newcastle United	1	L 0-1		56,595

The Cups

Date	Round	Venue	Opponents	Opponent Division	Score	Scorers	Att
1924-25							
10th Jan	1	(h)	Leeds United	1	W 3-0	Shone 2, Hopkin	39,000
31st Jan	2	(a)	Bristol City	3 Sth	W 1-0	Rawlings	29,362
21st Feb	3	(h)	Birmingham City	1	W 2-1	Rawlings, Shone	44,000
7th Mar	4	(a)	Southampton	2	L 0-1		21,501
1925-26							
9th Jan	3	(a)	Southampton	2	D 0-0		18,031
13th Jan	3 Rep	(h)	Southampton	2	W 1-0	Forshaw	42,000
30th Jan	4	(a)	Fulham	2	L 1-3	Forshaw	36,381
1926-27							
8th Jan	3	(a)	Bournemouth	3 Sth	D 1-1	Hodgson	13,243
12th Jan	3 Rep	(h)	Bournemouth	3 Sth	W 4-1	Hopkin, Chambers 3	36,800
29th Jan	4	(h)	Southport	3 Nth	W 3-1	Hodgson, Chambers, Edmed	51,600
19th Feb	5	(a)	Arsenal	1	L 0-2		43,000
1927-28							
14th Jan	3	(h)	Darlington	3 Nth	W 1-0	Chambers	28,500
28th Jan	4	(a)	Cardiff City	1	L 1-2	Edmed (pen)	20,000
1928-29							
12th Jan	3	(a)	Bristol City	2	W 2-0	Salisbury, Hodgson	28,500
26th Jan	4	(h)	Bolton Wanderers	1	D 0-0		55,055
30th Jan	4 Rep	(a)	Bolton Wanderers	1	L 2-5 aet	Lindsay, Hodgson	41,808
1929-30							
11th Jan	3	(h)	Cardiff City	2	L 1-2	McPherson	50,141
1930-31							
10th Jan	3	(h)	Birmingham City	1	L 0-2		40,500
1931-32							
9th Jan	3	(a)	Everton	1	W 2-1	Gunson, Hodgson	57,090
23rd Jan	4	(a)	Chesterfield	2	W 4-2	Barton 4	28,393
13th Feb	5	(h)	Grimsby Town	1	W 1-0	Gunson	49,479
27th Feb	6	(h)	Chelsea	1	L 0-2		57,804
1932-33							
14th Jan	3	(a)	West Bromwich Alb.	1	L 0-2		29,170
1933-34							
13th Jan	3	(h)	Fulham	2	D 1-1	Hodgson	45,619
17th Jan	3 Rep	(a)	Fulham	2	W 3-2 aet	Hanson, Bradshaw, S.Roberts	28,319
27th Jan	4	(h)	Tranmere Rovers (match played at Anfield)	3 Nth	W 3-1	English 2, Nieuwenhuys	61,036
17th Feb	5	(h)	Bolton Wanderers	2	L 0-3		54,912
1934-35							
12th Jan	3	(a)	Yeovil & Petters	Non Lge	W 6-2	Nieuwenhuys, Wright, Hodgson 2, Roberts 2	13,000
26th Jan	4	(a)	Blackburn Rovers	1	L 0-1		49,546

Date	Round	Venue	Opponents	Opponent Division	Score	Scorers	Att
1935-36							
11th Jan	3	(h)	Swansea Town	2	W 1-0	Wright	33,494
25th Jan	4	(h)	Arsenal	1	L 0-2		53,720
1936-37							
16th Jan	3	(a)	Norwich City	2	L 0-3		26,800
1937-38							
8th Jan	3	(a)	Crystal Palace	3 Sth	D 0-0		33,000
12th Jan	3 Rep	(h)	Crystal Palace	3 Sth	W 3-1 aet	Shafto, Collins o.g., Fagan (pen)	35,919
22nd Jan	4	(a)	Sheffield United	2	D 1-1	Hanson	50,264
26th Jan	4 Rep	(h)	Sheffield United	2	W 1-0	Johnson o.g.	48,297
12th Feb	5	(h)	Huddersfield Town	1	L 0-1		57,682
1938-39							
7th Jan	3	(h)	Luton Town	2	W 3-0	Balmer 2, Paterson	40,431
21st Jan	4	(h)	Stockport County	3 Nth	W 5-1	Nieuwenhuys 2, Eastham, Balmer 2	39,407
11th Feb	5	(a)	Wolverhampton W.	1	L 1-4	Fagan (pen)	61,315
1945-46							
5th Jan	3 Leg 1	(a)	Chester	3 Nth	W 2-0	Liddell, Fagan	12,000
9th Jan	3 Leg 2	(h)	Chester	3 Nth	W 2-1	Fagan 2	11,207
26th Jan	4 Leg 1	(a)	Bolton Wanderers	1	L 0-5		39,692
30th Jan	4 Leg 2	(h)	Bolton Wanderers	1	W 2-0	Balmer, Nieuwenhuys	35,247
1946-47							
11th Jan	3	(a)	Walsall	3 Sth	W 5-2	Foulkes o.g., Done, Liddell, Balmer 2	18,379
25th Jan	4	(h)	Grimsby Town	1	W 2-0	Stubbins, Done	42,265
8th Feb	5	(h)	Derby County	1	W 1-0	Balmer	44,493
1st Mar	6	(h)	Birmingham City	2	W 4-1	Stubbins 3, Balmer	51,911
29th Mar	S.F.	Ewood Pk	Burnley	2	D 0-0 aet		52,570
12th Apr	S.F. Rep	Maine Rd	Burnley	2	L 0-1		72,000
1947-48							
10th Jan	3	(h)	Nottingham Forest	2	W 4-1	Priday, Stubbins 2, Liddell	48,569
24th Jan	4	(a)	Manchester United	1	L 0-3		74,721
			(match played at Goodison Park due to bomb damage)				
1948-49							
8th Jan	3	(a)	Nottingham Forest	2	D 2-2 aet	Fagan, Done	35,000
15th Jan	3 Rep	(h)	Nottingham Forest	2	W 4-0	Payne, Balmer 2, Stubbins	52,218
29th Jan	4	(h)	Notts County	3 Sth	W 1-0	Liddell	61,003
12th Feb	5	(a)	Wolverhampton W.	1	L 1-3	Done	54,983
1949-50							
7th Jan	3	(a)	Blackburn Rovers	2	D 0-0		52,468
11th Jan	3 Rep	(h)	Blackburn Rovers	2	W 2-1	Payne, Fagan	52,221
28th Jan	4	(h)	Exeter City	3 Sth	W 3-1	Baron, Fagan, Payne	45,209
11th Feb	5	(a)	Stockport County	3 Nth	W 2-1	Fagan, Stubbins	27,833
4th Mar	6	(h)	Blackpool	1	W 2-1	Fagan, Liddell	53,973
25th Mar	S.F.	Maine Rd	Everton	1	W 2-0	Paisley, Liddell	72,000
29th Apr	Final	Wembley	Arsenal	1	L 0-2		98,249

The Cups

Date	Round	Venue	Opponents	Opponent Division	Score	Scorers	Att
1950-51							
6th Jan	3	(a)	Norwich City	3 Sth	L 1-3	Balmer	34,641
1951-52							
12th Jan	3	(h)	Workington Town	3 Nth	W 1-0	Payne	52,581
2nd Feb	4	(h)	Wolverhampton W.	1	W 2-1	Paisley, Done	61,905
23rd Feb	5	(a)	Burnley	1	L 0-2		52,070
1952-53							
10th Jan	3	(a)	Gateshead	3 Nth	L 0-1		15,193
1953-54							
9th Jan	3	(a)	Bolton Wanderers	1	L 0-1		45,341
1954-55							
8th Jan	3	(a)	Lincoln City	2	D 1-1	Evans	15,399
12th Jan	3 Rep	(h)	Lincoln City	2	W 1-0 aet	Evans	32,179
29th Jan	4	(a)	Everton	1	W 4-0	Liddell, A'Court, Evans 2	72,000
19th Feb	5	(h)	Huddersfield Town	1	L 0-2		57,115
1955-56							
7th Jan	3	(h)	Accrington Stanley	3 Nth	W 2-0	Liddell 2	48,385
28th Jan	4	(h)	Scunthorpe United	3 Nth	D 3-3	Liddell 2, Payne	53,393
6th Feb	4 Rep	(a)	Scunthorpe United	3 Nth	W 2-1 aet	Liddell, Arnell	19,500
18th Feb	5	(a)	Manchester City	1	D 0-0		70,640
22nd Feb	5 Rep	(h)	Manchester City	1	L 1-2	Arnell	57,528
1956-57							
5th Jan	3	(a)	Southend United	3 Sth	L 1-2	Wheeler	18,253
1957-58							
4th Jan	3	(h)	Southend United	3 Sth	D 1-1	Smith o.g.	43,454
8th Jan	3 Rep	(a)	Southend United	3 Sth	W 3-2	Molyneux, White, Rowley	20,000
25th Jan	4	(h)	Northampton Town	3 Sth	W 3-1	Liddell, Collins o.g., Bimpson	56,939
15th Feb	5	(a)	Scunthorpe United	3 Nth	W 1-0	Murdoch	23,000
1st Mar	6	(a)	Blackburn Rovers	2	L 1-2	Murdoch	51,000
1958-59							
15th Jan	3	(a)	Worcester City	Non Lge	L 1-2	Twentyman (pen)	15,011
1959-60							
9th Jan	3	(h)	Leyton Orient	2	W 2-1	Hunt 2	40,343
30th Jan	4	(h)	Manchester United	1	L 1-3	Wheeler	56,736
1960-61							
7th Jan	3	(h)	Coventry City	3	W 3-2	Hunt, Lewis, Harrower	50,909
28th Jan	4	(h)	Sunderland	2	L 0-2		46,185
1st Feb	4 Rep	(h)	Burnley	1	W 2-1 aet	St John, Moran (pen)	57,906
16th Mar	5	(a)	Arsenal	1	W 2-1	Melia, Moran (pen)	55,245
30th Mar	6	(h)	West Ham United	1	W 1-0	Hunt	49,036
27th Apr	S.F.	H'borough	Leicester City	1	L 0-1		65,000

Liverpool skipper Ron Yeats is held aloft by jubilant team-mates during the lap of honour, as the Reds' players celebrate a first FA Cup triumph in 1965

The Cups

Date	Round	Venue	Opponents	Opponent Division	Score	Scorers	Att
1961-62							
6th Jan	3	(h)	Chelsea	1	W 4-3	St John 2, Hunt, A'Court	48,455
27th Jan	4	(a)	Oldham Athletic	4	W 2-1	St John 2	42,000
17th Feb	5	(h)	Preston North End	2	D 0-0		54,967
20th Feb	5 Rep	(a)	Preston North End	2	D 0-0 aet		37,831
26th Feb	5 Rep (2)	Old Trafford	Preston North End	2	L 0-1		43,944
1962-63							
9th Jan	3	(a)	Wrexham	3	W 3-0	Hunt, Lewis, Melia	29,992
26th Jan	4	(a)	Burnley	1	D 1-1	Lewis	49,885
21st Feb	4 Rep	(h)	Burnley	1	W 2-1 aet	St John, Moran (pen)	57,906
16th Mar	5	(a)	Arsenal	1	W 2-1	Melia, Moran (pen)	55,245
30th Mar	6	(h)	West Ham United	1	W 1-0	Hunt	49,036
27th Apr	S.F.	Hillsborough	Leicester City	1	L 0-1		65,000
1963-64							
4th Jan	3	(h)	Derby County	2	W 5-0	Arrowsmith 4, Hunt	46,460
25th Jan	4	(h)	Port Vale	3	D 0-0		52,327
27th Jan	4 Rep	(a)	Port Vale	3	W 2-1 aet	Hunt, Thompson	42,179
15th Feb	5	(a)	Arsenal	1	W 1-0	St John	61,295
29th Feb	6	(h)	Swansea Town	2	L 1-2	Thompson	52,608
1964-65							
9th Jan	3	(a)	West Bromwich Alb.	1	W 2-1	Hunt, St John	28,360
30th Jan	4	(h)	Stockport County	4	D 1-1	Milne	51,587
3rd Feb	4 Rep	(a)	Stockport County	4	W 2-0	Hunt 2	24,080
20th Feb	5	(a)	Bolton Wanderers	2	W 1-0	Callaghan	52,207
6th Mar	6	(a)	Leicester City	1	D 0-0		39,356
10th Mar	6 Rep	(h)	Leicester City	1	W 1-0	Hunt	53,324
27th Mar	S.F.	Villa Park	Chelsea	1	W 2-0	Thompson, Stevenson (pen)	67,686
1st May	Final	Wembley	Leeds United	1	W 2-1 aet	Hunt, St John	100,000
1965-66							
22nd Jan	3	(h)	Chelsea	1	L 1-2	Hunt	54,097
1966-67							
28th Jan	3	(a)	Watford	3	D 0-0		33,000
1st Feb	3 Rep	(h)	Watford	3	W 3-1	St John, Hunt, Lawler	54,451
18th Feb	4	(h)	Aston Villa	1	W 1-0	St John	52,447
11th Mar	5	(a)	Everton	1	L 0-1		64,851
			(a further 40,149 watched on closed-circuit TV at Anfield)				
1967-68							
27th Jan	3	(a)	Bournemouth	3	D 0-0		24,388
30th Jan	3 Rep	(h)	Bournemouth	3	W 4-1	Hateley, Thompson, Hunt, Lawler	54,075
17th Feb	4	(a)	Walsall	3	D 0-0		21,066
19th Feb	4 Rep	(h)	Walsall	3	W 5-2	Hateley 4, Strong	39,113
9th Mar	5	(a)	Tottenham Hotspur	1	D 1-1	Hateley	54,005
12th Mar	5 Rep	(h)	Tottenham Hotspur	1	W 2-1	Hunt, Smith (pen)	53,658
30th Mar	6	(a)	West Bromwich Alb.	1	D 0-0		53,062
8th Apr	6 Rep	(h)	West Bromwich Alb.	1	D 1-1 aet	Hateley	54,273
18th Apr	6 Rep (2)	Maine Rd	West Bromwich Alb.	1	L 1-2	Hateley	56,000

Date	Round	Venue	Opponents	Opponent Division	Score	Scorers	Att
1968-69							
4th Jan	3	(h)	Doncaster Rovers	4	W 2-0	Hunt, Callaghan	48,330
25th Jan	4	(h)	Burnley	1	W 2-1	Smith (pen), Hughes	53,677
1st Mar	5	(a)	Leicester City	1	D 0-0		42,002
3rd Mar	5 Rep	(h)	Leicester City	1	L 0-1		54,666
1969-70							
7th Jan	3	(a)	Coventry City	1	D 1-1	Graham	33,688
12th Jan	3 Rep	(h)	Coventry City	1	W 3-0	Ross, Thompson, Graham	51,261
24th Jan	4	(h)	Wrexham	4	W 3-1	Graham 2, St John	54,096
7th Feb	5	(h)	Leicester City	2	D 0-0		53,785
11th Feb	5 Rep	(a)	Leicester City	2	W 2-0	Evans 2	42,100
21st Feb	6	(a)	Watford	2	L 0-1		34,047
1970-71							
2nd Jan	3	(h)	Aldershot	4	W 1-0	McLaughlin	45,500
23rd Jan	4	(h)	Swansea Town	3	W 3-0	Toshack, St John, Lawler	47,229
13th Feb	5	(h)	Southampton	1	W 1-0	Lawler	50,226
6th Mar	6	(h)	Tottenham Hotspur	1	D 0-0		54,731
16th Mar	6 Rep	(a)	Tottenham Hotspur	1	W 1-0	Heighway	56,283
27th Mar	S.F.	Old Trafford	Everton	1	W 2-1	Evans, Hall	62,144
8th May	Final	Wembley	Arsenal	1	L 1-2 aet	Heighway	100,000
1971-72							
15th Jan	3	(a)	Oxford United	2	W 3-0	Keegan 2, Lindsay	18,000
5th Feb	4	(h)	Leeds United	1	D 0-0		56,300
9th Feb	4 Rep	(a)	Leeds United	1	L 0-2		45,821
1972-73							
13th Jan	3	(a)	Burnley	2	D 0-0		35,730
16th Jan	3 Rep	(h)	Burnley	2	W 3-0	Toshack 2, Cormack	56,124
3rd Feb	4	(h)	Manchester City	1	D 0-0		56,296
7th Feb	4 Rep	(a)	Manchester City	1	L 0-2		49,572
1973-74							
5th Jan	3	(h)	Doncaster Rovers	4	D 2-2	Keegan 2	31,483
8th Jan	3 Rep	(a)	Doncaster Rovers	4	W 2-0	Heighway, Cormack	22,499
26th Jan	4	(h)	Carlisle United	2	D 0-0		47,211
29th Jan	4 Rep	(a)	Carlisle United	2	W 2-0	Boersma, Toshack	21,262
16th Feb	5	(h)	Ipswich Town	1	W 2-0	Hall, Keegan	45,340
9th Mar	6	(a)	Bristol City	2	W 1-0	Toshack	37,671
30th Mar	S.F.	Old Trafford	Leicester City	1	D 0-0		60,000
3rd Apr	S.F. Rep	Villa Park	Leicester City	1	W 3-1	Hall, Keegan, Toshack	55,619
4th May	Final	Wembley	Newcastle United	1	W 3-0	Keegan 2, Heighway	100,000
1974-75							
4th Jan	3	(h)	Stoke City	1	W 2-0	Heighway, Keegan	48,723
25th Jan	4	(a)	Ipswich Town	1	L 0-1		34,708
1975-76							
3rd Jan	3	(a)	West Ham United	1	W 2-0	Keegan, Toshack	32,363
24th Jan	4	(a)	Derby County	1	L 0-1		38,200

The Cups

Date	Round	Venue	Opponents	Opponent Division	Score	Scorers	Att
1976-77							
8th Jan	3	(h)	Crystal Palace	3	D 0-0		44,730
11th Jan	3 Rep	(a)	Crystal Palace	3	W 3-2	Keegan, Heighway 2	42,644
29th Jan	4	(h)	Carlisle United	2	W 3-0	Keegan, Toshack, Heighway	45,358
26th Feb	5	(h)	Oldham Athletic	2	W 3-1	Keegan, Case, Neal (pen)	52,455
19th Mar	6	(h)	Middlesbrough	1	W 2-0	Fairclough, Keegan	55,881
23rd Apr	S.F.	Maine Rd	Everton	1	D 2-2	McDermott, Case	52,637
27th Apr	S.F. Rep	Maine Rd	Everton	1	W 3-0	Neal (pen), Case, Kennedy	52,579
21st May	Final	Wembley	Manchester United	1	L 1-2	Case	100,000
1977-78							
7th Jan	3	(a)	Chelsea	1	L 2-4	Johnson, Dalglish	45,449
1978-79							
10th Jan	3	(a)	Southend United	3	D 0-0		31,033
17th Jan	3 Rep	(h)	Southend United	3	W 3-0	Case, Dalglish, R.Kennedy	37,797
30th Jan	4	(h)	Blackburn Rovers	2	W 1-0	Dalglish	43,432
28th Feb	5	(h)	Burnley	2	W 3 0	Johnson 2, Souness	47,161
10th Mar	6	(a)	Ipswich Town	1	W 1-0	Dalglish	31,322
31st Mar	S.F.	Maine Rd	Manchester United	1	D 2-2	Dalglish, Hansen	52,584
4th Apr	S.F. Rep	Goodison	Manchester United	1	L 0-1		53,069
1979-80							
5th Jan	3	(h)	Grimsby Town	3	W 5-0	Souness, Johnson 3, Case	49,706
26th Jan	4	(a)	Nottingham Forest	1	W 2-0	Dalglish, McDermott (pen)	33,277
16th Feb	5	(h)	Bury	3	W 2-0	Fairclough 2	43,769
8th Mar	6	(a)	Tottenham Hotspur	1	W 1-0	Mc Dermott	48,033
12th Apr	S.F.	Hillsborough	Arsenal	1	D 0-0		50,174
16th Apr	S.F. Rep	Villa Park	Arsenal	1	D 1-1 aet	Fairclough	40,679
28th Apr	S.F.Rep (2)	Villa Park	Arsenal	1	D 1-1 aet	Dalglish	42,975
1st May	S.F.Rep (3)	Highfield Rd	Arsenal	1	L 0-1		35,335
1980-81							
3rd Jan	3	(h)	Altrincham	Non Lge	W 4-1	McDermott, Dalglish 2, R.Kennedy	37,170
24th Jan	4	(a)	Everton	1	L 1-2	Case	53,804
1981-82							
2nd Jan	3	(a)	Swansea City	1	W 4-0	Hansen, Rush 2, Lawrenson	24,179
23rd Jan	4	(a)	Sunderland	1	W 3-0	Dalglish 2, Rush	28,582
13th Feb	5	(a)	Chelsea	2	L 0-2		41,422
1982-83							
8th Jan	3	(a)	Blackburn Rovers	2	W 2-1	Hodgson, Rush	21,967
29th Jan	4	(h)	Stoke City	1	W 2-0	Dalglish, Rush	36,666
20th Feb	5	(h)	Brighton	1	L 1-2	Johnston	44,868
1983-84							
6th Jan	3	(h)	Newcastle United	2	W 4-0	Robinson, Rush 2, Johnston	33,566
29th Jan	4	(a)	Brighton	2	L 0-2		19,057

Date	Round	Venue	Opponents	Opponent Division	Score	Scorers	Att
1984-85							
5th Jan	3	(h)	Aston Villa	1	W 3-0	Rush 2, Wark	36,877
27th Jan	4	(h)	Tottenham Hotspur	1	W 1-0	Rush	27,905
16th Feb	5	(a)	York City	3	D 1-1	Rush	13,485
20th Feb	5 Rep	(h)	York City	3	W 7-0	Whelan 2, Wark 3, Neal, Walsh	43,010
10th Mar	6	(a)	Barnsley	2	W 4-0	Rush 3, Whelan	19,838
13th Apr	S.F.	Goodison	Manchester United	1	D 2-2 aet	Whelan, Walsh	51,690
17th Apr	S.F. Rep	Maine Rd	Manchester United	1	L 1-2	McGrath o.g.	45,775
1985-86							
4th Jan	3	(h)	Norwich City	2	W 5-0	MacDonald, Walsh, McMahon, Whelan, Wark	29,082
26th Jan	4	(a)	Chelsea	1	W 2-1	Rush, Lawrenson	33,625
15th Feb	5	(a)	York City	3	D 1-1	Molby (pen)	12,443
18th Feb	5 Rep	(h)	York City	3	W 3-1 aet	Wark, Molby, Dalglish	29,362
11th Mar	6	(h)	Watford	1	D 0-0		36,775
17th Mar	6 Rep	(a)	Watford	1	W 2-1 aet	Molby (pen), Rush	28,097
5th Apr	S.F.	Tottenham	Southampton	1	W 2-0 aet	Rush 2	44,605
10th May	Final	Wembley	Everton	1	W 3-1	Rush 2, Johnston	98,000
1986-87							
11th Jan	3	(a)	Luton Town	1	D 0-0		11,085
26th Jan	3 Rep	(h)	Luton Town	1	D 0-0 aet		34,822
28th Jan	3 Rep (2)	(a)	Luton Town	1	L 0-3		14,687
1987-88							
9th Jan	3	(a)	Stoke City	2	D 0-0		31,979
12th Jan	3 Rep	(h)	Stoke City	2	W 1-0	Beardsley	39,147
31st Jan	4	(a)	Aston Villa	2	W 2-0	Barnes, Beardsley	46,324
21st Feb	5	(a)	Everton	1	W 1-0	Houghton	48,270
13th Mar	6	(a)	Manchester City	2	W 4-0	Houghton, Beardsley (pen) Johnston, Barnes	44,077
9th Apr	S.F.	Hillsborough	Nottingham Forest	1	W 2-1	Aldridge 2 (1 pen)	51,627
14th May	Final	Wembley	Wimbledon	1	L 0-1		98,203
1988-89							
7th Jan	3	(a)	Carlisle United	4	W 3-0	Barnes, McMahon 2	18,556
29th Jan	4	(a)	Millwall	1	W 2-0	Aldridge, Rush	23,615
18th Feb	5	(a)	Hull City	2	W 3-2	Barnes, Aldridge 2	20,058
18th Mar	6	(h)	Brentford	3	W 4-0	McMahon, Barnes, Beardsley 2	42,376
7th May	S.F.	Old Trafford	Nottingham Forest	1	W 3-1	Aldridge, Laws o.g.	38,000
20th May	Final	Wembley	Everton	1	W 3-2aet	Aldridge, Rush 2	82,800
1989-90							
6th Jan	3	(a)	Swansea City	3	D 0-0		16,098
9th Jan	3 Rep	(h)	Swansea City	3	W 8-0	Barnes 2, Whelan, Rush 3, Beardsley, Nicol	29,194
28th Jan	4	(a)	Norwich City	1	D 0-0		23,152
31st Jan	4 Rep	(h)	Norwich City	1	W 3-1	Nicol, Barnes, Beardsley (pen)	29,339
17th Feb	5	(h)	Southampton	1	W 3-0	Rush, Beardsley, Nicol	35,961
11th Mar	6	(a)	QPR	1	D 2-2	Barnes, Rush	21,057
14th Mar	6 Rep	(h)	QPR	1	W 1-0	Beardsley	38,090
8th Apr	S.F.	Villa Park	Crystal Palace	1	L 3-4 aet	Rush, McMahon, Barnes (pen)	38,389

The Cups

Date	Round	Venue	Opponents	Opponent Division	Score	Scorers	Att
1990-91							
5th Jan	3	(a)	Blackburn Rovers	2	D 1-1	Atkins o.g.	18,524
8th Jan	3 Rep	(h)	Blackburn Rovers	2	W 3-0	Houghton, Rush, Staunton	34,175
26th Jan	4	(h)	Brighton	2	D 2-2	Rush 2	32,670
30th Jan	4 Rep	(a)	Brighton	2	W 3-2 aet	McMahon 2, Rush	14,392
17th Feb	5	(h)	Everton	1	D 0-0		38,323
20th Feb	5 Rep	(a)	Everton	1	D 4-4 aet	Beardsley 2, Rush, Barnes	37,766
27th Feb	5 Rep (2)	(a)	Everton	1	L 0-1		40,201
1991-92							
6th Jan	3	(a)	Crewe Alexandra	4	W 4-0	McManaman, Barnes 3 (1 pen)	7,400
5th Feb	4	(a)	Bristol Rovers	2	D 1-1	Saunders	9,464
11th Feb	4 Rep	(h)	Bristol Rovers	2	W 2-1	McManaman, Saunders	30,142
16th Feb	5	(a)	Ipswich Town	2	D 0-0		26,140
26th Feb	5 Rep	(h)	Ipswich Town	2	W 3-2 aet	Houghton, Molby, McManaman	27,335
8th Mar	6	(h)	Aston Villa	1	W 1-0	Thomas	29,109
5th Apr	S.F.	Highbury	Portsmouth	2	D 1-1 aet	Whelan	41,869
13th Apr	S.F. Rep	Villa Park	Portsmouth	2	W 0-0 aet		40,077
			(Liverpool won 3-1 on penalties)				
9th May	Final	Wembley	Sunderland	2	W 2-0	Thomas, Rush	79,544
1992-93							
3rd Jan	3	(a)	Bolton Wanderers	2	D 2-2	Winstanley o.g., Rush	21,502
13th Jan	3 Rep	(h)	Bolton Wanderers	2	L 0-2		34,790
1993-94							
19th Jan	3	(a)	Bristol City	1	D 1-1	Rush	21,718
25th Jan	3 Rep	(h)	Bristol City	1	L 0-1		36,720
1994-95							
7th Jan	3	(a)	Birmingham City	2	D 0-0		25,326
18th Jan	3 Rep	(h)	Birmingham City	2	W 1-1aet	Redknapp	36,275
			(Liverpool won 2-0 on penalties)				
28th Jan	4	(a)	Burnley	1	D 0-0		20,551
7th Feb	4 Rep	(h)	Burnley	1	W 1-0	Barnes	32,109
19th Feb	5	(h)	Wimbledon	Prem	D 1-1	Fowler	25,124
28th Feb	5 Rep	(a)	Wimbledon	Prem	W 2-0	Barnes, Rush	12,553
11th Mar	6	(h)	Tottenham Hotspur	Prem	L 1-2	Fowler	39,592
1995-96							
6th Jan	3	(h)	Rochdale	3	W 7-0	Fowler, Collymore 3, Valentine o.g., Rush, McAteer	28,126
18th Feb	4	(a)	Shrewsbury Town	2	W 4-0	Collymore, Walton o.g., Fowler, McAteer	7,752
28th Feb	5	(h)	Charlton Athletic	1	W 2-1	Fowler, Collymore	36,818
10th Mar	6	(a)	Leeds United	Prem	D 0-0		34,632
20th Mar	6 Rep	(h)	Leeds United	Prem	W 3-0	McManaman 2, Fowler	30,812
31st Mar	S.F	Old Trafford	Aston Villa	Prem	W 3-0	Fowler 2, McAteer	39,072
11th May	Final	Wembley	Manchester United	Prem	L 0-1		79,007
1996-97							
4th Jan	3	(h)	Burnley	2	W 1-0	Collymore	33,252
26th Jan	4	(a)	Chelsea	Prem	L 2-4	Fowler, Collymore	27,950

Date	Round	Venue	Opponents	Opponent Division	Score	Scorers	Att
1997-98							
3rd Jan	3	(h)	Coventry City	Prem	L 1-3	Redknapp	33,888
1998-99							
3rd Jan	3	(a)	Port Vale	1	W 3-0	Owen (pen), Ince, Fowler	16,557
24th Jan	4	(a)	Manchester United	Prem	L 1-2	Owen	54,591
1999-2000							
12th Dec	3	(a)	Huddersfield Town	1	W 2-0	Camara, Matteo	23,678
10th Jan	4	(h)	Blackburn Rovers	1	L 0-1		32,839
2000-01							
6th Jan	3	(h)	Rotherham United	2	W 3-0	Heskey 2, Hamann	30,689
27th Jan	4	(a)	Leeds United	Prem	W 2-0	Barmby, Heskey	37,108
18th Feb	5	(h)	Manchester City	Prem	W 4-2	Litmanen (pen), Heskey, Smicer (pen), Babbel	36,231
11th Mar	6	(a)	Tranmere Rovers	1	W 4-2	Murphy, Owen, Gerrard, Fowler (pen)	16,334
8th Apr	S.F.	Villa Park	Wycombe W.	2	W 2-1	Heskey, Fowler	40,037
12th May	Final	Cardiff	Arsenal	Prem	W 2-1	Owen 2	74,200
2001-02							
5th Jan	3	(h)	Birmingham City	1	W 3-0	Owen 2, Anelka	40,875
27th Jan	4	(a)	Arsenal	Prem	L 0-1		38,092
2002-03							
5th Jan	3	(a)	Manchester City	Prem	W 1-0	Murphy (pen)	28,586
26th Jan	4	(a)	Crystal Palace	1	D 0-0		26,054
5th Feb	4 Rep	(h)	Crystal Palace	1	L 0-2		35,109
2003-04							
4th Jan	3	(a)	Yeovil Town	3	W 2-0	Heskey, Murphy (pen)	9,348
24th Jan	4	(h)	Newcastle United	Prem	W 2-1	Cheyrou 2	41,365
15th Feb	5	(h)	Portsmouth	Prem	D 1-1	Owen	34,669
22nd Feb	5 Rep	(a)	Portsmouth	Prem	L 0-1		19,529
2004-05							
18th Jan	3	(a)	Burnley	Champ	L 0-1		19,033
2005-06							
7th Jan	3	(a)	Luton Town	Champ	W 5-3	Gerrard, Sinama-Pongolle 2, Alonso 2	10,170
29th Jan	4	(a)	Portsmouth	Prem	W 2-1	Gerrard (pen), Riise	17,247
18th Feb	5	(h)	Manchester United	Prem	W 1-0	Crouch	44,039
21st Mar	6	(a)	Birmingham City	Prem	W 7-0	Hyypia, Crouch 2, Morientes, Riise, Tebily o.g., Cisse	27,378
22nd Apr	S.F.	Old Trafford	Chelsea	Prem	W 2-1	Riise, Garcia	64,575
13th May	Final	Cardiff	West Ham United (Liverpool won 3-1 on penalties)	Prem	W 3-3 aet	Cisse, Gerrard 2	74,000
2006-07							
6th Jan	3	(h)	Arsenal	Prem	L 1-3	Kuyt	43,619

The Cups

Steve Heighway jumps in delight after scoring in the 1974 FA Cup final (top) – while Pepe Reina saves from Paul Konchesky in the 2006 FA Cup final penalty shootout

THE LEAGUE CUP

Date	Round	Venue	Opponents	Opponent Division	Score	Scorers	Att
1960-61							
19th Oct	2	(h)	Luton Town	2	D 1-1	Leishman	10,502
24th Oct	2 Rep	(a)	Luton Town	2	W 5-2	Lewis 2, Hickson, Hunt 2	6,125
16th Nov	3	(h)	Southampton	2	L 1-2	Hunt	14,036
1967-68							
13th Sept	2	(h)	Bolton Wanderers	2	D 1-1	Thompson	45,957
27th Sept	2 Rep	(a)	Bolton Wanderers	2	L 2-3	Smith (pen), Callaghan	31,500
1968-69							
4th Sept	2	(h)	Sheffield United	2	W 4-0	Hunt, Lawler, Callaghan, Thompson	32,358
25th Sept	3	(h)	Swansea Town	4	W 2-0	Lawler, Hunt	31,051
15th Oct	4	(a)	Arsenal	1	L 1-2	Lawler	39,299
1969-70							
3rd Sept	2	(a)	Watford	2	W 2-1	Slater o.g., St John	21,149
24th Sept	3	(a)	Manchester City	1	L 2-3	A.Evans, Graham	28,019
1970-71							
8th Sept	2	(a)	Mansfield Town	3	D 0-0		12,532
22nd Sept	2 Rep	(h)	Mansfield Town	3	W 3-2 aet	Hughes, Smith (pen), A.Evans	31,087
6th Oct	3	(a)	Swindon Town	2	L 0-2		23,992
1971-72							
7th Sept	2	(h)	Hull City	2	W 3-0	Lawler, Heighway, Hall (pen)	31,612
5th Oct	3	(h)	Southampton	1	W 1-0	Heighway	28,964
27th Oct	4	(a)	West Ham United	1	L 1-2	Graham	40,878
1972-73							
5th Sept	2	(a)	Carlisle United	2	D 1-1	Keegan	16,257
19th Sept	2 Rep	(h)	Carlisle United	2	W 5-1	Keegan, Boersma 2, Lawler, Heighway	22,128
3rd Oct	3	(a)	West Bromwich Alb.	1	D 1-1	Heighway	17,756
10th Oct	3 Rep	(h)	West Bromwich Alb.	1	W 2-1 aet	Hughes, Keegan	26,461
31st Oct	4	(h)	Leeds United	1	D 2-2	Keegan, Toshack	44,609
22nd Nov	4 Rep	(a)	Leeds United	1	W 1-0	Keegan	34,856
4th Dec	5	(h)	Tottenham Hotspur	1	D 1-1	Hughes	48,677
6th Dec	5 Rep	(a)	Tottenham Hotspur	1	L 1-3	Callaghan	34,565
1973-74							
8th Oct	2	(a)	West Ham United	1	D 2-2	Cormack, Heighway	25,823
29th Oct	2 Rep	(h)	West Ham United	1	W 1-0	Toshack	26,002
21st Nov	3	(a)	Sunderland	2	W 2-0	Keegan, Toshack	36,208
27th Nov	4	(a)	Hull City	2	D 0-0		19,748
4th Dec	4 Rep	(h)	Hull City	2	W 3-1	Callaghan 3	17,120
19th Dec	5	(a)	Wolverhampton W.	1	L 0-1		15,242
1974-75							
10th Sept	2	(h)	Brentford	4	W 2-1	Kennedy, Boersma	21,413
8th Oct	3	(a)	Bristol City	2	D 0-0		25,573
16th Oct	3 Rep	(h)	Bristol City	2	W 4-0	Heighway 2, Kennedy 2	23,694
12th Nov	4	(h)	Middlesbrough	1	L 0-1		24,906

The Cups

Date	Round	Venue	Opponents	Opponent Division	Score	Scorers	Att
1975-76							
10th Sept	2	(a)	York City	2	W 1-0	Lindsay (pen)	9,421
7th Oct	3	(h)	Burnley	1	D 1-1	Case	24,607
14th Oct	3 Rep	(a)	Burnley	1	L 0-1		20,022
1976-77							
31st Aug	2	(h)	West Bromwich Alb.	1	D 1-1	Callaghan	23,378
6th Sept	2 Rep	(a)	West Bromwich Alb.	1	L 0-1		22,662
1977-78							
30th Aug	2	(h)	Chelsea	1	W 2-0	Dalglish, Case	33,170
26th Oct	3	(h)	Derby County	1	W 2-0	Fairclough 2	30,400
29th Nov	4	(h)	Coventry City	1	D 2-2	Fairclough, Neal (pen)	33,817
20th Dec	4 Rep	(a)	Coventry City	1	W 2-0	Case, Dalglish	36,105
17th Jan	5	(a)	Wrexham	3	W 3-1	Dalglish 3	25,641
7th Feb	S.F.Leg 1	(h)	Arsenal	1	W 2-1	Dalglish, Kennedy	44,764
14th Feb	S.F.Leg 2	(a)	Arsenal	1	D 0-0		49,561
18th Mar	Final	Wembley	Nottingham Forest	1	D 0-0 aet		100,000
22nd Mar	Final Rep.	Old Trafford	Nottingham Forest	1	L 0-1		54,375
1978-79							
28th Aug	2	(a)	Sheffield United	2	L 0-1		35,753
1979-80							
29th Aug	2 Leg 1	(a)	Tranmere Rovers	4	D 0-0		16,759
4th Sept	2 Leg 2	(h)	Tranmere Rovers	4	W 4-0	Thompson, Dalglish 2, Fairclough	24,785
25th Sept	3	(h)	Chesterfield	3	W 3-1	Fairclough, Dalglish, McDermott	20,960
30th Oct	4	(h)	Exeter City	3	W 2-0	Fairclough 2	21,019
5th Dec	5	(a)	Norwich City	1	W 3-1	Johnson 2, Dalglish	23,000
22nd Jan	S.F.Leg 1	(a)	Nottingham Forest	1	L 0-1		32,234
12th Feb	S.F.Leg 2	(h)	Nottingham Forest	1	D 1-1	Fairclough	50,880
1980-81							
27th Aug	2 Leg 1	(a)	Bradford City	4	L 0-1		16,232
2nd Sept	2 Leg 2	(h)	Bradford City	4	W 4-0	Dalglish 2, R.Kennedy, Johnson	21,017
23rd Sept	3	(h)	Swindon Town	3	W 5-0	Lee 2, Dalglish, Cockerill o.g., Fairclough	16,566
28th Oct	4	(h)	Portsmouth	3	W 4-1	Dalglish, Johnson 2, Souness	32,021
5th Dec	5	(h)	Birmingham City	1	W 3-1	Dalglish, McDermott, Johnson	30,236
14th Jan	S.F.Leg 1	(a)	Manchester City	1	W 1-0	R.Kennedy	48,045
10th Feb	S.F.Leg 2	(h)	Manchester City	1	D 1-1	Dalglish	46,711
14th Mar	Final	Wembley	West Ham United	2	D 1-1aet	A.Kennedy	100,000
1st Apr	Final Rep	Villa Park	West Ham United	2	W 2-1	Dalglish, Hansen	36,693
1981-82							
7th Oct	2 Leg 1	(h)	Exeter City	3	W 5-0	Rush 2, McDermott, Dalglish, Whelan	11,478
28th Oct	2 Leg 2	(a)	Exeter City	3	W 6-0	Rush 2, Dalglish, Neal, Sheedy, Marker o.g.	11,740
10th Nov	3	(h)	Middlesbrough	1	W 4-1	Sheedy, Rush, Johnson 2	16,145
1st Dec	4	(a)	Arsenal	1	D 0-0		37,917
8th Dec	4 Rep	(h)	Arsenal	1	W 3-0 aet	Johnston, McDermott (pen), Dalglish	21,375
12th Jan	5	(h)	Barnsley	2	D 0-0		33,707
19th Jan	5 Rep	(a)	Barnsley	2	W 3-1	Souness, Johnson, Dalglish	29,639

Date	Round	Venue	Opponents	Opponent Division	Score	Scorers	Att
1981-82 (cont)							
2nd Feb	S.F.Leg 1	(a)	Ipswich Town	1	W 2-0	McDermott, Rush	26,690
9th Feb	S.F.Leg 2	(h)	Ipswich Town	1	D 2-2	Rush, Dalglish	34,933
13th Mar	Final	Wembley	Tottenham Hotspur	1	W 3-1 aet	Whelan 2, Rush	100,000
1982-83							
5th Oct	2 Leg 1	(a)	Ipswich Town	1	W 2-1	Rush 2	19,328
26th Oct	2 Leg 2	(h)	Ipswich Town	1	W 2-0	Whelan, Lawrenson	17,698
11th Nov	3	(h)	Rotherham United	2	W 1-0	Johnston	20,412
30th Nov	4	(h)	Norwich City	1	W 2-0	Lawrenson, Fairclough	13,235
18th Jan	5	(h)	West Ham United	1	W 2-1	Hodgson, Souness	23,953
8th Feb	S.F.Leg 1	(h)	Burnley	2	W 3-0	Souness, Neal (pen), Hodgson	33,520
15th Feb	S.F.Leg 2	(a)	Burnley	2	L 0-1		20,000
26th Mar	Final	Wembley	Manchester United	1	W 2-1 aet	Kennedy, Whelan	100,000
1983-84							
5th Oct	2 Leg 1	(a)	Brentford	3	W 4-1	Rush 2, Robinson, Souness	17,859
25th Oct	2 Leg 2	(h)	Brentford	3	W 4-0	Souness (pen), Hodgson, Dalglish, Robinson	9,902
8th Nov	3	(a)	Fulham	2	D 1-1	Rush	20,142
22nd Nov	3 Rep	(h)	Fulham	2	D 1-1 aet	Dalglish	15,783
29th Nov	3 Rep (2)	(a)	Fulham	2	W 1-0 aet	Souness	20,905
20th Dec	4	(a)	Birmingham City	1	D 1-1	Souness	17,405
22nd Dec	4 Rep	(h)	Birmingham City	1	W 3-0	Nicol, Rush 2 (1 pen)	11,638
17th Jan	5	(a)	Sheffield Wed.	2	D 2-2	Nicol, Neal (pen)	49,357
25th Jan	5 Rep	(h)	Sheffield Wed.	2	W 3-0	Rush 2, Robinson	40,485
7th Feb	S.F.Leg 1	(h)	Walsall	3	D 2-2	Whelan 2	31,073
14th Feb	S.F.Leg 2	(a)	Walsall	3	W 2-0	Rush, Whelan	19,591
25th Mar	Final	Wembley	Everton	1	D 0-0 aet		100,000
28th Mar	Final Rep	Maine Rd	Everton	1	W 1-0	Souness	52,089
1984-85							
24th Sept	2 Leg 1	(a)	Stockport County	4	D 0-0		11,169
9th Oct	2 Leg 2	(h)	Stockport County	4	W 2-0 aet	Robinson, Whelan	13,422
31st Oct	3	(a)	Tottenham Hotspur	1	L 0-1		38,690
1985-86							
24th Sept	2 Leg 1	(h)	Oldham Athletic	2	W 3-0	McMahon 2, Rush	16,150
9th Oct	2 Leg 2	(a)	Oldham Athletic	2	W 5-2	Whelan 2, Wark, Rush, MacDonald	7,719
29th Oct	3	(h)	Brighton	2	W 4-0	Walsh 3, Dalglish	15,291
26th Nov	4	(h)	Manchester United	1	W 2-1	Molby 2 (1 pen)	41,291
21st Jan	5	(h)	Ipswich Town	1	W 3-0	Walsh, Whelan, Rush	19,762
12th Feb	S.F.Leg 1	(a)	QPR	1	L 0-1		15,051
5th Mar	S.F.Leg 2	(h)	QPR	1	D 2-2	McMahon, Johnston	23,863
1986-87							
23rd Sept	2 Leg 1	(h)	Fulham	3	W 10-0	Rush 2, Wark 2, Whelan, McMahon 4, Nicol	13,498
7th Oct	2 Leg 2	(a)	Fulham	3	W 3-2	McMahon, Parker o.g., Molby (pen)	7,864
29th Oct	3	(h)	Leicester City	1	W 4-1	McMahon 3, Dalglish	20,248
19th Nov	4	(a)	Coventry City	1	D 0-0		26,385
26th Nov	4 Rep	(h)	Coventry City	1	W 3-1	Molby 3 (3 pens)	19,179
21st Jan	5	(a)	Everton	1	W 1-0	Rush	53,325
11th Feb	S.F.Leg 1	(a)	Southampton	1	D 0-0		22,818

The Cups

Date	Round	Venue	Opponents	Opponent Division	Score	Scorers	Att
1986-87 (cont)							
11th Feb	S.F.Leg 1	(a)	Southampton	1	D 0-0		22,818
25th Feb	S.F.Leg 2	(h)	Southampton	1	W 3-0	Whelan, Dalglish, Molby	38,481
5th Apr	Final	Wembley	Arsenal	1	L 1-2	Rush	96,000
1987-88							
23rd Sept	2 Leg 1	(a)	Blackburn Rovers	2	D 1-1	Nicol	13,924
6th Oct	2 Leg 2	(h)	Blackburn Rovers	2	W 1-0	Aldridge	28,994
28th Oct	3	(h)	Everton	1	L 0-1		44,071
1988-89							
28th Sept	2 Leg 1	(h)	Walsall	2	W 1-0	Gillespie	18,084
12th Oct	2 Leg 2	(a)	Walsall	2	W 3-1	Barnes, Rush, Molby (pen)	12,015
2nd Nov	3	(h)	Arsenal	1	D 1-1	Barnes	31,951
9th Nov	3 Rep	(a)	Arsenal	1	D 0-0		54,029
23rd Nov	3 Rep (2)	Villa Park	Arsenal	1	W 2-1	McMahon, Aldridge	21,708
30th Nov	4	(a)	West Ham United	1	L 1-4	Aldridge (pen)	26,971
1989-90							
19th Sept	2 Leg 1	(h)	Wigan Athletic	3	W 5-2	Hysen, Rush 2, Beardsley, Barnes	19,231
4th Oct	2 Leg 2	(a)	Wigan Athletic (match played at Anfield)	3	W 3-0	Staunton 3	17,954
25th Oct	3	(a)	Arsenal	1	L 0-1		40,814
1990-91							
25th Sept	2 Leg 1	(h)	Crewe Alexandra	3	W 5-1	McMahon, Gillespie, Houghton, Rush 2	17,228
9th Oct	2 Leg 2	(a)	Crewe Alexandra	3	W 4-1	Rush 3, Staunton	7,200
31st Oct	3	(a)	Manchester United	1	L 1-3	Houghton	42,033
1991-92							
25th Sept	2 Leg 1	(h)	Stoke City	3	D 2-2	Rush 2	18,389
9th Oct	2 Leg 2	(a)	Stoke City	3	W 3-2	McManaman, Saunders, Walters	22,335
29th Oct	3	(h)	Port Vale	2	D 2-2	McManaman, Rush	21,553
20th Nov	3 Rep	(a)	Port Vale	2	W 4-1	McManaman, Walters, Houghton, Saunders	18,725
3rd Dec	4	(a)	Peterborough Utd	3	L 0-1		14,114
1992-93							
22nd Sept	2 Leg 1	(h)	Chesterfield	3	D 4-4	Rosenthal, Hutchison, Walters, Wright	12,533
6th Oct	2 Leg 2	(a)	Chesterfield	3	W 4-1	Hutchison, Redknapp, Walters, Rush	10,632
28th Oct	3	(a)	Sheffield United	Prem	D 0-0		17,856
11th Nov	3 Rep	(h)	Sheffield United	Prem	W 3-0	McManaman 2, Marsh (pen)	17,654
1st Dec	4	(h)	Crystal Palace	Prem	D 1-1	Marsh (pen)	18,525
16th Dec	4 Rep	(a)	Crystal Palace	Prem	L 1-2 aet	Marsh (pen)	19,622

Date	Round	Venue	Opponents	Opponent Division	Score	Scorers	Att
1993-94							
22nd Sept	2 Leg 1	(a)	Fulham	2	W 3-1	Rush, Clough, Fowler	13,599
5th Oct	2 Leg 2	(h)	Fulham	2	W 5-0	Fowler 5	12,541
27th Oct	3	(h)	Ipswich Town	Prem	W 3-2	Rush 3	19,058
1st Dec	4	(h)	Wimbledon	Prem	D 1-1	Molby (pen)	19,290
14th Dec	4 Rep	(a)	Wimbledon	Prem	L 2-2 aet	Ruddock, Segers o.g.	11,343
			(Liverpool lost 3-4 on penalties)				
1994-95							
21st Sept	2 Leg 1	(h)	Burnley	1	W 2-0	Scales, Fowler	23,359
5th Oct	2 Leg 2	(a)	Burnley	1	W 4-1	Redknapp 2, Fowler, Clough	19,032
25th Oct	3	(h)	Stoke City	1	W 2-1	Rush 2	32,060
30th Nov	4	(a)	Blackburn Rovers	Prem	W 3-1	Rush 3	30,115
11th Jan	5	(h)	Arsenal	Prem	W 1-0	Rush	36,004
15th Feb	S.F.Leg 1	(h)	Crystal Palace	Prem	W 1-0	Fowler	25,480
8th Mar	S.F.Leg 2	(a)	Crystal Palace	Prem	W 1-0	Fowler	18,224
2nd Apr	Final	Wembley	Bolton Wanderers	1	W 2-1	McManaman 2	75,595
1995-96							
20th Sept	2 Leg 1	(h)	Sunderland	1	W 2-0	McManaman, Thomas	25,579
4th Oct	2 Leg 2	(a)	Sunderland	1	W 1-0	Fowler	20,560
25th Oct	3	(h)	Manchester City	Prem	W 4-0	Scales, Fowler, Rush, Harkness	29,394
29th Nov	4	(h)	Newcastle United	Prem	L 0-1		40,077
1996-97							
23rd Oct	3	(a)	Charlton Athletic	1	D 1-1	Fowler	15,000
13th Nov	3 Rep	(h)	Charlton Athletic	1	W 4-1	Wright, Redknapp, Fowler 2	20,714
27th Nov	4	(h)	Arsenal	Prem	W 4-2	McManaman, Fowler 2 (1 pen) Berger	32,814
8th Jan	5	(a)	Middlesbrough	Prem	L 1-2	McManaman	28,670
1997-98							
15th Oct	3	(a)	West Bromwich Alb.	1	W 2-0	Berger, Fowler	21,986
18th Nov	4	(h)	Grimsby Town	2	W 3-0	Owen 3	28,515
7th Jan	5	(a)	Newcastle United	Prem	W 2-0 aet	Owen, Fowler	33,207
27th Jan	S.F.Leg 1	(h)	Middlesbrough	1	W 2-1	Redknapp, Fowler	33,438
18th Feb	S.F.Leg 2	(a)	Middlesbrough	1	L 0-2		29,828
1998-99							
27th Oct	3	(h)	Fulham	2	W 3-1	Morgan o.g., Fowler (pen), Ince	22,296
10th Nov	4	(h)	Tottenham Hotspur	Prem	L 1-3	Owen	20,772
1999-2000							
14th Sept	2 Leg 1	(a)	Hull City	3	W 5-1	Murphy 2, Meijer 2, Staunton	10,034
21st Sept	2 Leg 2	(h)	Hull City	3	W 4-2	Murphy, Maxwell, Riedle 2	24,318
13th Oct	3	(a)	Southampton	Prem	L 1-2	Owen	13,822
2000-01							
1st Nov	3	(h)	Chelsea	Prem	W 2-1 aet	Murphy, Fowler	29,370
29th Nov	4	(a)	Stoke City	2	W 8-0	Ziege, Smicer, Babbel, Fowler 3 (1 pen), Hyypia, Murphy	27,109
13th Dec	5	(h)	Fulham	1	W 3-0 aet	Owen, Smicer, Barmby	20,144
10th Jan	S.F.Leg 1	(a)	Crystal Palace	1	L 1-2	Smicer	25,933
24th Jan	S.F.Leg 2	(h)	Crystal Palace	1	W 5-0	Smicer, Murphy 2, Biscan, Fowler	41,854
25th Feb	Final	Cardiff	Birmingham City	1	W 1-1 aet	Fowler	73,500
			(Liverpool won 5-4 on penalties)				

The Cups

Date	Round	Venue	Opponents	Opponent Division	Score	Scorers	Att
2001-02							
9th Oct	3	(h)	Grimsby Town	1	L 1-2 aet	McAllister (pen)	32,672
2002-03							
6th Nov	3	(h)	Southampton	Prem	W 3-1	Berger, Diouf, Baros	35,870
4th Dec	4	(h)	Ipswich Town (Liverpool won 5-4 on penalties)	1	W 1-1	Diouf (pen)	26,305
18th Dec	5	(a)	Aston Villa	Prem	W 4-3	Murphy 2, Baros, Gerrard	38,530
8th Jan	S.F.Leg 1	(a)	Sheffield United	1	L 1-2	Mellor	30,095
21st Jan	S.F.Leg 2	(h)	Sheffield United	1	W 2-0 aet	Diouf, Owen	43,837
2nd Mar	Final	Cardiff	Manchester United	Prem	W 2-0	Gerrard, Owen	74,500
2003-04							
29th Oct	3	(a)	Blackburn Rovers	Prem	W 4-3	Murphy (pen), Heskey 2, Kewell	16,918
3rd Dec	4	(h)	Bolton Wanderers	Prem	L 2-3	Murphy, Smicer	33,185
2004-05							
26th Oct	3	(a)	Millwall	Champ	W 3-0	Diao, Baros 2	17,655
10th Nov	4	(h)	Middlesbrough	Prem	W 2-0	Mellor 2	28,176
1st Dec	5	(a)	Tottenham Hotspur (Liverpool won 4-3 on penalties)	Prem	W 1-1 aet	Sinama-Pongolle (pen)	36,100
11th Jan	S.F.Leg 1	(h)	Watford	Champ	W 1-0	Gerrard	35,739
25th Jan	S.F.Leg 2	(a)	Watford	Champ	W 1-0	Gerrard	19,797
27th Feb	Final	Cardiff	Chelsea	Prem	L 2-3 aet	Riise, Nunez	71,622
2005-06							
25th Oct	3	(a)	Crystal Palace	Champ	L 1-2	Gerrard	19,673
2006-07							
25th Oct	3	(h)	Reading	Prem	W 4-3	Fowler, Riise, Paletta, Crouch	42,445
8th Nov	4	(a)	Birmingham City	Champ	W 1-0	Agger	23,061
9th Jan	5	(h)	Arsenal	Prem	L 3-6	Fowler, Gerrard, Hyypia	42,614

Left to right: John Arne Riise, Jerzy Dudek and Stephane Henchoz delight in Liverpool 2003 League Cup triumph over Manchester United

CLUB WORLD CHAMPIONSHIP

Date	Round	Venue	Opponents	Opponent Country	Score	Scorers	Att
1981							
13th Dec	Final	Tokyo	Flamengo	Bra	L 0-3		62,000
1984							
9th Dec	Final	Tokyo	Independiente	Arg	L 0-1		62,000
2005							
15th Dec	S.F.	Yokohama	Saprissa	CRi	W 3-0	Crouch 2, Gerrard	43,902
18th Dec	Final	Yokohama	Sao Paulo	Bra	L 0-1		66,821

THE CHARITY SHIELD (FA COMMUNITY SHIELD)

Date	Round	Venue	Opponents	Opponent Division	Score	Scorers	Att
1922							
10th May		Old Trafford	Huddersfield Town	1	L 0-1		20,000
1964							
15th Aug		Anfield	West Ham United	1	D 2-2	Wallace, Byrne	38,858
1965							
14th Aug		Old Trafford	Manchester United	1	D 2-2	Stevenson, Yeats	48,502
1966							
13th Aug		Goodison P	Everton	1	W 1-0	Hunt	63,329
1971							
7th Aug		Filbert St	Leicester City	1	L 0-1		25,014
1974							
10th Aug		Wembley	Leeds United (Liverpool won 6-5 on penalties)	1	W 1-1	Boersma	67,000
1976							
14th Aug		Wembley	Southampton	2	W 1-0	Toshack	76,500
1977							
13th Aug		Wembley	Manchester United	1	D 0-0		82,000
1979							
11th Aug		Wembley	Arsenal	1	W 3-1	McDermott 2, Dalglish	92,000
1980							
9th Aug		Wembley	West Ham United	2	W 1-0	McDermott	90,000
1982							
21st Aug		Wembley	Tottenham Hotspur	1	W 1-0	Rush	82,500
1983							
20th Aug		Wembley	Manchester United	1	L 0-2		92,000
1984							
18th Aug		Wembley	Everton	1	L 0-1		100,000
1986							
16th Aug		Wembley	Everton	1	D 1-1	Rush	88,231
1988							
20th Aug		Wembley	Wimbledon	1	W 2-1	Aldridge 2	54,887
1989							
12th Aug		Wembley	Arsenal	1	W 1-0	Beardsley	63,149
1990							
18th Aug		Wembley	Manchester United	1	D 1-1	Barnes	66,558
1992							
12th Aug		Wembley	Leeds United	Prem	L 3-4	Rush, Saunders, Strachan o.g.	61,291
2001							
12th Aug		Cardiff	Manchester United	Prem	W 2-1	McAllister (pen), Owen	70,227
2002							
11th Aug		Cardiff	Arsenal	Prem	L 0-1		67,337
2006							
13th Aug		Cardiff	Chelsea	Prem	W 2-1	Riise, Crouch	56,275

The Liverpool squad pose for a team shot following the FA Community Shield triumph over Chelsea at the start of last season

SCREEN SPORT SUPER CUP

Date	Round	Venue	Opponents	Opponent Division	Score	Scorers	Att
1985-86							
			Group stage				
17th Sept	Group	(h)	Southampton	1	W 2-1	Molby, Dalglish	16,189
22nd Oct	Group	(a)	Southampton	1	D 1-1	Walsh	10,503
3rd Dec	Group	(h)	Tottenham Hotspur	1	W 2-0	MacDonald, Walsh	14,855
14th Jan	Group	(a)	Tottenham Hotspur	1	W 3-0	Rush 2, Lawrenson	10,078
5th Feb	SF Leg 1	(a)	Norwich City	1	D 1-1	Dalglish	15,330
6th May	SF Leg 2	(h)	Norwich City	1	W 3-1	MacDonald, Molby (pen), Johnston	26,696
1986-87							
16th Sept	F Leg 1	(h)	Everton	1	W 3-1	Rush 2, McMahon	20,660
30th Sept	F Leg 2	(a)	Everton	1	W 4-1	Rush 3, Nicol	26,068

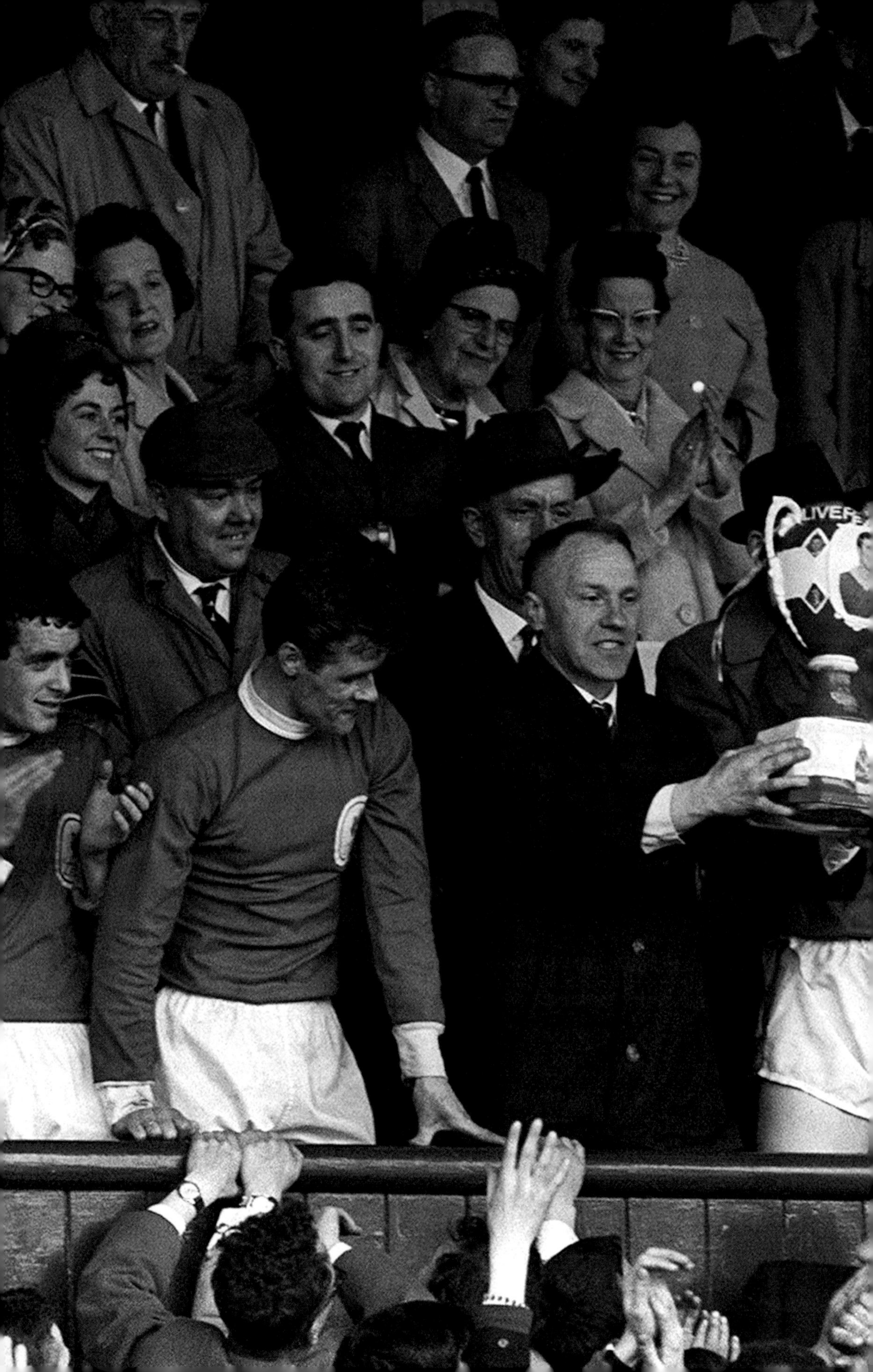

THE RECORDS

THE MARATHON MEN

CORRECT AT END OF MAY 2007 – Games played includes substitute appearances

OVERALL APPEARANCES (500+ GAMES)

1	Ian Callaghan	857
2	Ray Clemence	665
=	Emlyn Hughes	665
4	Ian Rush	660
5	Phil Neal	650
6	Tommy Smith	638
7	Bruce Grobbelaar	628
8	Alan Hansen	620
9	Chris Lawler	549
10	Billy Liddell	534
11	Kenny Dalglish	515

Tommy Smith and Ian Callaghan, in the top 6

LEAGUE APPEARANCES (400+ GAMES)

1	Ian Callaghan	640
2	Billy Liddell	492
3	Emlyn Hughes	474
4	Ray Clemence	470
5	Ian Rush	469
6	Tommy Smith	467
7	Phil Neal	455
8	Bruce Grobbelaar	440
9	Alan Hansen	434
10	Elisha Scott	430
11	Chris Lawler	406
12	Roger Hunt	404

Billy Liddell, second to Cally

EUROPE APPEARANCES (40+ GAMES)

1	Jamie Carragher	91
2	Ian Callaghan	89
3	Tommy Smith	85
4	**Sami Hyypia**	81
5	Ray Clemence	80
6	Emlyn Hughes	79
7	**Steven Gerrard**	78
8	Phil Neal	74
9	**John Arne Riise**	69
10	Steve Heighway	67
11	Chris Lawler	66
12	Dietmar Hamann	61
13	Kenny Dalglish	51
14	Ray Kennedy	50
=	Michael Owen	50
=	Phil Thompson	50
17	Alan Hansen	46
=	Danny Murphy	46
19	Emile Heskey	45
20	Robbie Fowler	44
=	**Steve Finnan**	44
=	Peter Thompson	44

John Arne Riise, now in the top 10

FA CUP APPEARANCES (40+ GAMES)

1	Ian Callaghan	79
2	Bruce Grobbelaar	62
=	Emlyn Hughes	62
4	Ian Rush	61
5	Alan Hansen	58
6	Ray Clemence	54
7	Tommy Smith	52
8	John Barnes	51
9	Steve Nicol	50
=	Ron Yeats	50
11	Ian St John	49
12	Chris Lawler	47

LEAGUE CUP APPEARANCES (40+ GAMES)

1	Ian Rush	78
2	Bruce Grobbelaar	70
3	Alan Hansen	68
4	Phil Neal	66
5	Kenny Dalglish	59
6	Ray Clemence	55
7	Mark Lawrenson	50
=	Ronnie Whelan	50
9	Emlyn Hughes	46
10	Alan Kennedy	45
=	Graeme Souness	45
12	Phil Thompson	43
13	Ian Callaghan	42
=	Steve Nicol	42

John Barnes - At No. 8 on the list of most FA Cup appearances for the Reds

Emlyn Hughes and Kenny Dalglish, amongst the names on the League Cup appearance list

THE RECORD GOALSCORERS

CORRECT AT END OF MAY 2007 - Games played includes substitute appearances

OVERALL (100+ GOALS)

#	Name	TIME WITH CLUB	GAMES	GOALS
1	Ian Rush	1980-87 & 1988-96	660	346
2	Roger Hunt	1959-1970	492	286
3	Gordon Hodgson	1925-1936	377	241
4	Billy Liddell	1945-1961	534	228
5	Robbie Fowler	1993-2001 & 2006-07	369	183
6	Kenny Dalglish	1977-1990	515	172
7	Michael Owen	1997-2004	297	158
8	Harry Chambers	1919-1928	339	151
9	Jack Parkinson	1899-1914	222	130
10	Sam Raybould	1899-1907	226	128
11	Dick Forshaw	1919-1927	288	124
12	Ian St John	1961-1971	425	118
13	Jack Balmer	1935-1952	310	110
14	John Barnes	1987-1997	407	108
15	Kevin Keegan	1971-1977	323	100

LEAGUE (100+ GOALS)

#	Name	TIME WITH CLUB	GAMES	GOALS
1	Roger Hunt	1959-1970	404	245
2	Gordon Hodgson	1925-1936	358	233
3	Ian Rush	1980-87 & 1988-96	469	229
4	Billy Liddell	1945-1961	492	215
5	Harry Chambers	1919-1928	310	135
6	Robbie Fowler	1993-2001 & 2006-07	266	128
7	Jack Parkinson	1899-1914	203	125
8	Sam Raybould	1899-1907	211	119
9	Michael Owen	1997-2004	216	118
=	Kenny Dalglish	1979-1990	355	118
11	Dick Forshaw	1919-1927	266	117

EUROPE (11+ GOALS)

#	Name	TIME WITH CLUB	GAMES	GOALS
1	Michael Owen	1997-2004	50	22
2	Ian Rush	1980-87 & 1988-96	38	20
3	**Steven Gerrard**	**1998-**	**78**	**19**
4	Roger Hunt	1959-1970	31	17
5	Terry McDermott	1974-1982	34	15
6	Robbie Fowler	1993-2001 & 2006-07	44	14
7	Jimmy Case	1974-1981	35	13
=	Emile Heskey	2000-2004	45	13
9	Kevin Keegan	1971-1977	40	12
=	Ray Kennedy	1974-1982	50	12
11	Luis Garcia	2004-2007	32	11
=	Kenny Dalglish	1979-1990	51	11
=	Chris Lawler	1962-1975	66	11
=	Steve Heighway	1970-1981	67	11
=	Phil Neal	1974-1985	74	11

The Records

EUROPEAN CUP (7+ GOALS)

		TIME WITH CLUB	GAMES	GOALS
1	**Steven Gerrard**	1998-	53	15
2	Ian Rush	1980-87 & 1988-96	25	14
3	Terry McDermott	1974-1982	31	12
4	Roger Hunt	1959-1970	14	10
=	Luis Garcia	2004-2007	31	10
=	Kenny Dalglish	1977-1990	47	10
=	Phil Neal	1974-1985	57	10
8	Michael Owen	1997-2004	16	9
9	David Johnson	1976-1982	20	8
10	Ian St John	1961-1971	13	7
=	Jimmy Case	1975-1981	22	7
=	Djibril Cisse	2004-2007	22	7
=	**Peter Crouch**	2005-	22	7

FA CUP (10+ GOALS)

		TIME WITH CLUB	GAMES	GOALS
1	Ian Rush	1980-87 & 1988-96	61	39
2	Roger Hunt	1959-1970	44	18
3	Harry Chambers	1919-1928	28	16
=	John Barnes	1987-1997	51	16
5	Kevin Keegan	1971-1977	28	14
6	Kenny Dalglish	1979-1990	37	13
=	Billy Liddell	1945-1961	42	13
8	Jack Balmer	1935-1952	21	12
=	Robbie Fowler	1993-2001 & 2006-07	24	12
=	Ian St John	1961-1971	49	12
11	Peter Beardsley	1987-1991	25	11
=	Billy Lacey	1911-1924	28	11
13	Willie Fagan	1937-1952	24	10

LEAGUE CUP (9+ GOALS)

		TIME WITH CLUB	GAMES	GOALS
1	Ian Rush	1980-87 & 1988-96	78	48
2	Robbie Fowler	1993-2001 & 2006-07	35	29
3	Kenny Dalglish	1979-1990	59	27
4	Ronnie Whelan	1980-1994	50	14
5	Steve McMahon	1985-1991	27	13
6	Danny Murphy	1997-2004	16	11
7	David Fairclough	1975-1983	20	10
=	Steve McManaman	1990-1999	33	10
9	Michael Owen	1997-2004	14	9
=	David Johnson	1976-1982	19	9
=	Jan Molby	1984-1996	28	9
=	Graeme Souness	1978-1984	45	9

ROBBIE FOWLER'S GOALS FOR LIVERPOOL

To salute the LFC career of Robbie Fowler, we produce a comprehensive list of every goal 'God' scored for the Reds:

GOAL NUMBER	DATE	OPPONENTS	VENUE	COMPETITION	RESULT
SEASON 1993/94					
1	22/9/93	FULHAM	CRAVEN COTTAGE	LEAGUE CUP	WON 3-1
2, 3, 4, 5, 6	5/10/93	FULHAM	ANFIELD	LEAGUE CUP	WON 5-0
7	16/10/93	OLDHAM ATH.	ANFIELD	LEAGUE	WON 2-1
8, 9, 10	30/10/93	SOUTHAMPTON	ANFIELD	LEAGUE	WON 4-2
11	28/11/93	ASTON VILLA	ANFIELD	LEAGUE	WON 2-1
12	4/12/93	SHEFF WED	HILLSBOROUGH	LEAGUE	LOST 1-3
13, 14	18/12/93	TOTTENHAM H.	WHITE HART LANE	LEAGUE	DREW 3-3
15	15/01/94	OLDHAM ATH.	BOUNDARY PARK	LEAGUE	WON 3-0
16	13/03/94	EVERTON	ANFIELD	LEAGUE	WON 2-1
17	23/04/94	WEST HAM UTD	UPTON PARK	LEAGUE	WON 2-1
18	7/5/94	ASTON VILLA	VILLA PARK	LEAGUE	LOST 1-2
SEASON 1994/95					
19	20/8/94	CRYSTAL PALACE	SELHURST PARK	LEAGUE	WON 6-1
20, 21, 22	28/8/94	ARSENAL	ANFIELD	LEAGUE	WON 3-0
23	31/8/94	SOUTHAMPTON	THE DELL	LEAGUE	WON 2-0
24	21/9/94	BURNLEY	ANFIELD	LEAGUE CUP	WON 2-0
25	5/10/94	BURNLEY	TURF MOOR	LEAGUE CUP	WON 4-1
26, 27	8/10/94	ASTON VILLA	ANFIELD	LEAGUE	WON 3-2
28	15/10/94	BLACKBURN ROV.	EWOOD PARK	LEAGUE	LOST 2-3
29	22/10/94	WIMBLEDON	ANFIELD	LEAGUE	WON 3-0
30, 31	29/10/94	IPSWICH TOWN	PORTMAN ROAD	LEAGUE	WON 3-1
32	5/11/94	NOTTINGHAM F.	ANFIELD	LEAGUE	WON 1-0
33, 34	9/11/94	CHELSEA	ANFIELD	LEAGUE	WON 3-1
35	26/11/94	TOTTENHAM H.	ANFIELD	LEAGUE	DREW 1-1
36	26/12/94	LEICESTER CITY	FILBERT STREET	LEAGUE	WON 2-1
37	28/12/94	MANCHESTER CITY	ANFIELD	LEAGUE	WON 2-0
38	31/12/94	LEEDS UNITED	ELLAND ROAD	LEAGUE	WON 2-0
39, 40	2/1/95	NORWICH CITY	ANFIELD	LEAGUE	WON 4-0
41	4/2/95	NOTTINGHAM F.	CITY GROUND	LEAGUE	DREW 1-1
42	15/2/95	CRYSTAL PALACE	ANFIELD	LEAGUE CUP	WON 1-0
43	19/2/95	WIMBLEDON	ANFIELD	FA CUP	DREW 1-1
44	4/3/95	NEWCASTLE UTD	ANFIELD	LEAGUE	WON 2-0
45	8/3/95	CRYSTAL PALACE	SELHURST PARK	LEAGUE CUP	WON 1-0
46	11/3/95	TOTTENHAM H.	ANFIELD	FA CUP	LOST 1-2
47	5/4/95	SOUTHAMPTON	ANFIELD	LEAGUE	WON 3-1
48	12/4/95	ARSENAL	HIGHBURY	LEAGUE	WON 1-0
49	17/4/95	LEICESTER CITY	ANFIELD	LEAGUE	WON 2-0
SEASON 1995/96					
50	26/8/95	TOTTENHAM H.	WHITE HART LANE	LEAGUE	WON 3-1
51	16/9/95	BLACKBURN ROV.	ANFIELD	LEAGUE	WON 3-0
52, 53, 54, 55	23/9/95	BOLTON W.	ANFIELD	LEAGUE	WON 5-2
56, 57	1/10/95	MANCHESTER UTD	OLD TRAFFORD	LEAGUE	DREW 2-2
58	4/10/95	SUNDERLAND	ROKER PARK	LEAGUE CUP	WON 1-0
59	25/10/95	MANCHESTER CITY	ANFIELD	LEAGUE CUP	WON 4-0
60, 61	28/10/95	MANCHESTER CITY	ANFIELD	LEAGUE	WON 6-0
62	18/11/95	EVERTON	ANFIELD	LEAGUE	LOST 1-2
63, 64	17/12/95	MANCHESTER UTD	ANFIELD	LEAGUE	WON 2-0
65, 66, 67	23/12/95	ARSENAL	ANFIELD	LEAGUE	WON 3-1
68, 69	1/1/96	NOTTINGHAM F.	ANFIELD	LEAGUE	WON 4-2
70	6/1/96	ROCHDALE	ANFIELD	FA CUP	WON 7-0
71, 72	20/1/96	LEEDS UNITED	ANFIELD	LEAGUE	WON 5-0
73	31/1/96	ASTON VILLA	VILLA PARK	LEAGUE	WON 2-1
74	11/2/96	QPR	LOFTUS ROAD	LEAGUE	WON 2-1
75	18/2/96	SHREWSBURY T.	GAY MEADOW	FA CUP	WON 4-0
76	28/2/96	CHARLTON ATH.	ANFIELD	FA CUP	WON 2-1
77, 78	3/3/96	ASTON VILLA	ANFIELD	LEAGUE	WON 3-0
79	16/3/96	CHELSEA	ANFIELD	LEAGUE	WON 2-0
80	20/3/96	LEEDS UNITED	ANFIELD	FA CUP	WON 3-0
81, 82	31/3/96	ASTON VILLA	OLD TRAFFORD	FA CUP	WON 3-0
83, 84	3/4/96	NEWCASTLE UTD	ANFIELD	LEAGUE	WON 4-3
85	16/4/96	EVERTON	GOODISON PARK	LEAGUE	DREW 1-1

ROBBIE FOWLER'S GOALS FOR LIVERPOOL

GOAL NUMBER	DATE	OPPONENTS	VENUE	COMPETITION	RESULT
SEASON 1996/97					
86	17/8/96	MIDDLESBROUGH	RIVERSIDE STADIUM	LEAGUE	DREW 3-3
87	21/9/96	CHELSEA	ANFIELD	LEAGUE	WON 5-1
88	17/10/96	SION	STADE DE TOURBILLON	EUROPE	WON 2-1
89	23/10/96	CHARLTON ATH.	THE VALLEY	LEAGUE CUP	DREW 1-1
90, 91	27/10/96	DERBY COUNTY	ANFIELD	LEAGUE	WON 2-1
92, 93	31/10/96	SION	ANFIELD	EUROPE	WON 6-3
94, 95	13/11/96	CHARLTON ATH.	ANFIELD	LEAGUE CUP	WON 4-1
96	20/11/96	EVERTON	ANFIELD	LEAGUE	DREW 1-1
97, 98	27/11/96	ARSENAL	ANFIELD	LEAGUE CUP	WON 4-2
99, 100, 101, 102	14/12/96	MIDDLESBROUGH	ANFIELD	LEAGUE	WON 5-1
103	17/12/96	NOTTINGHAM F.	ANFIELD	LEAGUE	WON 4-2
104	23/12/96	NEWCASTLE UTD	ST. JAMES' PARK	LEAGUE	DREW 1-1
105	18/1/97	ASTON VILLA	ANFIELD	LEAGUE	WON 3-0
106	26/1/97	CHELSEA	STAMFORD BRIDGE	FA CUP	LOST 2-4
107	19/2/97	LEEDS UNITED	ANFIELD	LEAGUE	WON 4-0
108	6/3/97	SK BRANN	BRANN STADION	EUROPE	DREW 1-1
109, 110	10/3/97	NEWCASTLE UTD	ANFIELD	LEAGUE	WON 4-3
111	15/3/97	NOTTINGHAM F.	CITY GROUND	LEAGUE	DREW 1-1
112, 113	20/3/97	SK BRANN	ANFIELD	EUROPE	WON 3-0
114	6/4/97	COVENTRY CITY	ANFIELD	LEAGUE	LOST 1-2
115	13/4/97	SUNDERLAND	ROKER PARK	LEAGUE	WON 2-1
116	24/4/97	PARIS ST GERMAIN	ANFIELD	EUROPE	WON 2-0
SEASON 1997/98					
117	22/9/97	ASTON VILLA	ANFIELD	LEAGUE	WON 3-0
118	27/9/97	WEST HAM UNITED	UPTON PARK	LEAGUE	LOST 1-2
119	5/10/97	CHELSEA	ANFIELD	LEAGUE	WON 4-2
120	15/10/97	WEST BROM	THE HAWTHORNS	LEAGUE CUP	WON 2-0
121, 122	25/10/97	DERBY COUNTY	ANFIELD	LEAGUE	WON 4-0
123	1/11/97	BOLTON W.	REEBOK STADIUM	LEAGUE	DREW 1-1
124	4/11/97	RC STRASBOURG	ANFIELD	EUROPE	WON 2-0
125	6/12/97	MANCHESTER UTD	ANFIELD	LEAGUE	LOST 1-3
126, 127	26/12/97	LEEDS UNITED	ANFIELD	LEAGUE	WON 3-1
128	7/1/98	NEWCASTLE UTD	ST.JAMES' PARK	LEAGUE CUP	WON 2-0
129	27/1/98	MIDDLESBROUGH	ANFIELD	LEAGUE CUP	WON 2-1
SEASON 1998/99					
130, 131	19/9/98	CHARLTON ATH.	ANFIELD	LEAGUE	DREW 3-3
132, 133	29/9/98	FC KOSICE	ANFIELD	EUROPE	WON 5-0
134	27/10/98	FULHAM	ANFIELD	LEAGUE CUP	WON 3-1
135	14/11/98	LEEDS UNITED	ANFIELD	LEAGUE	LOST 1-3
136, 137, 138	21/11/98	ASTON VILLA	VILLA PARK	LEAGUE	WON 4-2
139	3/1/99	PORT VALE	VALE PARK	F.A.CUP	WON 3-0
140, 141, 142	16/1/99	SOUTHAMPTON	ANFIELD	LEAGUE	WON 7-1
143	20/2/99	WEST HAM UNITED	ANFIELD	LEAGUE	DREW 2-2
144, 145	13/3/99	DERBY COUNTY	PRIDE PARK	LEAGUE	LOST 2-3
146, 147	3/4/99	EVERTON	ANFIELD	LEAGUE	WON 3-2
SEASON 1999/2000					
148	7/8/99	SHEFFIELD WED.	HILLSBOROUGH	LEAGUE	WON 2-1
149	28/8/99	ARSENAL	ANFIELD	LEAGUE	WON 2-0
150	28/12/99	WIMBLEDON	ANFIELD	LEAGUE	WON 3-1
SEASON 2000/01					
151	1/11/00	CHELSEA	ANFIELD	LEAGUE CUP	WON 2-1
152	19/11/00	TOTTENHAM H.	WHITE HART LANE	LEAGUE	LOST 1-2
153, 154, 155	29/11/00	STOKE CITY	BRITANNIA STADIUM	LEAGUE CUP	WON 8-0
156	23/12/00	ARSENAL	ANFIELD	LEAGUE	WON 4-0
157	24/1/01	CRYSTAL PALACE	ANFIELD	LEAGUE CUP	WON 5-0
158, 159	3/2/01	WEST HAM UNITED	ANFIELD	LEAGUE	WON 3-0
160	25/2/01	BIRMINGHAM CITY	MILLENNIUM STADIUM	LEAGUE CUP	WON 1-1(5-4 ON PENS)
161	11/3/01	TRANMERE ROVERS	PRENTON PARK	FA CUP	WON 4-2
162	31/3/01	MANCHESTER UTD	ANFIELD	LEAGUE	WON 2-0
163	8/4/01	WYCOMBE W.	VILLA PARK	FA CUP	WON 2-1
164	22/4/01	TOTTENHAM H.	ANFIELD	LEAGUE	WON 3-1
165	16/5/01	ALAVES	WESTFALENSTADION	EUROPE	WON 5-4

ROBBIE FOWLER'S GOALS FOR LIVERPOOL

GOAL NUMBER	DATE	OPPONENTS	VENUE	COMPETITION	RESULT
SEASON 2000/01 (cont)					
166, 167	19/5/01	CHARLTON ATH.	THE VALLEY	LEAGUE	WON 4-0
SEASON 2001/02					
168	21/8/01	FC HAKA	ANFIELD	EUROPE	WON 4-1
169, 170, 171	20/10/01	LEICESTER CITY	FILBERT STREET	LEAGUE	WON 4-1
SEASON 2005/06					
172	15/3/06	FULHAM	ANFIELD	LEAGUE	WON 5-1
173	1/4/06	WEST BROM	THE HAWTHORNS	LEAGUE	WON 2-0
174	9/4/06	BOLTON W.	ANFIELD	LEAGUE	WON 1-0
175	16/4/06	BLACKBURN ROV.	EWOOD PARK	LEAGUE	WON 1-0
176	7/5/06	PORTSMOUTH	FRATTON PARK	LEAGUE	WON 3-1
SEASON 2006/07					
177	19/8/06	SHEFFIELD UNITED	BRAMALL LANE	LEAGUE	DREW 1-1
178	25/10/06	READING	ANFIELD	LEAGUE CUP	WON 4-3
179, 180	5/12/06	GALATASARAY	ATATURK STADIUM	EUROPE	LOST 2-3
181	9/1/07	ARSENAL	ANFIELD	LEAGUE CUP	LOST 3-6
182, 183	24/2/07	SHEFFIELD UNITED	ANFIELD	LEAGUE	WON 4-0

The following two tables are final tables for the teams Robbie faced during his Liverpool career, and the goals he scored:

ROBBIE FOWLER'S LIVERPOOL EUROPEAN GOALS

	GAMES	GOALS
BRANN BERGEN	2	3
FC SION	2	3
GALATASARAY	1	2
FC KOSICE	2	2
CD ALAVES	1	1
FC HAKA	2	1
PARIS ST GERMAIN	2	1
RC STRASBOURG	2	1
BAYERN MUNICH	1	0
BOAVISTA	1	0
BORDEAUX	1	0
BORUSSIA DORTMUND	1	0
CELTIC	1	0
CHELSEA	1	0
DYNAMO KIEV	1	0
MY PA '47	1	0
PSV EINDHOVEN	1	0
BENFICA	2	0
BRONDBY	2	0
CELTA VIGO	2	0
FC PORTO	2	0
RAPID BUCHAREST	2	0
ROMA	2	0
SLOVAN LIBEREC	2	0
SPARTAK VLADIKAVKAZ	2	0
VALENCIA	2	0
FC BARCELONA	3	0
TOTAL	**44**	**14**

ROBBIE FOWLER'S LIVERPOOL DOMESTIC GOALS

	LEAGUE		FA CUP		LEAGUE CUP		TOTAL	
	GAMES	GOALS	GAMES	GOALS	GAMES	GOALS	GAMES	GOALS
ASTON VILLA	15	12	1	2	-	-	16	14
ARSENAL	13	9	1	0	3	3	17	12
FULHAM	3	1	-	-	4	7	7	8
CHARLTON ATHLETIC	8	4	1	1	2	3	11	8
SOUTHAMPTON	12	8	-	-	-	-	12	8
LEEDS UNITED	13	7	3	1	-	-	16	8
TOTTENHAM HOTSPUR	11	6	1	1	1	0	13	7
CHELSEA	14	5	1	1	1	1	16	7
NEWCASTLE UNITED	15	6	-	-	2	1	17	7
BOLTON WANDERERS	6	6	-	-	1	0	7	6
DERBY COUNTY	7	6	-	-	-	-	7	6
NOTTINGHAM FOREST	7	6	-	-	-	-	7	6
MIDDLESBROUGH	9	5	-	-	3	1	12	6
MANCHESTER UNITED	12	6	2	0	-	-	14	6
EVERTON	17	6	-	-	-	-	17	6
LEICESTER CITY	9	5	-	-	-	-	9	5
WEST HAM UNITED	12	5	-	-	-	-	12	5
CRYSTAL PALACE	3	1	-	-	3	3	6	4
MANCHESTER CITY	7	3	1	0	1	1	9	4
STOKE CITY	-	-	-	-	2	3	2	3
SHEFFIELD UNITED	4	3	-	-	-	-	4	3
BLACKBURN ROVERS	10	3	-	-	1	0	11	3
WIMBLEDON	10	2	2	1	2	0	14	3
OLDHAM ATHLETIC	2	2	-	-	-	-	2	2
WEST BROMWICH ALBION	1	1	-	-	1	1	2	2
NORWICH CITY	3	2	-	-	-	-	3	2
BURNLEY	-	-	2	0	2	2	4	2
IPSWICH TOWN	5	2	-	-	1	0	6	2
SUNDERLAND	5	1	-	-	2	1	7	2
SHEFFIELD WEDNESDAY	10	2	-	-	-	-	10	2
PORT VALE	-	-	1	1	-	-	1	1
ROCHDALE	-	-	1	1	-	-	1	1
SHREWSBURY TOWN	-	-	1	1	-	-	1	1
TRANMERE ROVERS	-	-	1	1	-	-	1	1
WYCOMBE WANDERERS	-	-	1	1	-	-	1	1
READING	1	0	-	-	1	1	2	1
PORTSMOUTH	3	1	-	-	-	-	3	1
BIRMINGHAM CITY	1	0	2	0	2	1	5	1
QUEENS PARK RANGERS	5	1	-	-	-	-	5	1
COVENTRY CITY	9	1	1	0	-	-	10	1
BRISTOL CITY	-	-	1	0	-	-	1	0
SWINDON TOWN	1	0	-	-	-	-	1	0
WIGAN ATHLETIC	1	0	-	-	-	-	1	0
WATFORD	2	0	-	-	-	-	2	0
TOTAL	**266**	**128**	**24**	**12**	**35**	**29**	**325**	**169**

THE OLDEST/YOUNGEST

Oldest player

	Final game	Age
Ted Doig	April 11 1908	41 years & 165 days

Oldest player (post-War)

Kenny Dalglish	May 1 1990	39 years & 58 days
Billy Liddell	August 31 1960	38 years & 234 days
Gary McAllister	May 11 2002	37 years & 137 days
Paul Jones	January 17 2004	36 years & 274 days
Bruce Grobbelaar	February 19 1994	36 years & 136 days
Phil Taylor	December 25 1953	36 years & 98 days
Jack Balmer	February 16 1952	36 years & 10 days
Ian Callaghan	February 4 1978	35 years 300 days
Berry Nieuwenhuys	February 1 1947	35 years 88 days
Bob Paisley	March 13 1954	35 years 49 days

Youngest player (post-War)

	Debut	Age
Max Thompson	May 8 1974	17 years & 128 days
Michael Owen	May 6 1997	17 years & 144 days
Johnny Morrissey	September 23 1957	17 years & 158 days
Reginald Blore	October 17 1959	17 years & 213 days
Phil Charnock	September 16 1992	17 years & 215 days

Youngest player to score on debut

Michael Owen	May 6 1997	17 years & 144 days

Young and old...Michael Owen and Kenny Dalglish

MOST GOALS IN A LEAGUE SEASON

Name	Season	Division	Games	Goals	Goal average
Roger Hunt	1961/62	2	41	41	1
Gordon Hodgson	1930/31	1	40	36	1.11
Ian Rush	1983/84	1	41	32	1.28
Sam Raybould	1902/03	1	33	31	1.06
Roger Hunt	1963/64	1	41	31	1.32
Jack Parkinson	1909/10	1	31	30	1.03
Gordon Hodgson	1928/29	1	38	30	1.27
Billy Liddell	1954/55	2	40	30	1.33
Ian Rush	1986/87	1	42	30	1.4
Roger Hunt	1965/66	1	37	29	1.28
John Evans	1954/55	2	38	29	1.31
Robbie Fowler	1995/96	Prem	38	28	1.36
Dick Forshaw	1925/26	1	32	27	1.19
Gordon Hodgson	1934/35	1	34	27	1.26
Billy Liddell	1955/56	2	39	27	1.44
Gordon Hodgson	1931/32	1	39	26	1.5
John Aldridge	1987/88	1	36	26	1.38
George Allan	1895/96	2	20	25	0.8
Roger Hunt	1964/65	1	40	25	1.6
Roger Hunt	1967/68	1	40	25	1.6
Robbie Fowler	1994/95	Prem	42	25	1.68

MOST GOALS IN A SEASON - ALL COMPETITIONS

Name	Season	Games	Goals	Goal average
Ian Rush	1983/84	65	47	1.38
Roger Hunt	1961/62	46	42	1.1
Ian Rush	1986/87	57	40	1.43
Roger Hunt	1964/65	58	37	1.57
Gordon Hodgson	1930/31	41	36	1.14
Robbie Fowler	1995/96	53	36	1.47
John Evans	1954/55	42	33	1.27
Roger Hunt	1963/64	46	33	1.39
Ian Rush	1985/86	56	33	1.7
Sam Raybould	1902/03	34	32	1.06
Gordon Hodgson	1928/29	41	32	1.28
Billy Liddell	1955/56	44	32	1.38
Roger Hunt	1965/66	46	32	1.44
Billy Liddell	1954/55	44	31	1.42
Robbie Fowler	1996/97	44	31	1.42
John Aldridge	1988/89	47	31	1.52
Ian Rush	1982/83	51	31	1.65
Robbie Fowler	1994/95	57	31	1.84
Kenny Dalglish	1977/78	62	31	2
Jack Parkinson	1909/10	32	30	1.07
Ian Rush	1981/82	49	30	1.63
Roger Hunt	1967/68	57	30	1.9

DEBUT GOALSCORERS

(SINCE RETURNING TO TOP-FLIGHT IN 1962)

Player	Date	Opponents	Competition	Goals scored	Result
Bobby Graham	14/9/64	Reykjavik (h)	European Cup	1	Won 6-1
John Sealey	26/4/65	Wolverhampton W. (a)	League	1	Won 3-1
Alun Evans	21/9/68	Leicester City (h)	League	1	Won 4-0
Alec Lindsay	16/9/69	Dundalk (h)	Fairs Cup	1	Won 10-0
Kevin Keegan	14/8/71	Nottingham Forest (h)	League	1	Won 3-1
Ray Kennedy	31/8/74	Chelsea (a)	League	1	Won 3-0
Sammy Lee	8/4/78	Leicester City (h)	League	1	Won 3-2
Ronnie Whelan	3/4/81	Stoke City (h)	League	1	Won 3-0
John Wark	31/3/84	Watford (a)	League	1	Won 2-0
David Speedie	3/2/91	Manchester United (a)	League	1	Drew 1-1
Nigel Clough	14/8/93	Sheffield Wed. (h)	League	2	Won 2-0
Robbie Fowler	22/9/93	Fulham (a)	League Cup	1	Won 3-1
Stan Collymore	19/8/95	Sheffield Wed. (h)	League	1	Won 1-0
Michael Owen	6/5/97	Wimbledon (a)	League	1	Lost 1-2
Titi Camara	7/8/99	Sheffield Wed. (a)	League	1	Won 2-1
Leyton Maxwell	21/9/99	Hull City (h)	League Cup	1	Won 4-2
Abel Xavier	9/2/02	Ipswich Town (a)	League	1	Won 6-0
Craig Bellamy	9/8/06	Maccabi Haifa (h)	European Cup	1	Won 2-1
Mark Gonzalez	9/8/06	Maccabi Haifa (h)	European Cup	1	Won 2-1
Gabriel Paletta	25/10/06	Reading (h)	League Cup	1	Won 4-3

* Kenny Dalglish scored at Middlesbrough on 20.08.77 but had played in the Charity Shield a week earlier.

SUPER SUBS

LIVERPOOL'S MOST PROLIFIC GOALSCORING SUBSTITUTES

	League	FA Cup	Lge Cup	Europe	Others	Total
David Fairclough	7	2	7	2	0	18
Djibril Cisse	2	1	0	4	0	7
Michael Owen	4	0	1	1	0	6
Ian Rush	2	3	0	1	0	6
Vladimir Smicer	4	0	1	1	0	6
Robbie Fowler	3	1	0	1	0	5
Emile Heskey	3	1	1	0	0	5
David Johnson	3	0	1	1	0	5
Milan Baros	1	0	2	1	0	4
Phil Boersma	0	0	2	2	0	4
Jimmy Case	2	1	0	1	0	4
Luis Garcia	4	0	0	0	0	4
Craig Johnston	2	1	1	0	0	4
Jari Litmanen	3	0	0	1	0	4
Danny Murphy	4	0	0	0	0	4
Ronny Rosenthal	4	0	0	0	0	4
Florent Sinama-Pongolle	1	2	0	1	0	4

LIVERPOOL HAT-TRICK MEN

FULL RECORD OF LIVERPOOL HAT-TRICKS

17	Gordon Hodgson
16	Ian Rush
12	Roger Hunt
10	Robbie Fowler, Michael Owen
8	Dick Forshaw, Jack Parkinson
6	Sam Raybould
5	Harry Chambers, Billy Liddell
4	George Allan, Joe Hewitt
3	John Aldridge, Jack Balmer, Kenny Dalglish, Tony Hateley, Fred Howe, Albert Stubbins, John Toshack, John Wark
2	John Barnes, Harold Barton, Frank Becton, Jimmy Case, William Devlin, Cyril Done, John Evans, Dick Johnson, Terry McDermott, Steve McMahon, Malcolm McVean, Fred Pagnam, Henry Race, Robert Robinson, Jimmy Ross, Antonio Rowley, Ian St John, Dean Saunders, Graeme Souness, Paul Walsh
1	Alan Arnell, Alf Arrowsmith, Milan Baros, Peter Beardsley, Patrik Berger, Louis Bimpson, Phil Boersma, Ian Callaghan, Stan Collymore, **Peter Crouch,** Alun Evans, David Fairclough, Gary Gillespie, **Steven Gerrard,** Bobby Graham, Jimmy Harrower, Emile Heskey, Dave Hickson, 'Sailor' Hunter, David Johnson, Kevin Keegan, Kevin Lewis, Andy McGuigan, William McPherson, Arthur Metcalfe, Jan Molby, Steve Nicol, Ronald Orr, Tom Reid, Michael Robinson, Ronny Rosenthal, Danny Shone, Jimmy Smith, Steve Staunton, James Stewart, James Stott, John Walker, Jimmy Walsh, Mark Walters, Johnny Wheeler, Ronnie Whelan, Jack Whitham, Dave Wright

83 players have scored a total of 212 hat-tricks

BIGGEST-EVER VICTORIES

Date	Opponents	Venue	Competition	Score
17th Sept 1974	Stromsgodset	Home	European Cup Winners' Cup	Won 11-0
16th Sept 1969	Dundalk	Home	Inter Cities' Fairs Cup	Won 10-0
23rd Sept 1986	Fulham	Home	League Cup	Won 10-0
18th Feb 1896	Rotherham Utd	Home	League	Won 10-1
1st Oct 1980	Oulu Palloseura	Home	European Cup	Won 10-1
29th Oct 1892	Newtown	Home	FA Cup	Won 9-0
12th Sept 1989	Crystal Palace	Home	League	Won 9-0
26th Dec 1928	Burnley	Home	League	Won 8-0
7th Nov 1967	TSV Munich 1860	Home	Inter Cities' Fairs Cup	Won 8-0
9th Jan 1990	Swansea City	Home	FA Cup	Won 8-0
29th Nov 2000	Stoke City	Away	League Cup	Won 8-0
6th Dec 1902	Grimsby Town	Home	League	Won 9-2
8th Apr 1905	Port Vale	Home	League	Won 8-1
29th Feb 1896	Burton Swifts	Away	League	Won 7-0
28th Mar 1896	Crewe A	Away	League	Won 7-0
4th Jan 1902	Stoke City	Home	League	Won 7-0
2nd Sept 1978	Tottenham H	Home	League	Won 7-0
21st Mar 2006	Birmingham City	Away	FA Cup	Won 7-0

BIGGEST-EVER DEFEATS

Date	Opponents	Venue	Competition	Score
11th Dec 1954	Birmingham C	Away	League	Lost 9-1
10th Nov 1934	Huddersfield T	Away	League	Lost 8-0
1st Jan 1934	Newcastle Utd	Away	League	Lost 9-2
7th May 1932	Bolton W	Away	League	Lost 8-1
1st Sept 1934	Arsenal	Away	League	Lost 8-1
7th Dec 1912	Sunderland	Away	League	Lost 7-0
1st Sept 1930	West Ham United	Away	League	Lost 7-0
19th Apr 1930	Sunderland	Home	League	Lost 6-0
28th Nov 1931	Arsenal	Away	League	Lost 6-0
11th Sept 1935	Manchester City	Away	League	Lost 6-0
26th Sept 1953	Charlton Athletic	Away	League	Lost 6-0

Robbie Fowler on target in the 8-0 demolition of Stoke City in 2000

THE INDIVIDUAL HONOURS

FOOTBALL WRITERS FOOTBALLER OF THE YEAR

		Honours won (that season)
1974	Ian Callaghan	FA Cup
1976	Kevin Keegan	First Division, UEFA Cup
1977	Emlyn Hughes	First Division, European Cup, Charity Shield
1979	Kenny Dalglish	First Division
1980	Terry McDermott	First Division, Charity Shield
1983	Kenny Dalglish	First Division, League Cup, Charity Shield
1984	Ian Rush	First Division, League Cup, European Cup
1988	John Barnes	First Division
1989	Steve Nicol	FA Cup, Charity Shield
1990	John Barnes	First Division, Charity Shield

PFA PLAYER OF THE YEAR

1980	Terry McDermott	First Division, Charity Shield
1983	Kenny Dalglish	First Division, League Cup, Charity Shield
1984	Ian Rush	First Division, League Cup, European Cup
1988	John Barnes	First Division
2006	Steven Gerrard	FA Cup, European Super Cup

PFA YOUNG PLAYER OF THE YEAR

1983	Ian Rush	First Division, League Cup, Charity Shield
1995	Robbie Fowler	League Cup
1996	Robbie Fowler	
1998	Michael Owen	
2001	Steven Gerrard	FA Cup, League Cup, UEFA Cup

EUROPEAN FOOTBALLER OF THE YEAR

2001	Michael Owen	FA Cup, League Cup, UEFA Cup

MANAGER OF THE YEAR

1973	Bill Shankly	First Division, UEFA Cup
1976	Bob Paisley	First Division, UEFA Cup
1977	Bob Paisley	First Division, European Cup, European Super Cup, Charity Shield
1979	Bob Paisley	First Division
1980	Bob Paisley	First Division, Charity Shield
1982	Bob Paisley	First Division, League Cup
1983	Bob Paisley	First Division, League Cup, Charity Shield
1984	Joe Fagan	First Division, League Cup, European Cup
1986	Kenny Dalglish	First Division, FA Cup
1988	Kenny Dalglish	First Division
1990	Kenny Dalglish	First Division, Charity Shield

PLAYER WITH MOST MEDALS

20	Phil Neal (8 League, 1 FA Cup runner-up, 4 League Cup, 1 runner-up, 5 European, 1 runner-up)

CLEAN SHEET RECORDS

MOST CLEAN SHEETS IN A SEASON (ALL COMPS)

SEASON	CLEAN SHEETS	GAMES PLAYED
1978/79	34	54
1970/71	34	62
1983/84	34	67
2005/06	33	62
1977/78	32	62
1981/82	31	62
1973/74	30	61
1975/76	29	59
1984/85	29	64
1971/72	28	53
2006/07	28	58
2001/02	28	59
2000/01	28	63
1987/88	27	50
1979/80	27	60
1982/83	27	60
1976/77	27	62
1995/96	26	53
1972/73	26	66
1968/69	25	51
1994/95	25	57
1974/75	24	53
1986/87	24	57
1980/81	24	63
1985/86	24	63
1991/92	24	64
1922/23	23	46
1965/66	23	53
2002/03	23	60

HIGHEST % OF CLEAN SHEETS IN SEASON (ALL COMPS)

SEASON	%	CLEAN SHEETS	GAMES PLAYED
1978/79	62.96	34	54
1970/71	54.84	34	62
1987/88	54.00	27	50
2005/06	53.23	33	62
1971/72	52.83	28	53
1977/78	51.61	32	62
1983/84	50.75	34	67
1893/94	50.00	16	32
1922/23	50.00	23	46
1981/82	50.00	31	62
1973/74	49.18	30	61
1975/76	49.15	29	59
1995/96	49.06	26	53
1968/69	49.02	25	51
2006/07	48.28	28	58
2001/02	47.46	28	59
1984/85	45.31	29	64
1974/75	45.28	24	53
1898/99	45.00	18	40
1979/80	45.00	27	60
1982/83	45.00	27	60

MOST CLEAN SHEETS KEPT BY LIVERPOOL IN A LEAGUE SEASON

SEASON	CLEAN SHEETS	GAMES	SEASON	CLEAN SHEETS	GAMES
1978/79	28	42	1968/69	21	42
1975/76	23	42	1987/88	21	40
1977/78	23	42	1981/82	20	42
1970/71	22	42	1983/84	20	42
1971/72	22	42	2006/07	20	38
2005/06	22	38			
1922/23	21	42			

CLEAN SHEET RECORDS

CLEAN SHEETS AND GOALS CONCEDED BY LIVERPOOL (GOALKEEPERS IN FIRST 50 (FULL) LEAGUE GAMES)

The criteria for qualification for this table is as follows:
Goalkeepers have to play the full game for the clean sheet to be awarded.
However, if injured, substituted or sent-off having conceded during that game the appearance counts.

	CLEAN SHEETS	GOALS CONCEDED	DATE OF 50TH START UNDER CRITERIA
JOSE REINA	28	36	9th December 2006
RAY CLEMENCE	25	33	10th April 1971
BRUCE GROBBELAAR	25	39	2nd October 1982
JERZY DUDEK	25	41	1st December 2002
HARRY STORER	18	57	25th December 1897
TED DOIG	18	62	4th April 1908
SANDER WESTERVELD	17	50	19th November 2000
MIKE HOOPER	17	59	9th January 1993
SAM HARDY	15	56	26th December 1906
CYRIL SIDLOW	15	58	7th February 1948
DAVID JAMES	14	59	8th October 1994
TOMMY LAWRENCE	14	60	26th December 1963
WILLIAM PERKINS	14	67	16th February 1901
ELISHA SCOTT	14	70	13th November 1920
CHARLIE ASHCROFT	13	69	13th September 1952
BERT SLATER	13	71	26th December 1960
TOMMY YOUNGER	12	67	28th September 1957
DOUG RUDHAM	10	88	1st September 1959
KENNY CAMPBELL	10	91	4th October 1913
RUSSELL CROSSLEY	8	87	6th April 1953
ARTHUR RILEY	8	95	30th March 1929

MOST CONSECUTIVE LEAGUE CLEAN SHEETS AT ANFIELD

9	4th November 2006 – 24th February 2007
8	1st January 1920 – 3rd April 1920
8	31st August 1957 – 27th November 1957
8	3rd May 1977 – 22nd October 1977
8	20th March 1979 – 21st August 1979
8	15th October 2005 – 14th January 2006
6	12th September 1896 – 21st November 1897
6	6th January 1923 – 24th March 1923
6	14th April 1973 – 8th September 1973
6	29th September 1987 – 24th November 1987

NATIONALITIES

The signing of Ukraine striker Andriy Voronin adds a new nationality to the list for the 2007/08 season, while Brazil, Holland, Israel and Spain should also see additions in the form of Lucas Leiva, Ryan Babel, Yossi Benayoun and Fernando Torres respectively.

A clutch of youth players will also be looking to break into the list including Sebastian Leto (Argentina), Jordy Brouwer (Holland), and Ronald Huth (Paraguay).

Below is a comprehensive list of those players to have represented Liverpool in a first-team game:

COUNTRIES REPRESENTED	PLAYERS
Argentina	4 - Mauricio Pellegrino, Gabriel Paletta, Javier Mascherano, Emiliano Insua
Australia	1 - Harry Kewell
Brazil	1 - Fabio Aurelio
Cameroon	1 - Rigobert Song
Chile	1 - Mark Gonzalez
Croatia	1 - Igor Biscan
Czech Republic	3 - Patrik Berger, Vladimir Smicer, Milan Baros
Denmark	3 - Jan Molby, Torben Piechnik, Daniel Agger
Finland	2 - Sami Hyypia, Jari Litmanen
France	10 - Jean-Michel Ferri, Pegguy Arphexad, Bernard Diomede, Gregory Vignal, Nicolas Anelka, Bruno Cheyrou, Patrice Luzi, Anthony Le Tallec, Florent Sinama-Pongolle, Djibril Cisse
Germany	5 - Karlheinz Riedle, Dietmar Hamann, Markus Babbel, Christian Ziege, Sean Dundee
Guinea	1 - Titi Camara
Holland	5 - Erik Meijer, Sander Westerveld, Bolo Zenden, Jan Kromkamp, Dirk Kuyt
Hungary	1 - Istvan Kozma
Israel	2 - Avi Cohen, Ronny Rosenthal
Italy	1 - Daniele Padelli
Mali	2 - Djimi Traore, Mohammed Sissoko
Morocco	1 - Nabil El Zhar
Norway	6 - Stig Inge Bjornebye, Oyvind Leonhardsen, Bjorn Tore Kvarme, Vegard Heggem, Frode Kippe, John Arne Riise
Poland	1 - Jerzy Dudek
Portugal	1 - Abel Xavier
Senegal	2 - El-Hadji Diouf, Salif Diao
South Africa	10 - Lance Carr, Hugh Gerhadi, Gordon Hodgson, Dirk Kemp, Berry Nieuwenhuys, Robert Priday, Arthur Riley, Doug Rudham, Charlie Thompson, Harman Van Den Berg
Spain	9 - Josemi, Luis Garcia, Xabi Alonso, Antonio Nunez, Fernando Morientes, Jose Reina, Antonio Barragan, Miki Roque, Alvaro Arbeloa
Sweden	1 - Glenn Hysen
Switzerland	1 - Stephane Henchoz
USA	2 - Brad Friedel, Zak Whitbread
Zimbabwe	1 - Bruce Grobbelaar

* Note Craig Johnston (born in South Africa) represented England at 'B' and U21 level and has not been included – likewise John Barnes (born in Jamaica) played for England.

Capped Liverpool players (July 2007)

England caps	Player
60	Michael Owen
59	Emlyn Hughes
57	STEVEN GERRARD
56	Ray Clemence
50	Phil Neal
48	John Barnes
42	Phil Thompson
35	Emile Heskey
34	Peter Beardsley
	JAMIE CARRAGHER,
	Roger Hunt
28	Kevin Keegan
25	Terry McDermott
24	Steve McManaman
22	Robbie Fowler
19	PETER CROUCH
17	Ray Kennedy,
	Steve McMahon,
	Jamie Redknapp
16	Peter Thompson
14	Sam Hardy, Sammy Lee,
	Gordon Milne
12	Paul Ince
9	Danny Murphy
8	Nick Barmby,
	Harry Chambers,
	Rob Jones
5	Alan A'Court,
	Tom Bromilow,
	David Johnson,
	Ephraim Longworth,
	Mark Wright
4	Ian Callaghan,
	Chris Lawler,
	Alec Lindsay
3	Jack Cox,
	Gordon Hodgson,
	Laurie Hughes,
	Larry Lloyd,
	Tommy Lucas,
	John Scales,
	Phil Taylor
2	Gerry Byrne, Bill Jones,
	Alan Kennedy, Jimmy Melia,
	Jack Parkinson
1	John Bamber, Frank Becton
	Thomas Bradshaw,
	Raby Howell,
	David James,
	Chris Kirkland,
	Neil Ruddock,
	Tommy Smith

Michael Owen

Roger Hunt

Capped Liverpool players (July 2007)

Scotland caps	Player
55	Kenny Dalglish
37	Graeme Souness
28	Billy Liddell
27	Steve Nicol
26	Alan Hansen
16	Tommy Younger
14	Ian St John
13	Gary Gillespie
8	Alex Raisbeck
3	Ken Campbell, Tommy Lawrence, John Wark
2	Jimmy McDougall, Frank McGarvey, Don MacKinlay, Ron Yeats
1	George Allan, Billy Dunlop, Jock McNab, Tom Miller, Hugh Morgan

Wales caps	Player
67	Ian Rush
26	John Toshack
18	Joey Jones
16	Maurice Parry
11	Craig Bellamy
10	Ernest Peake
8	George Lathom, Dean Saunders
7	Cyril Sidlow
5	Ray Lambert, Richard Morris, Edward Parry
3	John Hughes
1	Lee Jones, Robert Matthews

Northern Ireland caps	(3 players only)
27	Elisha Scott
12	Billy Lacey
3	David McMullan

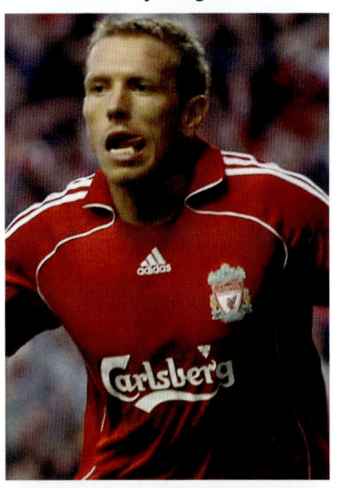

Republic of Ireland caps	Player
51	Ronnie Whelan
38	Steve Staunton
34	Ray Houghton
33	Steve Heighway
25	Phil Babb
24	STEVE FINNAN, Mark Lawrenson
19	John Aldridge
17	Mark Kennedy
15	Jim Beglin
14	Jason McAteer
5	Michael Robinson
1	Ken De Mange

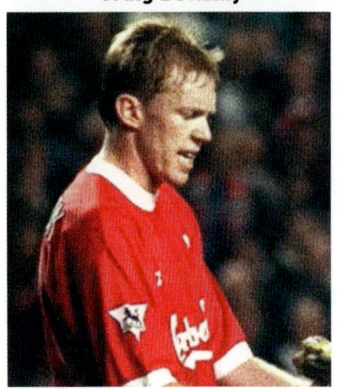

Kenny Dalglish

Craig Bellamy

Steve Staunton

Home International Goalscorers while Liverpool players (July 2007)

England goals	Player
26	Michael Owen
18	Roger Hunt
12	PETER CROUCH, STEVEN GERRARD
8	John Barnes
7	Kevin Keegan
6	Peter Beardsley
5	Harry Chambers, Robbie Fowler, Emile Heskey, Phil Neal
3	David Johnson, Ray Kennedy, Terry McDermott
2	Frank Becton, Sammy Lee
1	Alan A'Court, Nick Barmby, Gordon Hodgson, Emlyn Hughes, Chris Lawler, Jimmy Melia, Danny Murphy, Jamie Redknapp, Phil Thompson

Scotland goals	Player
13	Kenny Dalglish
8	Ian St John
6	Billy Liddell
4	Graeme Souness
2	Tom Miller

Northern Ireland goals	(1 player only)
2	Billy Lacey

Wales goals	Player
26	Ian Rush
8	John Toshack
4	Craig Bellamy
2	Dean Saunders
1	Ernest Peake

Republic of Ireland goals	Player
3	Ray Houghton, Mark Lawrenson, Ronnie Whelan
2	Steve Staunton
1	John Aldridge, Jason McAteer

Ian Rush, prolific for both Liverpool and Wales

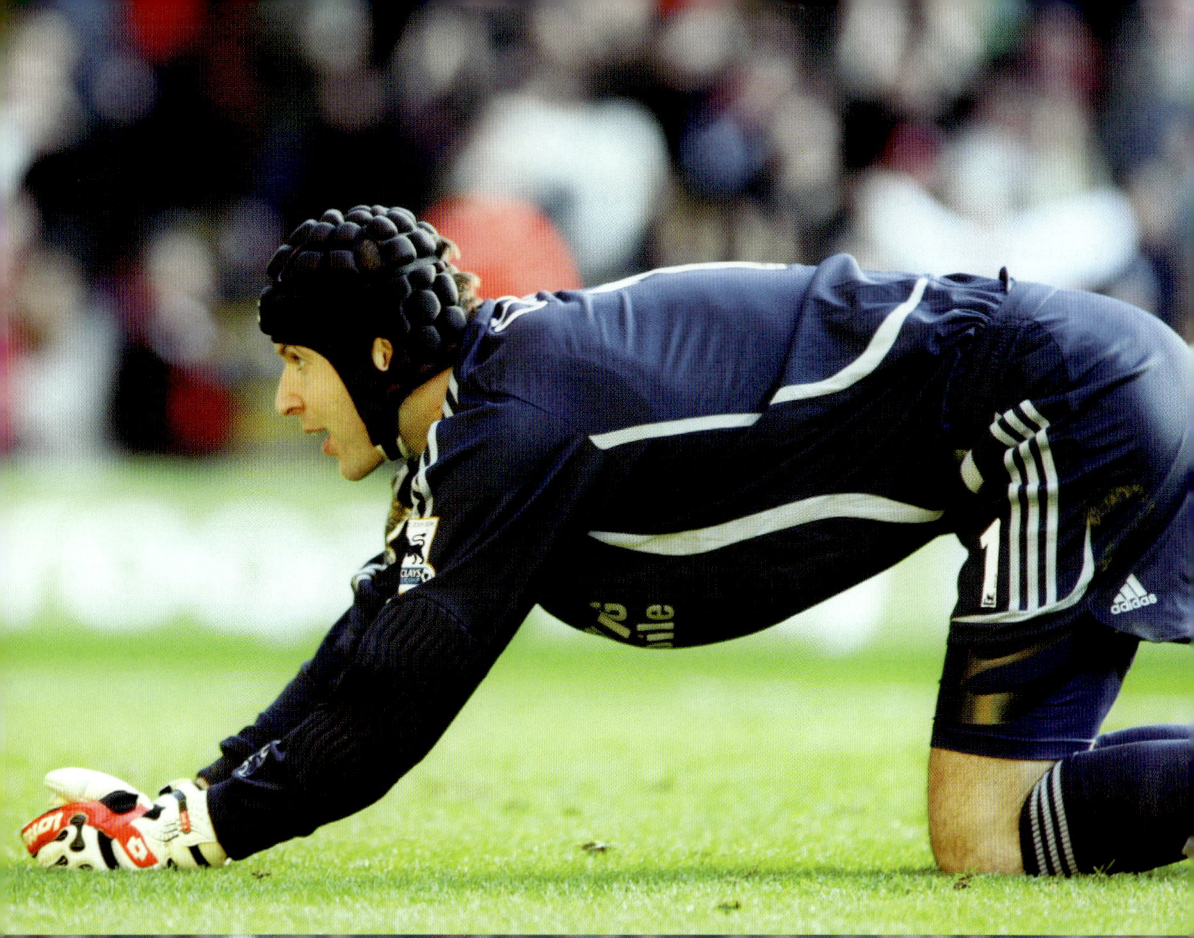

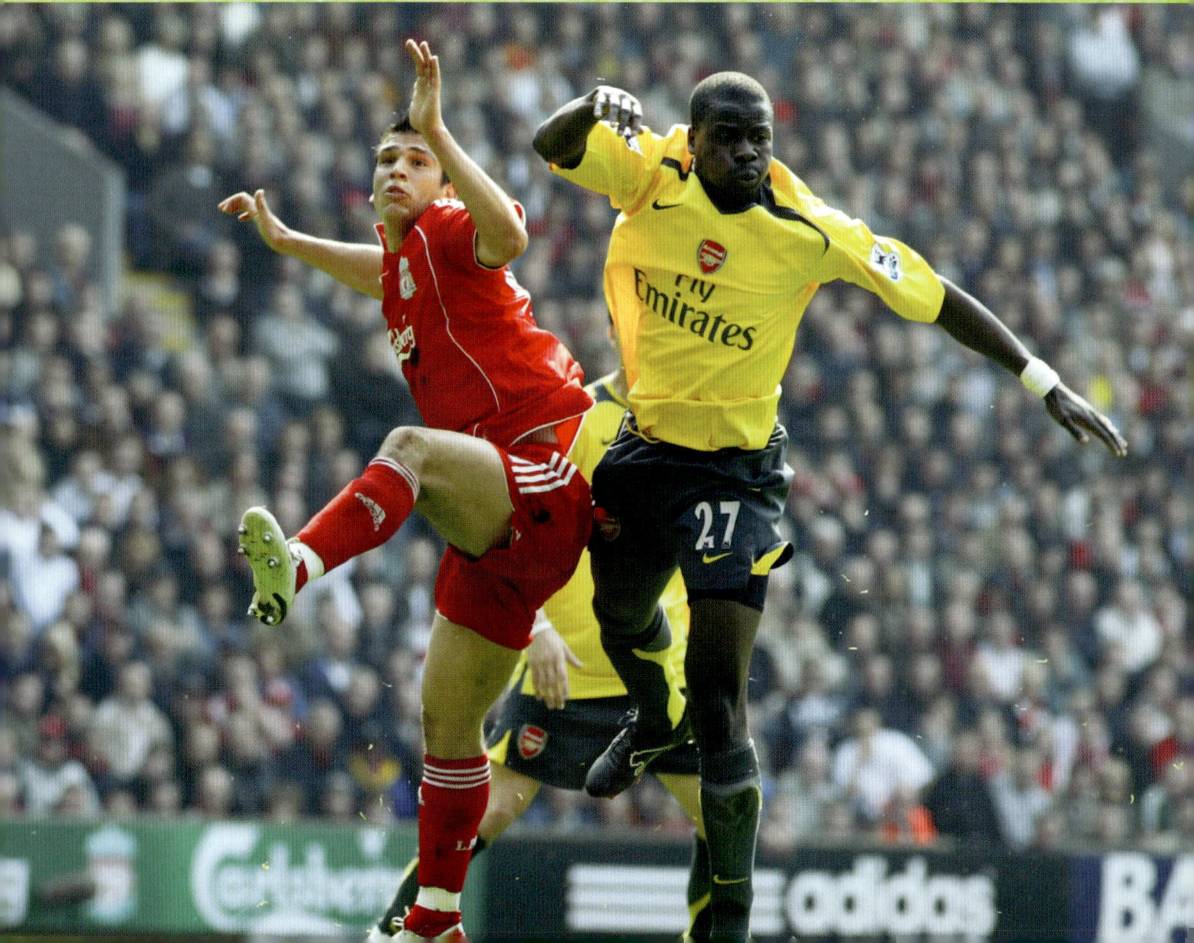
Fly Emirates
27
adidas

PREMIERSHIP OPPONENTS

ARSENAL

FINAL STANDINGS 06-07

		W	D	L	PTS
3	Liverpool	20	8	10	68
4	**Arsenal**	**19**	**11**	**8**	**68**
5	Tottenham	17	9	12	60

ALL-TIME RECORD

(League matches only)

	PL	W	D	L
Home:	83	48	14	21
Away:	83	20	26	37
Overall:	166	68	40	58

LAST 2 MEETINGS (LEAGUE)

31/03/2007
Liverpool   4-1   Arsenal
Crouch 4, 35, 81   Gallas 73
Agger 60

12/11/2006
Arsenal   3-0   Liverpool
Flamini 41, Toure 56,
Gallas 80

CLUB DETAILS

Nickname: The Gunners
Ground: Emirates Stadium, capacity 60,432 (away allocation 3,000)
Manager: Arsene Wenger (app. 30/09/96)
Assistant: Pat Rice
Year formed: 1886

USEFUL INFORMATION

Website: www.arsenal.com
Address: Emirates Stadium, Highbury House, 75 Drayton Park N5 1BU
Switchboard: 0207 704 4000

TRAVEL INFORMATION

By Tube: The nearest station is Arsenal (Piccadilly Line), around three minutes walk from the ground. Finsbury Park and Highbury & Islington are also within a 10-minute walking distance.

By Bus: Main bus stops are located on Holloway Road, Nag's Head, Seven Sisters Road, Blackstock Road and Highbury Corner. Regular services will take you to within 10 minutes walk of the ground.

ASTON VILLA

FINAL STANDINGS 06-07

		W	D	L	PTS
10	Blackburn	15	7	16	52
11	**Aston Villa**	**11**	**17**	**10**	**50**
12	Middlesbro	12	10	16	46

ALL-TIME RECORD

(League matches only)

	PL	W	D	L
Home:	82	52	16	14
Away:	82	25	20	37
Overall:	164	77	36	51

LAST 2 MEETINGS

18/03/2007
Aston Villa   0-0   Liverpool

28/10/2006
Liverpool   3-1   Aston Villa
Kuyt 31, Crouch 38,   Agbonlahor 56
Garcia 44

CLUB DETAILS

Nickname: The Villans
Ground: Villa Park, capacity 42,573 (away allocation 3,000)
Manager: Martin O'Neill (app. 05/08/06)
Coaches: Steve Walford, John Robertson
Year formed: 1874

USEFUL INFORMATION

Website: www.avfc.co.uk
Address: Villa Park, Trinity Road, Birmingham B6 6HE
Switchboard: 0871 423 8100

TRAVEL INFORMATION

By Train: Witton station is a 5-minute walk from the ground, while Aston is 15 minutes away. From New Street Station, a taxi should take 15 minutes.

By Bus: The number 7 West Midlands Travel Bus runs from Birmingham City Centre directly to the ground (Witton). To check services check at: www.travelwm.co.uk .

Premiership Opponents

BIRMINGHAM CITY

FINAL C'SHIP STANDINGS 06-07

		W	D	L	PTS
1	Sunderland	27	7	12	88
2	**Birmingham**	**26**	**8**	**12**	**86**
3	Derby	25	9	12	84

ALL-TIME RECORD

(League matches only)

	PL	W	D	L
Home:	47	31	9	7
Away:	47	15	11	21
Overall:	94	46	20	28

LAST 2 MEETINGS (LEAGUE)

01/02/2006
Liverpool 1-1 Birmingham
Gerrard 62 Alonso (o.g.) 88

24/09/2005
Birmingham 2-2 Liverpool
Warnock (o.g.) 72, Garcia 68, Cisse (p) 85
Pandiani 75

CLUB DETAILS

Nickname: Blues
Ground: St. Andrew's, capacity 30,009 (away allocation 2,500-4,500)
Manager: Steve Bruce (app. 12/12/01)
First-team coach: Eric Black
Year formed: 1875

USEFUL INFORMATION

Website: www.bcfc.co.uk
Address: St. Andrew's Stadium, Birmingham B9 4NH
Switchboard: 0844 557 1875

TRAVEL INFORMATION

By Train: The nearest local railway station is Bordesley, which is a 10-minute walk. Mainline station Birmingham New Street will cost around £6 in a taxi.
By Bus: Numerous routes serve the ground from the city centre, including numbers 96, 97, 58 and 60 - details can be found at www.networkwestmidlands.com .

BLACKBURN ROVERS

FINAL STANDINGS 06-07

		W	D	L	PTS
9	Portsmouth	14	12	12	54
10	**Blackburn**	**15**	**7**	**16**	**52**
11	Aston Villa	11	17	10	50

ALL-TIME RECORD

(League matches only)

	PL	W	D	L
Home:	59	34	16	9
Away:	59	14	20	25
Overall:	118	48	36	34

LAST 2 MEETINGS

26/12/2006
Blackburn Rovers 1-0 Liverpool
McCarthy 49

14/10/2006
Liverpool 1-1 Blackburn Rovers
Bellamy 64 McCarthy 17

CLUB DETAILS

Nickname: Rovers
Ground: Ewood Park, capacity 31,367 (away allocation 4,000)
Manager: Mark Hughes (app. 15/09/04)
Assistant: Mark Bowen
Year formed: 1875

USEFUL INFORMATION

Website: www.rovers.co.uk
Address: Ewood Park, Bolton Road, Blackburn, Lancashire BB2 4JF
Switchboard: 08701 113232

TRAVEL INFORMATION

By Train: Blackburn station is a mile and a half away, while Mill Hill is 1 mile from the stadium. Direct trains run from Manchester Victoria, Salford Crescent and Preston.
By Bus: The central bus station is next to the railway station. Services 3, 3A, 3B, 46, and 346 all go from Blackburn to Darwen. Ewood Park is a mile and a half along the journey.

BOLTON WANDERERS

FINAL STANDINGS 06-07

		W	D	L	PTS
6	Everton	15	13	10	58
7	**Bolton**	**16**	**8**	**14**	**56**
8	Reading	16	7	15	55

ALL-TIME RECORD

(League matches only)

	PL	W	D	L
Home:	54	28	16	10
Away:	54	16	13	25
Overall:	108	44	29	35

LAST 2 MEETINGS

01/01/2007
Liverpool   3-0   Bolton Wanderers
Crouch 61, Gerrard 63,
Kuyt 83

30/09/2006
Bolton Wanderers 2-0   Liverpool
Speed 30, Campo 51

CLUB DETAILS

Nickname:	The Trotters
Ground:	Reebok Stadium, capacity 28,000 (away allocation 3-5,000)
Manager:	Sammy Lee (app. 30/04/07)
Coach:	Ricky Sbragia
Year formed:	1874

USEFUL INFORMATION

Website:	www.bwfc.co.uk
Address:	Reebok Stadium, Burnden Way, Lostock, Bolton BL6 6JW
Switchboard:	01204 673673

TRAVEL INFORMATION

By Train: Horwich Parkway station is 100 yards from the stadium, which is on the Manchester Airport to Preston and Blackpool North/Blackpool North and Preston to Manchester Airport line.

By Bus: The club operate regular buses to and from Bolton town centre.

CHELSEA

FINAL STANDINGS 06-07

		W	D	L	PTS
1	Man Utd	28	5	5	89
2	**Chelsea**	**24**	**11**	**3**	**83**
3	Liverpool	20	8	10	68

ALL-TIME RECORD

(League matches only)

	PL	W	D	L
Home:	64	43	13	8
Away:	64	15	13	36
Overall:	128	58	26	44

LAST 2 MEETINGS (LEAGUE)

20/01/2007
Liverpool   2-0   Chelsea
Kuyt 4, Pennant 18

17/09/2006
Chelsea   1-0   Liverpool
Drogba 42

CLUB DETAILS

Nickname:	The Blues
Ground:	Stamford Bridge, capacity 42,360 (away allocation 3,000)
Manager:	Avram Grant (app. 20/09/07)
Assistant:	Steve Clarke
Year formed:	1905

USEFUL INFORMATION

Website:	www.chelseafc.com
Address:	Stamford Bridge, Fulham Road, London SW6 1HS
Switchboard:	0870 300 2322

TRAVEL INFORMATION

By Tube: Fulham Broadway is on the District Line, around 5 minutes walk. Take a train to Earl's Court and change for Wimbledon-bound trains. West Brompton is a new railway station accessible from Clapham Junction.

By Bus: Numbers 14, 211 and 414 go along Fulham Road from central London via West Brompton train station.

Premiership Opponents

DERBY COUNTY

FINAL C'SHIP STANDINGS 06-07

		W	D	L	PTS
2	Birmingham	26	8	12	86
3	**Derby**	**25**	**9**	**12**	**84**
4	West Brom	22	10	14	76

ALL-TIME RECORD
(League matches only)

	PL	W	D	L
Home:	62	41	15	6
Away:	62	23	13	26
Overall:	124	64	28	32

LAST 2 MEETINGS

20/04/2002
Liverpool 2-0 Derby County
Owen 16, 90

01/12/2001
Derby County 0-1 Liverpool
                    Owen 6

CLUB DETAILS

Nickname: The Rams
Ground: Pride Park, capacity 33,600 (away allocation 3,000)
Manager: Billy Davies (app. 02/06/06)
Assistant: David Kelly
Year formed: 1884

USEFUL INFORMATION

Website: www.dcfc.co.uk
Address: Pride Park, Derby DE24 8XL
Switchboard: 0870 444 1884

TRAVEL INFORMATION

By Train: Derby Midland station is a 15-minute walk from Pride Park. When leaving the station use the footbridge directly into Pride Park.
By Bus: A regular shuttle service operates from the city centre.

EVERTON

FINAL STANDINGS 06-07

		W	D	L	PTS
5	Tottenham	17	9	12	60
6	**Everton**	**15**	**13**	**10**	**58**
7	Bolton	16	8	14	56

ALL-TIME RECORD
(League matches only)

	PL	W	D	L
Home:	88	37	28	23
Away:	88	28	27	33
Overall:	176	65	55	56

LAST 2 MEETINGS

03/02/2007
Liverpool 0-0 Everton

09/09/2006
Everton 3-0 Liverpool
Cahill 24,
Johnson 36, 90

CLUB DETAILS

Nickname: The Toffees
Ground: Goodison Park, capacity 40,260 (away allocation 3,000)
Manager: David Moyes (app. 15/03/02)
Assistant: Alan Irvine
Year formed: 1878

USEFUL INFORMATION

Website: www.evertonfc.com
Address: Goodison Park, Goodison Road, Liverpool L4 4EL
Switchboard: 0151 330 2200

TRAVEL INFORMATION

By Train: From Liverpool Central, take any train heading for Ormskirk or Kirkby and get off at Kirkdale - from there it is a 10-minute walk.
By Bus: From Queen's Square Bus Station in Liverpool city centre, numbers 1, 2, 19, 20, 311, 345 and 350 go past the stadium.

FULHAM

FINAL STANDINGS 06-07

		W	D	L	PTS
15	West Ham	12	5	21	41
16	**Fulham**	**8**	**15**	**15**	**39**
17	Wigan	10	8	20	38

ALL-TIME RECORD

(League matches only)

	PL	W	D	L
Home:	20	15	5	0
Away:	20	7	6	7
Overall:	40	22	11	7

LAST 2 MEETINGS

05/05/2007
Fulham   1-0   Liverpool
Dempsey 69

09/12/2006
Liverpool   4-0   Fulham
Gerrard 54,
Carragher 61,
Garcia 66, Gonzalez 90

CLUB DETAILS

Nickname: Cottagers
Ground: Craven Cottage, capacity 22,000 (away allocation 3,000)
Manager: Lawrie Sanchez (app. 11/04/07)
Assistant: Les Reed
Year formed: 1879

USEFUL INFORMATION

Website: www.fulhamfc.com
Address: Craven Cottage, Stevenage Road, Fulham, London SW6 6HH
Switchboard: 0870 442 1222

TRAVEL INFORMATION

By Tube: Alight at Putney Bridge (District line) from Central London. Turn left out of station and right down Ranleigh Gardens. At the end of the road (before the Eight Bells pub) turn left into Willow Bank and right through the underpass into Bishops Park. Walk along river to ground (note park is closed after night games).
By Bus: The numbers 74 and 220 both run along Fulham Palace Road.

MANCHESTER CITY

FINAL STANDINGS 06-07

		W	D	L	PTS
13	Newcastle	11	10	17	43
14	**Man City**	**11**	**9**	**18**	**42**
15	West Ham	12	5	21	41

ALL-TIME RECORD

(League matches only)

	PL	W	D	L
Home:	71	44	14	13
Away:	71	28	19	24
Overall:	142	72	33	37

LAST 2 MEETINGS

14/04/2007
Manchester City   0-0   Liverpool

25/11/2006
Liverpool   1-0   Manchester City
Gerrard 67

CLUB DETAILS

Nickname: Blues/The Citizens
Ground: City of Manchester Stadium, capacity 48,000 (away allocation 4,800)
Manager: Sven-Goran Eriksson (app. 06/07/07)
Assistant: Hans Backe
Year formed: 1887

USEFUL INFORMATION

Website: www.mcfc.co.uk
Address: City of Manchester Stadium, SportCity, Rowsley Street, Manchester M11 3FF
Switchboard: 0870 062 1894

TRAVEL INFORMATION

By Train: The nearest station is Ashburys (a 10-minute walk), which is a five-minute train ride from Piccadilly (which itself is a 20-25 minute walk).
By Bus: Numbers 216 and 217 are the main services from the city centre, but 53, 54, 185, 186, 230, 231, 232, 233, 234, 235, 236, 237, X36 and X37 also run to SportCity.

Premiership Opponents

MANCHESTER UNITED

FINAL STANDINGS 06-07

		W	D	L	PTS
1	**Man Utd**	**28**	**5**	**5**	**89**
2	Chelsea	24	11	3	83
3	Liverpool	20	8	10	68

ALL-TIME RECORD

(League matches only)

	PL	W	D	L
Home:	74	35	18	21
Away:	74	14	25	35
Overall:	148	49	43	56

LAST 2 MEETINGS

03/03/2007
Liverpool   0-1   Manchester Utd
                        O'Shea 90

22/10/2006
Manchester Utd 2-0   Liverpool
Scholes 39,
Ferdinand 66

CLUB DETAILS

Nickname: Red Devils
Ground: Old Trafford, capacity 76,312 (away allocation 3,000)
Manager: Sir Alex Ferguson (app. 06/11/86)
Assistant: Carlos Queiroz
Year formed: 1878

USEFUL INFORMATION

Website: www.manutd.com
Address: Old Trafford, Manchester M16 0RA
Switchboard: 0870 442 1994

TRAVEL INFORMATION

By Train: Special services run from Manchester Piccadilly to the clubs own railway station. There is also a Metrolink service, with the station located next to Lancashire County Cricket Club on Warwick Road, which leads up to Sir Matt Busby Way.
By Bus: Numbers 114, 230, 252 and 253 all run from the city centre to the ground.

MIDDLESBROUGH

FINAL STANDINGS 06-07

		W	D	L	PTS
11	Aston Villa	11	17	10	50
12	**Middlesbro**	**12**	**10**	**16**	**46**
13	Newcastle	11	10	17	43

ALL-TIME RECORD

(League matches only)

	PL	W	D	L
Home:	65	35	17	13
Away:	65	20	21	24
Overall:	130	55	38	37

LAST 2 MEETINGS

18/04/2007
Liverpool   2-0   Middlesbrough
Gerrard 58, 65 (p)

18/11/2006
Middlesbrough   0-0   Liverpool

CLUB DETAILS

Nickname: Boro
Ground: Riverside Stadium, capacity 35,100 (away allocation 4,000)
Manager: Gareth Southgate (app. 07/06/06)
Coach: Colin Cooper
Year formed: 1876

USEFUL INFORMATION

Website: www.mfc.co.uk
Address: Riverside Stadium, Middlesbrough, Cleveland TS3 6RS
Switchboard: 0844 499 6789

TRAVEL INFORMATION

By Train: Middlesbrough station is about 15 minutes walk from the stadium, served by trains from Darlington. Take the back exit from the station, turn right then after a couple of minutes right again into Wynward Way for the ground.
By Bus: Numbers 36, 37 and 38 go from the town centre close to the ground.

NEWCASTLE UNITED

FINAL STANDINGS 06-07

		W	D	L	PTS
12	Middlesbro	12	10	16	46
13	**Newcastle**	**11**	**10**	**17**	**43**
14	Man City	11	9	18	42

ALL-TIME RECORD

(League matches only)

	PL	W	D	L
Home:	72	47	14	11
Away:	72	20	23	29
Overall:	144	67	37	40

LAST 2 MEETINGS

10/02/2007
Newcastle   2-1   Liverpool
Martins 26,   Bellamy 6
Solano 70 (p)

20/09/2006
Liverpool   2-0   Newcastle
Kuyt 29, Alonso 79

CLUB DETAILS

Nickname: Magpies
Ground: St James' Park, capacity 52,387 (away allocation 3,000)
Manager: Sam Allardyce (app. 15/05/07)
Coaches: Steve Round, Terry McDermott, Nigel Pearson
Year formed: 1881

USEFUL INFORMATION

Website: www.nufc.co.uk
Address: St. James' Park, Newcastle-upon-Tyne NE1 4ST
Switchboard: 0191 201 8400

TRAVEL INFORMATION

By Train: St James' Park is a 10-minute walk from Newcastle Central Station. The stadium is also served by its own Metro station (St James' Metro).
By Bus: Any bus from the town centre heading towards Gallowgate takes you past the stadium.

PORTSMOUTH

FINAL STANDINGS 06-07

		W	D	L	PTS
8	Reading	16	7	15	55
9	**Portsmouth**	**14**	**12**	**12**	**54**
10	Blackburn	15	7	16	52

ALL-TIME RECORD

(League matches only)

	PL	W	D	L
Home:	27	13	10	4
Away:	27	8	4	15
Overall:	54	21	14	19

LAST 2 MEETINGS

28/04/2007
Portsmouth   2-1   Liverpool
Mwaruwari 27   Hyypia 59
Kranjcar 32

29/11/2006
Liverpool   0-0   Portsmouth

CLUB DETAILS

Nickname: Pompey
Ground: Fratton Park, capacity 20,200 (away allocation 2,000)
Manager: Harry Redknapp (app. 07/12/05)
Assistant: Tony Adams
Year formed: 1898

USEFUL INFORMATION

Website: www.pompeyfc.co.uk
Address: Fratton Park, Frogmore Road, Portsmouth, Hants PO4 8RA
Switchboard: 0239 273 1204

TRAVEL INFORMATION

By Train: Fratton Bridge Station is a 10-minute walk from the ground - on arrival by train you pass the ground on your left. Portsmouth mainline station is at least a 25-minute walk.
By Bus: 13, 17 and 18 all run to the ground, while other services that stop close to Fratton Park are the 3, 16, 16A, 24, 27 (all Fratton Bridge); 4, 4A, 6 (all Milton Road).

Premiership Opponents

READING

FINAL STANDINGS 06-07

		W	D	L	PTS
7	Bolton	16	8	14	56
8	**Reading**	16	7	15	55
9	Portsmouth	14	12	12	54

ALL-TIME RECORD
(League matches only)

	PL	W	D	L
Home:	1	1	0	0
Away:	1	1	0	0
Overall:	2	0	0	0

LAST 2 MEETINGS

07/04/2007
Reading 1-2 Liverpool
Gunnarsson 47 Arbeloa 15, Kuyt 86

04/11/2006
Liverpool 2-0 Reading
Kuyt 14, 73

CLUB DETAILS
Nickname: The Royals
Ground: Madejski Stadium, capacity 24,161 (away allocation 2,327)
Manager: Steve Coppell (app. 09/10/03)
Coaches: Kevin Dillon, Wally Downes
Year formed: 1871

USEFUL INFORMATION
Website: www.readingfc.co.uk
Address: Madejski Stadium, Junction 11, M4, Reading, Berkshire RG2 0FL
Switchboard: 0118 968 1100

TRAVEL INFORMATION
By Train: Reading Central is 3 miles away - but could take over an hour on foot. From the station a Fastrack Park & Ride is available - outside the main entrance turn right and they are 200 yards down the road.
By Bus: The shuttle bus services (Number 79) are provided between the stadium and the station, running from 1pm on a Saturday (for 3pm kick-offs).

SUNDERLAND

FINAL C'SHIP STANDINGS 06-07

		W	D	L	PTS
1	**Sunderland**	27	7	12	88
2	Birmingham	26	8	12	86
3	Derby	25	9	12	84

ALL-TIME RECORD
(League matches only)

	PL	W	D	L
Home:	70	34	18	18
Away:	70	26	13	31
Overall:	140	60	31	49

LAST 2 MEETINGS

30/11/2005
Sunderland 0-2 Liverpool
             Garcia 30, Gerrard 45

20/08/2005
Liverpool 1-0 Sunderland
Alonso 24

CLUB DETAILS
Nickname: The Black Cats
Ground: Stadium of Light, capacity 49,000 (away allocation 3,600)
Manager: Roy Keane (app. 30/08/06)
Head coach: Tony Loughlin
Year formed: 1879

USEFUL INFORMATION
Website: www.safc.com
Address: The Sunderland Stadium of Light, Sunderland SR5 1SU
Switchboard: 0191 551 5000

TRAVEL INFORMATION
By Train: Sunderland mainline station is a 10-15 minute walk. The Metro service also runs from here, with St. Peter's or the Stadium of Light stations nearest the stadium.
By Bus: Numbers 2, 3, 4, 12, 13, 15 and 16 all stop within a few minutes walk of the ground. All routes connect to the central bus station, Park Lane Interchange.

TOTTENHAM HOTSPUR

FINAL STANDINGS 06-07

		W	D	L	PTS
4	Arsenal	19	11	8	68
5	**Tottenham**	**17**	**9**	**12**	**60**
6	Everton	15	13	10	58

ALL-TIME RECORD

(League matches only)

	PL	W	D	L
Home:	64	41	18	5
Away:	64	19	15	30
Overall:	128	60	33	35

LAST 2 MEETINGS

30/12/2006
Tottenham H.   0-1   Liverpool
                                   Garcia 45

23/09/2006
Liverpool   3-0   Tottenham H.
Gonzalez 63, Kuyt 73,
Riise 89

CLUB DETAILS

Nickname: Spurs
Ground: White Hart Lane, capacity 36,240 (away allocation 3,500)
Manager: Martin Jol (app. 05/11/04)
Assistant: Chris Hughton
Year formed: 1882

USEFUL INFORMATION

Website: www.spurs.co.uk
Address: 748 High Road, Tottenham, London N17 0AP
Switchboard: 0208 365 5000

TRAVEL INFORMATION

By Tube: The nearest tube station is Seven Sisters (Victoria - a 25-minute walk), with trains running to Liverpool Street. The nearest mainline station is White Hart Lane, approx 5 minutes walk, on the Liverpool Street-Enfield Town line.
By Bus: A regular service runs from Seven Sisters past the stadium entrance (numbers 259, 279, 149).

WEST HAM UNITED

FINAL STANDINGS 06-07

		W	D	L	PTS
14	Man City	11	9	18	42
15	**West Ham**	**12**	**5**	**21**	**41**
16	Fulham	8	15	15	39

ALL-TIME RECORD

(League matches only)

	PL	W	D	L
Home:	50	34	13	3
Away:	50	18	15	17
Overall:	100	52	28	20

LAST 2 MEETINGS

30/01/2007
West Ham   1-2   Liverpool
Blanco 77   Kuyt 46, Crouch 53

26/08/2006
Liverpool   2-1   West Ham
Agger 42, Crouch 45   Zamora 12

CLUB DETAILS

Nickname: The Hammers
Ground: Upton Park, capacity 35,647 (away allocation 2,000)
Manager: Alan Curbishley (app. 13/12/06)
Assistant: Mervyn Day
Year formed: 1895

USEFUL INFORMATION

Website: www.whufc.com
Address: Boleyn Ground, Green Street, Upton Park, London E13 9AZ
Switchboard: 0208 548 2748

TRAVEL INFORMATION

By Tube: Upton Park is the closest tube station, around 45 minutes from Central London on the District (and also Hammersmith & City) line. When you exit the station turn right, the stadium is then a two-minute walk. East Ham and Plaistow Stations, which are further away, may also be worth using to avoid congestion after the match.
By Bus: Routes 5, 15, 58, 104, 115, 147, 330 and 376 all serve The Boleyn Ground.

Premiership Opponents

WIGAN ATHLETIC

FINAL STANDINGS 06-07

		W	D	L	PTS
16	Fulham	8	15	15	39
17	**Wigan**	**10**	**8**	**20**	**38**
18	Sheff Utd	10	8	20	38

ALL-TIME RECORD

(League matches only)

	PL	W	D	L
Home:	2	2	0	0
Away:	2	2	0	0
Overall:	4	4	0	0

LAST 2 MEETINGS

21/04/2007
Liverpool   2-0   Wigan
Kuyt 30, 68

02/12/2006
Wigan   0-4   Liverpool
                            Bellamy 9, 25, Kuyt 40,
                            McCulloch (o.g.) 45

CLUB DETAILS

Nickname:	The Latics
Ground:	JJB Stadium, capacity 25,023 (away allocation 5,000+)
Manager:	Chris Hutchings (app. 14/05/07)
Assistant:	Frank Barlow
Year formed:	1932

USEFUL INFORMATION

Website:	www.wiganlatics.co.uk
Address:	JJB Stadium, Robin Park, Newtown, Wigan WN5 0UZ
Switchboard:	01942 774000

TRAVEL INFORMATION

By Train: Wigan Wallgate and Wigan North Western are a 15-minute walk from the stadium. From either station head under the railway bridge and keep to the right - following the road (A49) for 10 minutes. The complex should soon be visible.

By Bus: No particular route, as the venue is within easy distance of the station.

Liverpool v Wigan Athletic, Anfield repeat confirmed for 2007-08 on New Year's Day

THIS IS
LIVERPOOL FOOTBALL CLUB
WILLIAMSON SQUARE
LIVERPOOL

LIVERPOOLFC.TV IN ASSOCIATION WITH OFFICIAL CLUB SPONSORS Carlsberg
LIVERPOOLFC.TV
LIVERPOOL FOOTBALL CLUB OFFICIAL WEBSITE
100% OFFICIAL
TEAM NEWS
Welcome back steven (stevenh@liverpoolfc.tv)
My Account
LogOut
MATCH SHOP BETTING INTERACTIVE MOBILE TICKETS TEAM HISTORY THE CLUB E-SEASON TICKET
HELP CONTACT US
July 27, 2007
NEWS HEADLINES
Leiva gets Djimi's shirt
Crouch wants to see in new stadium
Benitez happy with headache
Kuyt: Babel will shine at Anfield
Ticket Office improvements
Fantasy Football: Win £100k of...
LFC WEB SEARCH
TOP SEARCHES
1. Last Minute Holiday
2. Home Insurance
3. Cars
4. Remortgage
5. Home Loan
MORE NEWS
TICKET NEWS
HAVE YOU SEEN ?
Liverpool FC TV channel announcement
Win a footballer's weekend in Ibiza
Apply for an LFC Credit Card
LFC junior away kit
Check out our new season fixtures
LFC REVERSE AU
FIRST TROPHY OF THE SEASON?
SEASON TICKET
Live Match Coverage
Match Coverage Now Underway
Fans on new stadium
S China Highlights
FREE PREVIEW
BUY E-ST
TECH SUPPORT
NEXT MATCH
LAST MATCH
TABLES
SQUAD
PORTSMOUTH (a)
13:30 Fri 27th July
Barclays Asia Trophy
E-SEASON TICKET COVERAGE
LIVE AUDIO
LIVE VIDEO
DELAYED VIDEO
OPTIONS
HOW LOW WILL
MOBILE ZONE
ONLINE STORE
FANTASY FOOTBALL
LFC.TV BETTING

Carlsberg

CLUB ESSENTIALS

...cool, calm & collected

THE REAL BOB PAISLEY

The remarkable inside story of an Anfield legend — Told by his FAMILY

LIVERPOOL FOOTBALL CLUB · EST 1892 · LFC TV

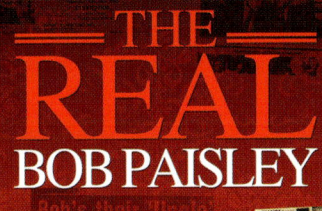

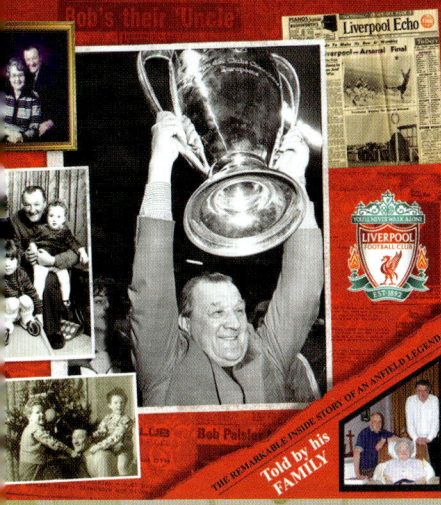

EXCLUSIVELY ON **SETANTA SPORTS**

THIS IS ANFIELD
Official Matchday Programme — £3.00

LIVERPOOL VS CHELSEA
BARCLAYS PREMIER LEAGUE, ANFIELD, KICK-OFF 4.00PM
19.08.07

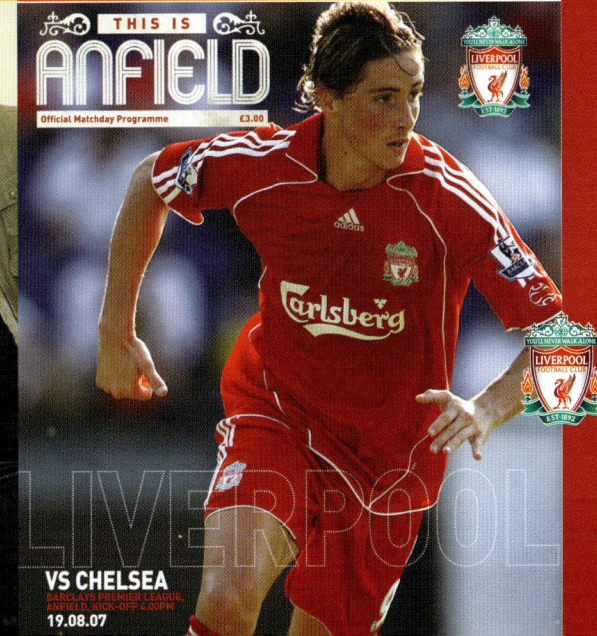

TICKETS

Address	Ticket Office, PO Box 204, Liverpool L69 4PQ
Telephone Number	24-Hour Ticket Information Line 0844 844 0844 Customer Services 0844 844 2005
Ticket Office Hours	Monday-Friday 8.15am-5.30pm Matchdays 9.15am to kick-off, then 15 minutes after end of game Non Match Saturdays/Sundays 9.15am-1.00pm

Prices	CAT B	CAT A
Kop	£32	£34
Over 65	£24	£25.50
Disabled and Visually Impaired	£24	£26
Main Stand	£34	£36
Over 65	£25.50	£27
Centenary	£34	£36
Over 65	£25.50	£27
Paddock	£34	£36
Over 65	£25.50	£27
Disabled and Visually Impaired	£26	£27
Anfield Road	£34	£36
Over 65	£25.50	£27
Combined 1 Adult/1 Child (16 or under)	£51	£54
Disabled and Visually Impaired	£26	£27

(Free for Disabled and Visually Impaired Assistants)

Category A matches
Arsenal, Aston Villa, Blackburn Rovers, Chelsea, Everton, Manchester City, Manchester United, Newcastle United and Tottenham Hotspur.

Family tickets
For adult/child combined tickets a ratio of two adults to one child, or two children to one adult is allowed. In the event that the number of children exceeds the ratio of 2:1 the additional tickets will be charged at the adult rate.

Buying tickets
General sales begin 18 days before a home fixture and are available through the credit card hotline (Monday-Friday 8.30am-5.30pm - a maximum of four tickets, minimum booking fee of 50p per ticket applies), postal application and for Fan Card holders, online (subject to a booking fee of £2.50 per ticket). A small number are often made available online on the date of general sale.

TICKETS

By post
State the match and number of tickets you require, with the correct remittance and a stamped addressed envelope, to LFC Ticket Office, PO Box 204, Liverpool L69 4PQ. You can pay by cheque, postal order, credit or debit card. Cheques must be made payable to Liverpool FC. If you want to pay by credit or debit card, include card number and expiry date, plus debit card issue number where applicable. If applications exceed the number of tickets, they will be allocated through a ballot.

By phone
You can apply for a maximum of four tickets, by calling the credit card hotline, quoting your credit or debit card number and expiry date. A minimum booking fee of 50p per ticket will be charged. Tickets booked more than three days before the match will be sent out by post, those booked after this must be collected from the credit card collections window at the ticket office, and you must produce the card used to book the tickets.

In person
Any remaining tickets will go on sale at the ticket office 11 days in advance. A maximum of four tickets may be purcased in one transaction (subject to change). However, tickets usually sell out through phone and postal bookings.

Away matches (Premiership)
Tickets go on sale first based on a priority system (i.e. to supporters who have attended the most away fixtures in the Premiership during season 2006-07 - and subsequently 2007-08). The number of matches attended will be determined from the information held on the ticket office database.

Cup matches
Ticket information concerning European and domestic Cup match allocations are made as soon as possible after each draw has taken place. Supporters are advised that they should quote their Fan Card number for all ticket purcahses, and to retain their ticket stubs for potential use for any additional fixtures allocated on a voucher system or in the ven of a home match being abandoned.

THE LFC FAN CARD

About the Fan Card
Fan Cards are used to record attendance and help prevent ticket fraud. If you do not have a Fan Card, you can purchase from the ticket office (for a one-off fee of £3.50 for a multi-season card). Season-ticket holders, Priority Ticket Scheme, Official Liverpool Supporters' Club and e-Season Ticket members all receive Fancard details automatically.

Buying Tickets
When purchasing tickets you must provide your Fan Card customer number either by handing your Fan Card to the ticket office, quoting it via the telephone booking line or by post, or using it to log in online. Further information may be requested for security reasons. Purchases made online will require your Fan Card customer number and password.
Only one ticket per match will be recorded on your Fan Card. If applying for tickets as a group it will be necessary for you to disclose each Fan Card customer number and the customer name.

What Happens If I Lose My Fan Card?
Please let the ticket office know immediately in writing. Your Fan Card will then be deactivated and a new Fan Card will be issued for a fee of £10. The data held on your lost or stolen Fan Card will be transferred onto your new Fan Card.

Should you change address, please inform the ticket office in writing, quoting your old address and enclosing a copy of a utility bill (gas, electric, water or telephone) to the ticket office.

GETTING TO ANFIELD

How to get there - by car
Follow the M62 until you reach the end of the motorway. Then follow the A5058 towards Liverpool for 3 miles, then turn left at the traffic lights into Utting Avenue (there is a McDonalds on the corner of this junction). Proceed for one mile and then turn right at The Arkles pub for the ground. It is recommended that you arrive at least two hours before kick-off in order to secure your parking spec. Otherwise, you can park in the streets around Goodison Park and walk across Stanley Park to Anfield, or you can park in a secure parking area at Goodison.

How to get there - by train
Kirkdale Station is the closest to Anfield (about a mile away), although Sandhills Station the stop before has the benefit of a bus service to the ground (Soccerbus). Both stations can be reached by first getting a train from Liverpool Lime Street (which is over 3 miles from the ground) to Liverpool Central (Merseyrail Northern Line), and then changing there for trains to Sandhills (2 stops away) or Kirkdale (3 stops). Note: only trains to Ormskirk or Kirkby go to Kirkdale station. A taxi from Liverpool Lime Street should cost between £5 and £7.

How to get there - Soccerbus
There are frequent shuttle buses from Sandhills Station, to Anfield for all Liverpool home Premiership and Cup matches. Soccerbus will run for two hours before each match (last bus from Sandhills Station is approximately 15 minutes before kick-off) and for 50 minutes after the final whistle (subject to availability). You can pay as you board the bus. Soccerbus is FREE for those who hold a valid TRIO, SOLO or SAVEAWAY ticket or Merseytravel Free Travel Pass.

How to get there - by bus
Take a 26 (or 27) from Paradise Street Bus Station or a 17B, 17C, 17D, or 217 from Queen Square bus station directly to the ground. The 68 and 168 which operate between Bootle and Aigburth and the 14 (from Queen Square) and 19 stop a short walk away.

How to get there - by air
Liverpool John Lennon Airport is around 10 miles from the ground, and taxis should be easily obtainable. Alternatively, you can catch the 80A bus to Garston Station and change at Sandhills for the Soccerbus service.

How to get there - on foot
From Kirkdale Station, turn right and then cross the railway bridge, where you will see the Melrose Abbey pub. Walk past up Westminster Road for around 1/3 of a mile before you arrive at the Elm Tree pub. Follow the road around the right-hand bend and then turn left into Bradwell Street. At the end of the road you will come to County Road (A59). Cross over at the traffic lights and then go down the road to the left of the Aldi superstore. At the end of this road you will reach Walton Lane (A580). You should be able to see Goodison Park on your left and Stanley Park in front of you. Cross Walton Lane and either enter Stanley Park, following the footpath through the park (keeping to the right) which will exit into Anfield Road. As an alternative to going through Stanley Park, bear right down Walton Lane and then turn left down the road at the end of Stanley Park to the ground.

To check bus and train times (8am-8pm, 7 days a week):

Traveline Merseyside   0870 608 2 608
Soccerbus   0151 330 1066

MUSEUM & STADIUM TOUR

Liverpool Football Club Museum & Stadium Tour Anfield is a real "Five Star" attraction. England's most successful football club has amassed a record 18 League Championships, a total of 14 League and FA Cups, plus three UEFA and European Super Cups apiece.
But its the five European Cups that place the club in an exclusive group who have won this most prestigious prize five times or more. Following "The Greatest football game ever" on 25 May 2005, Liverpool FC Museum has permanently added to it's collection the Champions League trophy.

Come on join the Rafa-lution
The Museum tells the story of England's most successful football club from the early days right up to the present day "Rafa-lution".
The stadium tour takes you behind the scenes at Anfield, visiting the dressing rooms, down the tunnel to the sound of the crowd, a chance to touch the "This Is Anfield" sign and sit in the dug-out. Tour places are limited, and demand is extremely high – please book well in advance of your visit.

Take the Red bus to Anfield!
During the 2007-8 season a special bus is operating on the No. 17 bus route from the City Centre to Anfield, celebrating the incredible European Cup success of Liverpool. Watch out for this, and also the amazing double decker open-top bus that runs daily between Liverpool and Preston – with a collage of the greatest Liverpool players involved in the club's European glories. These two buses were kindly sponsored by Stagecoach NorthWest, and have proved to be a fantastic way to celebrate the cultural heritage of Liverpool Football Club over these two important years.

Opening times:	Every day of the week from 10am until 5pm.
	Last admission to museum 4pm.
	On match days last admission is 1 hour before kick-off.
	NO STADIUM TOURS ON MATCH DAYS.
	Tours on day before a match will be MINI TOURS, at reduced prices.
Museum & Tour Prices:	Adults £10.00, Children/Student/OAPS £6.00, Family £25.00
Museum Prices:	Adults £5.00, Children/OAPS £3.00 Families, £13.00
	WE RECOMMEND BOOKING IN ADVANCE FOR STADIUM TOURS.
	THERE IS NO NEED TO PRE-BOOK A MUSEUM-ONLY VISIT.
	All times and prices subject to change at short notice.
	Due to operational reasons, tours can be cancelled at very short notice.
Booking hotline:	0151 260 6677

Important Security Information
We regret that we cannot accept suitcases and other large and bulky items into either the Museum or Stadium. There is no place to store such items in the ground.

Five European Cups and the Atletico Madrid centenary trophy – amongst the Museum sights

WEBSITE

LIVERPOOLFC.TV

Launched in October 2001, the club was the last top-flight side to launch an official site. But since then, it has become the most visited football club website in the world recording 30 million hits a year. These are some of the reasons why:

News: Get the latest, breaking news from the club.
Match: Full fixture list and results, match reports teamsheets and statistics.
Shop: Buy the latest LFC merchandise and other club related goods.
Interactive: Communicate with fellow fans, play LFC games and more.
Mobile: All phone-related fun including ringtones, realtones and SMS alerts.
Tickets: Latest availability, online sales, Anfield info and away travel planning.
Team: Want to know about your favourite player? It's all here…
History: The LFC story, interspersed with records and quotes.
Club: Includes all LFC-related initiatives and bodies.

Premium Content:

You can also sign up for our premium content package – your access all areas pass to the club's official website for as little as 11p per day.

The liverpoolfc.tv e-Season Ticket takes you right into the heart of Anfield with seven channels of web TV dedicated to the Reds.

You can enjoy highlights and goals from every one of our Premiership matches, watch interviews with the management staff and players direct from Melwood or enjoy the latest action from the reserve team.

Maybe you'd prefer to take a trip down memory lane with our retro channel featuring some of the greatest moments in the club's history, you can watch the supporters giving their views on the latest hot topics or enjoy our special features including the ground breaking 100 Days That Shook The Kop project.

Price: £39.99 for 12 months (direct debit - UK only),
£2.49 for 3 months then £4.49 thereafter.
£44.99 for 12 months (credit card), £4.49 a month.

e-Season ticket link: http://www.liverpoolfc.tv/preview/

Alternatively, log on to the home page and choose the shop option, scrolling down to the e-Season Ticket option.

The website homepage (above left) and e-Season Ticket console (above right)

LFC TV

LFC TV is the dedicated channel for British football's most successful football club.
For the first time in the club's 115-year history, supporters can now enjoy every minute of every Premiership and Champions League game from the comfort of their own homes.

With LFC TV positioned right at the heart of the club, the channel's flagship news programme 'LFC Now' has every angle covered – including exclusive interviews with the manager, former stars and, of course, the current players themselves.

Every Liverpool reserve-team game is broadcast live, giving fans a unique opportunity to cast an eye over the emerging talent knocking on the first-team dressing-room door.

And for an exclusive glimpse of the future, regular action and updates from the club's state-of-the-art Academy will reveal the progress of the youngsters hoping to lift trophies for the Reds when the current crop of stars have hung up their boots.

Many of the players who brought so much joy to fans on the way to earning legendary status at the club will be regular visitors to the LFC TV studios. The expert and, sometimes controversial, views of former heroes – trophy winners all – will form the backbone of the channel's innovative 'This is Anfield' show – a live, interactive football forum where the big issues are debated.

And it won't just be the professional pundits who have their say. 'This is Anfield' will provide a platform for the fans to make their views heard. It's the perfect opportunity for supporters to put forward their views and demonstrate why Liverpool followers are rightly considered by many to be the most passionate and knowledgeable in the world.

With five European Cups, seven FA Cups and a record 18 League Championships collected since the club was founded by John Houlding on March 15 1892, there's certainly plenty to talk about!

LFC TV is carried at no extra charge as part of the Setanta Sports Pack, a nine-channel offering, available on satellite. It is also be available to subscribers of Virgin Media's XL pack and subscribers to any other Virgin TV service who want to add the Setanta channels - including LFC TV - to their package will be able to do so for just £8 a month.

The channel is also broadcast live on www.liverpoolfc.tv as part of e-Season Ticket.

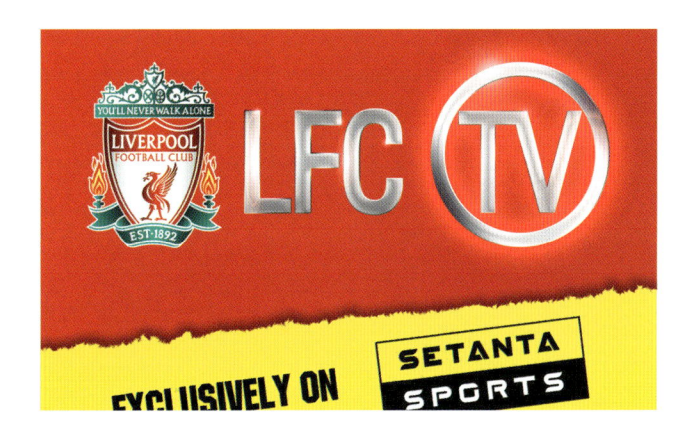

CLUB STORES

Selling everything from the new replica kits to the latest toys and games, both club stores provide Reds fans with a wealth of souvenirs. With the new adidas range having been unveiled, there remains a wealth of choice for the 2007-08 season.
Addresses and contact details are as follows:

Williamson Square Official Club Store
11 Williamson Square, Liverpool, L1 1EQ
United Kingdom
Tel +44 (0)151 330 3077
Opening times: Mon-Sat 9.00am - 5.30pm
Sundays 11.00am - 5.00pm

Chester Official Club Store
48 Eastgate Street, Chester, CH1 1LE
United Kingdom
Tel +44 (0)1244 344 608
Opening times: Mon-Sat 9.00am - 5.30pm
Sundays 11.00am - 5.00pm

Anfield Official Club Store
Telephone +44 (0)151 263 1760
Fax +44 (0)151 264 9088
Opening times Mon - Fri 9.00am - 5.00pm
Saturdays 9.00am - 5.00pm
Sundays 10.00am - 4.00pm
Match Saturdays 9.00am - 45 mins after game
Match Sundays 10.00am - 45 mins after game
Match Evenings 9.00am - 45 mins after game

Online Store
www.liverpoolfc.tv

Liverpool FC Order hotline: 0870 600 0532 **International calls:** +44 138 685 2035
Lines open 8am-9pm Mon-Sun

Inside the club shot in Williamson Square, Liverpool

MATCHDAY PROGRAMME AND OFFICIAL MAGAZINE

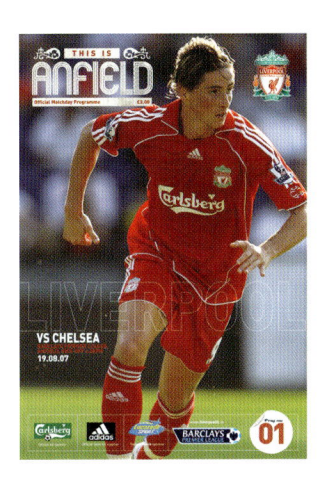

Official Matchday Programme

Liverpool's award-winning official matchday programme is written and produced in Liverpool by Sport Media on behalf of the club. The traditionally sized programme, now increased to 84 pages for 2007/08, includes regular features like the nostalgia-based The Files Of Anfield Road, exclusive Anfield news, features, a message from the manager plus captain's notes while for the new campaign their is a regular column by Gary McAllister.

How to subscribe

Phone: 0845 143 0001 (Monday-Friday 9am-5pm)
Website: www.liverpoolfc.tv/match/magazine
(Also available in braille and other formats - contact community department on 0151 264 2316 for details)

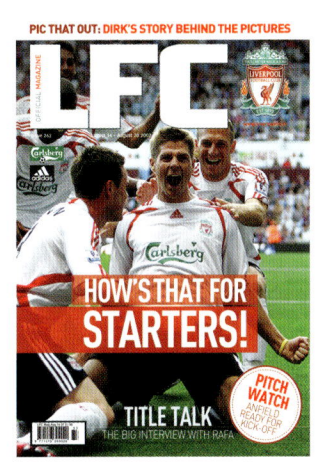

LFC Magazine

Liverpool are the only club boasting an official weekly magazine in the Premiership. The Sport Media-produced glossy LFC Magazine, priced £1.95, provides up-to-date news and views on all aspects of the club, from exclusive player interviews, match previews and reports to features on former players and famous Reds and stats. Popular back page feature asks fans to Spot The Kop Idol from a Liverpool crowd scene while regular columnists are chief executive Rick Parry, plus legendary duo Kenny Dalglish and Alan Hansen.

How to subscribe

Phone: 0845 143 0001 (Monday-Friday 9am-5pm)
Website: www.liverpoolfc.tv/match/magazine

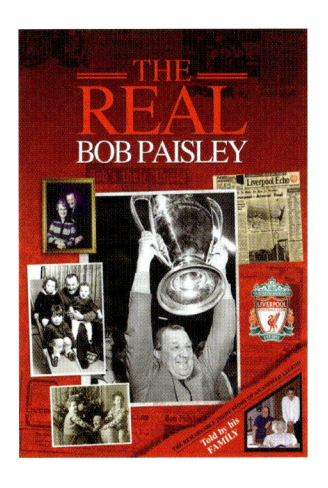

The Real Bob Paisley

This long overdue Sport Media publication celebrates the life and times of one of the most successful manager in British football history. The complete story paints an accurate profile of a very private man through the eyes of his family, those who knew him the best away from the glare of the public eye. His treasured family album is made public for the very first time, while tributes from some of the game's greatest names only serve to enhance his reputation as one of the finest servants the English game has ever seen.

How to order

Phone: 0845 143 0001 (Monday-Friday 9am-5pm)

ASSOCIATION OF INTERNATIONAL BRANCHES

There are almost 200 Association of International Branches, and several new ones are being formed each season. Benefits of affiliating include the chance to attend an exclusive Q&A session with a Reds legend, as well as meeting like-minded supporters in your area.
However, please note that new branches have restricted access to tickets.

If there isn't an AIB near you, why not form one. You'll need 25 supporters and will have to pay a small fee and sign up to AIB regulations. For further details or information on your nearest branch, please call: 0844 499 3000 or fax 0151 261 1695.

LIVERPOOL DISABLED SUPPORTERS ASSOCIATION

The aims and objectives of this association are to act in partnership with Liverpool Football Club to promote inclusiveness for the disabled fans of the club, the disabled fans of visiting clubs as well as those individuals who support disabled people and those with impairments. This association recognises that all fans should have an equal opportunity to participate in an enjoyable matchday experience and that people with disabilities and/or impairments must have their interests recognised and promoted by LFC with equal status to that of all other fans of the club.

The club's disability liaison officer Colin McCall continues to develop the LDSA, acting as a link between the club and its supporters. The LDSA and LFC concur with NADS guidelines that any relationship between club and supporters should be conducted in a harmonious manner by way of evolution, not revolution. The LDSA committee is made up of 10 members who are all Liverpool supporters and they meet once a month with the liaison officer to discuss disability issues at LFC.

If you would like any more information about the LDSA then please email LDSA@liverpoolfc.tv or write to LDSA, Liverpool Football Club, 69 Anfield Road, Liverpool, L4 0TH.

REDUC@TE

Since opening, thousands of children have now enjoyed the opportunity to learn in the exciting and inspirational environment of Liverpool Football Club. Staffed by a Centre Manager and students from the three Universities in Liverpool, Reduc@te aims to help children improve their skills in the key areas of literacy, numeracy and ICT. Resources are made available in Reduc@te on a daily basis and use football, sport and contemporary issues to help motivate young people to learn. Great emphasis is placed on rewarding achievement and building up the self-esteem of the children to give them more confidence when learning. Staff use the unique environment to make the educational experience as special as possible and groups are offered learning opportunities in the club shop, the LFC Museum, the Academy and around Anfield.

All of the curriculum materials are designed to be fun and enjoyable and study support groups attend after normal school hours on weekdays Monday to Thursday. Fridays are set aside for Special Needs schools or schools who wish to make a full day visit to the centre. Reduc@te is well equipped with ICT hardware and is always willing to embark on new and exciting projects. Recently primary schools have visited Reduc@te for French or Spanish lessons during the school day and a number of secondary schools attend Reduc@te for 'business days' where they focus on the off-field activities of the club for their GCSE and A-Level courses.

Further details on Reduc@te may be obtained from the Centre Manager, Keith White:
Tel: 0151 263 1313   **Email:** krwhite.lfc.study@talk21.com or Reducate@liverpoolfc.tv

OFFICIAL LIVERPOOL SUPPORTERS CLUB

The Official Liverpool Supporters Club boasts of over 30,000 members from all over the world. Our dedicated supporters come from all walks of life and a variety of countries, but the one constant is the passion that each and every one has for this great club.
The OLSC offers two membership schemes; adult and junior, which are priced at £32.00 (inc p/p) and £22.00 (inc p/p) respectively.

The adult membership contains an exclusive interview with Liverpool colossus, Jamie Carragher. In the DVD entitled "23 Carra Gold", Jamie tells us all about his life and times at Liverpool FC and talks us through some of his most memorable games over the last 10 years. Members also receive a uniquely designed mobile phone holder/desk tidy which displays handy club telephone numbers as well as keeping your mobile phone and LFC pen and pencil to hand. All of this comes in an LFC folder, in which you can store your quarterly Member's magazines.

Our Junior members receive a fantastic array of LFC goodies, which will delight any young LFC fan. There's a drawstring bag, which holds an OLSC sun hat, a personalised OLSC certificate, pencil case and pencil, a noisy OLSC hand clapper to help to cheer on the Reds, a giant hand inflatable to show your support, a Member's badge and a coin holder to keep your money safe. Junior Members are automatically entered into a draw to be a Mascot, to lead out the Reds at an away fixture. There's also a draw to attend the Christmas party held here at Anfield!

Every member, whether adult or junior receives 20% discount on Museum entry or the combined Stadium/Museum visit, 10% in our club stores (a second form of identification is required), free entry into our reserve games, an exclusive discount on subscription to the LFC Magazine and a free monthly Megadraw. Members are automatically entered into the draw to win tickets, signed shirts, signed footballs, and a whole host of exciting prizes.

To join this exciting and fantastic membership scheme, please call 0844 499 3000 or log onto www.liverpoolfc.tv/olsc. You can download a form or join online instantly.

Adult Membership for 07/08 (£32 including p&p)	Junior Membership for 07/08 (£22 including p&p)
• "23 Carra Gold" DVD	• Free Fan Card (if required)
• Free LFC Fan Card (if required)	• Personalised LFC loyalty certificate
• An LFC exclusive desk tidy	• Member's sun hat (for OLSC members only)
• LFC pen and pencil	• Exclusive OLSC football clapper
• A folder in which to keep Member magazines	• OLSC inflatable giant hand to cheer on the Reds!
• Official Member's quarterly magazine	• OLSC pencils and pencil case
• 10% discount in our club store	• Handy OLSC coin holder for your pocket money
• Free monthly draw for all members	• Exclusive Member's badge
• 20% discount on Museum/Museum & Stadium Tour	• Enter the draw to attend the Junior Member's Christmas party at Anfield
• Free entry to reserve games	• Automatic entry to mascot draw (away fixture)
• Exclusive discount offer on LFC magazine	• An OLSC drawstring bag
	• Official Member's quarterly magazine
	• 10% discount in our club store
	• Free monthly draw for all members
	• 20% discount on Museum/Museum & Stadium Tour
	• Free entry to reserve games
	• Exclusive discount offer on LFC magazine

LIVERPOOL PR DEPARTMENT

Headed by former player, Brian Hall, the Public Relations department plays an important role in communicating with the huge international fan base that support our world renowned club. Thousands of letters are received and answered, with requests concerning just about every aspect of life at Liverpool Football Club.

Please Note: PR DO NOT DEAL WITH REQUESTS FOR MATCH DAY TICKETS.

The sheer volume of mail, especially for autographs, requires us to answer in a standard format with pre-printed signed photos of the team and individual players. P.R. produce a brochure which covers many aspects of club activities.

The demand for autographed items is enormous, so the club have to prioritise and focus on special needs and terminally ill youngsters/adults. Charities are also given priority for help with fundraising activities.

P.R. also organise visits to our training ground, Melwood, to meet staff and players for photos and autographs, again P.R. priorities as above. At the end of each season, the redundant matchday and training kits are distributed around the world to help support the wonderful work of the many Relief Agencies.

The national anti-racism campaigns, Show Racism the Red Card and Kick it Out, are supported each year through this department. Other strong and important social messages are also supported by the club through P.R. For example art competitions in schools are promoted using the influential images of our players, supporting "Kick Drugs into Touch", "Give Smoking the Boot" and other messages.

The club have supported the charity Football Aid for many years and 2007 was the most successful to date with £56,000 being raised. If you have ever dreamed of playing at Anfield then visit their website www.footballaid.com where dreams do come true.

Liverpool players on their Christmas visit to Alder Hey Children's Hospital

The highlight of the year is the annual visit to Alder Hey Children's Hospital in Liverpool. The department organise the visit by the first-team squad who see every child in the hospital and give them all a Christmas present from Liverpool Football Club. The visit is emotional but very rewarding for everyone concerned.

You can contact the Public Relations on either of the following:

Telephone Number:
0151 260 1433

Fax Number:
0151 264 2918

E-mail:
pr.department@liverpoolfc.tv

LFC IN THE COMMUNITY

Liverpool Football Club's community department has gone from strength to strength since it was formed in 2000. We are a dynamic and thriving area of the club that works very closely with the local community and are involved in a whole host of various activities both locally and world wide. Our main projects within the community are:

Truth 4 Youth Assemblies:
Taking our bully, racism and drug messages into schools across Merseyside. Due to the growing gun culture our message of "Shoot Goals not Guns" is proving to be of major importance.

Coaching 4 All:
Taking youngsters for football coaching in schools, after schools clubs and community centres.

Respect 4 All:
Providing football coaching in special needs schools and adult day centres. We also have 4 competitive disabled football teams.

Sweeperzone:
A hugely successful project with over 750 free matchday tickets given to various groups.

Charity 4 Others:
Sending old and unused kit to the poor and needy overseas.

Kick It, Kick Off:
Working with schools and Merseyside Police.

Young Person of the Year Award:
Awards evening, attended by a first-team player, to commend local youngsters.

Footie 4 Ladies:
With the successful Liverpool Ladies first team, reserve team and U16s.

Kickz:
A football initiative aimed at engaging young people.

Tactics 4 Families:
An initiative aimed at supporting families within the community. It is particularly targeted at parents as well as children.

For detailed information on the above please see our website www.liverpoolfc.tv/community and to get involved in any of the above schemes email us at community.department@liverpoolfc.tv

School initiatives are a key part of the work done by LFC in the Community

INSIDE ANFIELD

Hospitality

Heathcotes at Anfield is based at Liverpool Football Club, which has one of the regions most remarkable venues. The club is synonymous with achievement and success – great teams built on the perfect blend of skill, flair and determination, and this is highlighted in the service we offer.

Our experience in accommodating large numbers of hospitality guests – typically 2,500 people on match days – offers valuable reassurance that all events will run smoothly. And because of our considerable resources, we'll do our best to help if you are working to a tight deadline.

You'd be correct in thinking that any culinary experience that bears the name of Paul Heathcote has to be special. Under the direction of award-winning head chef Christian Grall you can enjoy a range of inspired menu options covering everything from conference luncheons to fine dining.

To find out details regarding conferencing, events and weddings and private events, further details can be obtained from the following contacts:

Telephone: 0151 263 7744
Email: events@liverpoolfc.tv
Website: www.liverpoolfc.tv/club/banqueting.htm

A view of The Paisley Suite at Anfield

LIVERPOOL IN THE MEDIA

LOCAL MEDIA

Liverpool Echo
Local evening daily, Monday-Saturday.
Saturday edition contains the 'Football Echo'.
Price: 45p

Liverpool Daily Post
Local morning daily, Monday-Saturday.
Price: 50p

LOCAL RADIO

BBC Radio Merseyside
Provides full coverage of all Liverpool first-team games, with Gary Gillespie the main summariser. Post-match fans' debate is a regular feature, while football is covered throughout the week, with Fridays usually previewing the weekend action.
Frequency: 95.8FM/1485AM

Radio City/Magic
Ian St John is a prominent figure of a Saturday during the football season, while full commentary on all Liverpool matches is provided with guest summarisers including John Aldridge, who also plays a popular agony uncle to fans on the station's post-match debate.
Frequency: 96.7FM/1548AM

Century FM
Coverage of all first-team games is available, with a daily football phone-in Monday-Friday (known as the 'Legends' phone-in), including Alan Kennedy.
Frequency: 105.4FM

OTHER UNOFFICIAL PUBLICATIONS

The KOP magazine
Important grass roots tabloid-style publication providing an alternative take on all things Red, established since 1994. On sale locally in newsagents or outside the ground on matchdays. Subscribe by calling 0845 143 0001.

Price: £1.50

The Liverpool Way
Alternative view of Liverpool FC since 1999, copies are available around Anfield on matchdays with the latest release, issue 59, costing £2.50.

Through The Wind And Rain
Long-running publication, available on matchday, priced £2.

Red All Over The Land
Having celebated its 10th anniversary, RAOTL is on sale at most home and away games. Including postage, the August/September 2007 issue (No. 124) could be ordered for £2.50.

Liverpool FC : The Official Guide 2008

2008	Jan	Feb	March	April	May	Jun
Monday						
Tuesday	1			1		
Wednesday	2			2		
Thursday	3			3	1	
Friday	4	1		4	2	
Saturday	5	2	1	5	3	
Sunday	6	3	2	6	4	1
Monday	7	4	3	7	5	2
Tuesday	8	5	4	8	6	3
Wednesday	9	6	5	9	7	4
Thursday	10	7	6	10	8	5
Friday	11	8	7	11	9	6
Saturday	12	9	8	12	10	7
Sunday	13	10	9	13	11	8
Monday	14	11	10	14	12	9
Tuesday	15	12	11	15	13	10
Wednesday	16	13	12	16	14	11
Thursday	17	14	13	17	15	12
Friday	18	15	14	18	16	13
Saturday	18	16	15	18	17	14
Sunday	20	17	16	20	18	15
Monday	21	18	17	21	18	16
Tuesday	22	18	18	22	20	17
Wednesday	23	20	18	23	21	18
Thursday	24	21	20	24	22	18
Friday	25	22	21	25	23	20
Saturday	26	23	22	26	24	21
Sunday	27	24	23	27	25	22
Monday	28	25	24	28	26	23
Tuesday	29	26	25	29	27	24
Wednesday	30	27	26	30	28	25
Thursday	31	28	27		29	26
Friday		29	28		30	27
Saturday			29		31	28
Sunday			30			29
Monday			31			30
Tuesday						
Wednesday						

2008 Yearplanner

July	Aug	Sept	Oct	Nov	Dec	
		1			1	Monday
		2			2	Tuesday
		3	1		3	Wednesday
		4	2		4	Thursday
	1	5	3		5	Friday
	2	6	4	1	6	Saturday
	3	7	5	2	7	Sunday
	4	8	6	3	8	Monday
	5	9	7	4	9	Tuesday
	6	10	8	5	10	Wednesday
	7	11	9	6	11	Thursday
	8	12	10	7	12	Friday
	9	13	11	8	13	Saturday
	10	14	12	9	14	Sunday
	11	15	13	10	15	Monday
	12	16	14	11	16	Tuesday
	13	17	15	12	17	Wednesday
	14	18	16	13	18	Thursday
	15	18	17	14	18	Friday
	16	20	18	15	20	Saturday
	17	21	18	16	21	Sunday
	18	22	20	17	22	Monday
	18	23	21	18	23	Tuesday
	20	24	22	18	24	Wednesday
	21	25	23	20	25	Thursday
	22	26	24	21	26	Friday
	23	27	25	22	27	Saturday
	24	28	26	23	28	Sunday
	25	29	27	24	29	Monday
	26	30	28	25	30	Tuesday
	27		29	26	31	Wednesday
	28		30	27		Thursday
	29		31	28		Friday
	30			29		Saturday
	31			30		Sunday
						Monday
						Tuesday

OTHER USEFUL CONTACTS

The Premier League
30, Gloucester Place, London W1U 8PL
Phone: 0207 864 9000
Email: info@premierleague.com

The Football Association
25 Soho Square, London W1D 4FA
Phone: 0207 745 4545

The Football League
Edward VII Quay, Navigation Way,
Preston, Lancashire
PR2 2YF
Phone: 01772 325800/
0870 442 0 1888
Email: fl@football-league.co.uk

Professional Footballers' Association
2, Oxford Court,
Bishopsgate,
Off Lower Mosley Street,
Manchester
M2 3WQ
Phone: 0161 236 0575
Emai: info@thepfa.co.uk

Hillsborough Family
Support Group
69, Anfield Road,
Liverpool
L4 0TH
Phone: 0151 264 2931
Email: hfsg@liverpoolfc.tv

LFC logo and crest are registered trade marks of
The Liverpool Football Club and Athletics Grounds.
Published in Great Britain in 2007 by: Trinity Mirror Sport Media, PO Box 48, Old Hall Street, Liverpool L69 3EB

All Rights Reserved. No part of this publication may be reproduced, stored in a retrieval system, or transmitted in any form, or by any means, electronic, mechanical, photocopying, recording or otherwise without the prior permission in writing of the copyright holders, nor be otherwise circulated in any form of binding or cover other than in which it is published and without a similar condition being imposed on the subsequent publisher.

ISBN: 1 9052 6633 3
978 1 9052 6633 3

Printed and finished by Scotprint, Haddington, Scotland